This Will Make It Taste Good

Also by
Vivian Howard
DEEP RUN ROOTS

A New
Path
to
Simple
Cooking

This Will Make It
Taste Good

Vivian Howard

PHOTOGRAPHS BY BAXTER MILLER

VORACIOUS

LITTLE, BROWN AND COMPANY

NEW YORK   BOSTON   LONDON

Voracious / Little, Brown and Company
Hachette Book Group
1290 Avenue of the Americas, New York, NY 10104
littlebrown.com

First Edition: October 2020

Voracious is an imprint of Little, Brown and Company,
a division of Hachette Book Group, Inc. The Voracious name and logo
are trademarks of Hachette Book Group, Inc.

The publisher is not responsible for websites (or their content)
that are not owned by the publisher.

The Hachette Speakers Bureau provides a wide
range of authors for speaking events. To find out more, go to
hachettespeakersbureau.com or call (866) 376-6591.

Photography by Baxter Miller

Interior design by Laura Palese

ISBN 978-0-316-38112-3
LCCN 2020936922

10 9 8 7 6 5 4 3 2 1

WOR

Printed in the United States of America

TO THE CORNERS WE FIND OURSELVES IN THAT FORCE NOVEL AND CREATIVE WAYS OUT

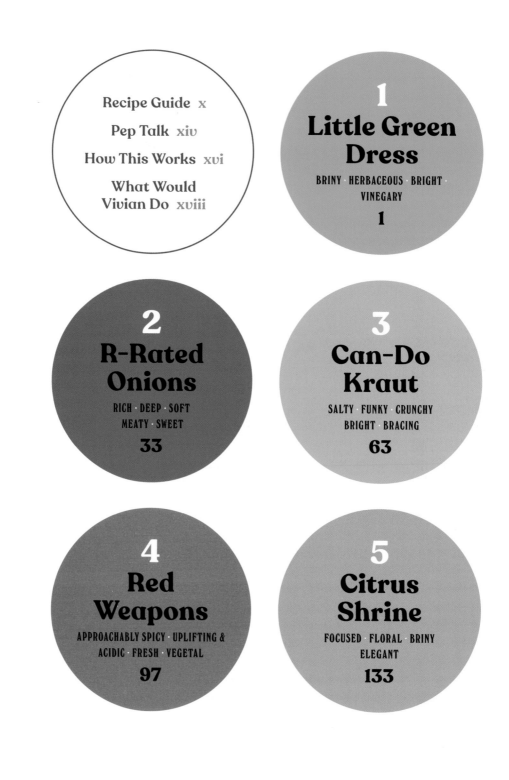

1

Little Green Dress

BRINY · HERBACEOUS · BRIGHT · VINEGARY

2

R-Rated Onions

RICH · DEEP · SOFT · MEATY · SWEET

3

Can-Do Kraut

SALTY · FUNKY · CRUNCHY · BRIGHT · BRACING

4

Red Weapons

APPROACHABLY SPICY · UPLIFTING & ACIDIC · FRESH · VEGETAL

5

Citrus Shrine

FOCUSED · FLORAL · BRINY · ELEGANT

Recipe Guide

IF YOU'RE LOOKING FOR VEGETARIAN OR GLUTEN-FREE RECIPES, more than half of the food in this book is one or both, so dive in. But note, Little Green Dress and V's Nuts contain anchovies in their whole form or in Worcestershire sauce. To make them and the recipes that use them vegetarian, remove the anchovies and swap the Worcestershire for the soy sauce of your preference. And go ahead and leave out the bread, croutons, or crackers to make many more dishes gluten-free.

IN PURSUIT OF DECADENCE

KIDS CAN'T RESIST

SNACKTASTIC

Pep Talk

MY FIRST COOKBOOK, *Deep Run Roots,* is a love letter to Eastern North Carolina, the place I've lived my whole life. It's as much a historical document as a cookbook, and of it I'm extremely proud. But *Deep Run Roots* really doesn't represent the way I cook at home most days. That's a little different than you might expect.

At home and at my home-away-from-home office (a place we affectionately call VHQ), I'm a modern day domestic engineer who calls on a roster of flavor heroes to make simple food fantastic food. These things, my kitchen MVPs, my tricks-to-delicious, are what this book is about.

If you come on this journey with me, if you go to the mat and make a hero or two, and then make a recipe or three that builds on that hero, I promise with every ounce of my highly accomplished self that you will be inspired.

This book will change the way you cook, the way you think about what's in your fridge, the way you see yourself in an apron. I swear on my dog Gracie's grave that you will be empowered, confident, dare I say even *nimble,* in your kitchen. Your journey to make your cooking taste good will shatter the chains of recipes you've struggled to follow. It will reshape, even streamline, the time you spend feeding yourself and the ones you love. Boring, bland dinners of basic Brussels sprouts and boneless skinless chicken breasts will be nothing more than limp dry memories in your house. You will emerge both kitchen magician and domestic god. You'll know what to do and when you need to do it to make breakfast, lunch, dinner, and all the nuggets in between remarkable moments in your day, because when I'm done with you, you'll be certain as a sultan that This Will Make It Taste Good.

The funny thing is that when I set out to write this cookbook I was bound and determined it was going to be "simple." The recipes would be exciting of course, but the nexus of it was that anybody anywhere could whippy-dippy-do them from start to finish in less than an hour. If you had no knife skills and cooking didn't bring you joy, then this book would be for you. If you're more Walmart than farmers' market, this book would be yours too. And of course if you love cooking and all things in the kitchen, you'd find plenty of joy in here too.

I'm happy to say that's where this book ended up, but it took a little while to figure out how to get there.

There were problems immediately with the lowest-common-denominator approach. Turns out that "simple" too often turns into "uninteresting" or "boring"—not exciting or fun. I broiled tomatoes and wished I could add deeply caramelized onions to the topping. I made vegetable soup and missed the onions' broth-defining depth there too. I stewed pots of beans in the name of easy and marveled at how basic they tasted. I seared fish and steak and wondered how to properly exalt both without an herb-y, punchy crown. I made lackluster dressings and pan sauces and offered store-bought suggestions for vegetable relish, pesto, and fruit preserves to help those sauces along.

My palate and my teacher's soul were not pleased. So I decided to do the thing that felt most natural. I decided to cook like I really cook.

I realized that my mission isn't to protect you from time in your kitchen, it's to help you make the most of it. So I resolved to open up my pantry and share the shelf full of tricks I use every day to make simple food taste good. I would be honest about how my experience as a chef shapes my experience cooking at home. I'd bring my green sauce, my furikake, and my preserved citrus out of the closet and expose their power. I'd give them names and bios that mirror their personality and demystify their purpose. I'd show you how to make them, organize them, store them, and exploit them to good end.

This book will change the way you cook.

Like a belt that lends me a waist when I'm feeling baggy, my little arsenal of condiments and components brighten, deepen, and define the food I cook. Recipes themselves, they make basic stuff taste complex. Damn right they deserve their own book!

I guess you'd call this "next-level meal prep" or "meal prep for people who want to cook food that tastes really freaking good." I mean, think about it. Why do meal-prep apostles suggest you roast asparagus on Sunday just to ruin them in the microwave on Wednesday? Why on the last night of your precious weekend do they want you to boil quinoa without a legit plan to make it taste good? Why is dry-grilled, boneless, skinless chicken breast a good way to save time? I appreciate the intention, but I'm here to tell you there's a better way to eat well without taking all night to cook dinner.

Trust me. Cancel your Sunday date with boiled quinoa and break out your blender in the name of a deep, rich, and round herb and garlic puree. Stop reheating broccoli that was oversteamed to start with and enlist your knife to craft a crown that makes broccoli shine. Forget portion bags and tiny Rubbermaid containers and say hello to jars and ice cube trays filled with colorful flavor treasures you feel proud of.

This will not be hard. I don't suggest you spend your free-from-quinoa time canning vegetables or butchering whole animals. Instead, I hope you lean into the way I cook at home and let my flavor heroes do the crafty part of the work. And just to be clear, these tricks-to-delicious are not hard to make. Rather, they're simple recipes like spiced nuts for texture and pickled tomatoes for just about everything else.

This is not about skill level, technique, or gadgets. This is about working smarter, not harder. You can do it.

How This Works

UNFOLDING IN FRONT OF YOU are ten chapters of recipes, each organized around one of my flavor heroes. Within each chapter I'll introduce you to each MVP's persona and function. You'll also learn how to prepare, store, and deploy that hero in a cornucopia of approachable ways. In addition to fully fleshed out, approachable, easy-to-shop-for recipes that call on that chapter's hero, you'll find "no brainer" suggestions for how to use it at the top of each chapter.

I suggest you start with one hero. Go deep, cooking several recipes that call on it so you can see the power a little forethought affords you. The recipes, even the heroes, are dead simple, and all but one's ingredients (Quirky Furki) can be found at any Walmart in our great nation. In short, nothing in this book is gonna have you searching the Internet for leaf lard or setting multiple timers in the name of precision. And because this book is practical at its core, you're gonna see a lot of chicken cooked in a bevy of ways because if you eat meat, you most likely eat chicken, and I find a lot of people need some guidance getting the bird right. Same goes for vegetables. Broccoli, cabbage, spinach, kale, squash, apples, and cauliflower look as good at Walmart as they do anywhere, so I call on them a lot.

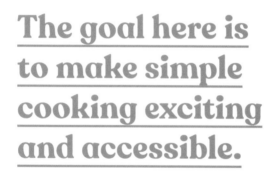

The goal here is to make simple cooking exciting and accessible.

If you're looking for interpretations of endive, white asparagus, and Guinea hen, look elsewhere. The goal here is to make simple cooking exciting and accessible. You can thank me when you see me.

Something else you'll notice is that the recipe names and their introductions are often, shall we say, inspired. Not necessarily a precise reflection of the ingredients they're made of, the recipe names in this book mirror what those dishes mean to me. Food is the language I use to talk about the fabric of my life, and that's what these recipes do.

There are stories, too, because I like to write them. They are a glimpse at the people, challenges, triumphs, and lessons learned that stock the pantry of who I am. Put it all together, and this is what makes my life taste good.

What Would Vivian Do?

Wag her finger in disapproval at anyone who uses anything other than **kosher salt, full-fat dairy, large eggs,** and **unsalted butter.**

Heap praise on everyone who has invested in a **high-powered blender** and a quality **12-inch cast-iron skillet.**

Add more accolades to all who have found a **10-inch chef's knife** that feels good in their hand and learned how to sharpen it.

Keep the olive oil game simple and just stock an extra virgin that tastes good and isn't pricey.

Stock all the vinegars. They don't go bad and are a relief to have around.

Grind her **black pepper** and the **rest of her spices** from whole.

Buy ground turkey and chicken that has some fat in it. Dry protein leaves her wondering what's the point.

Double, even triple the hero recipes and give them as gifts. She loves to please people.

Run out and get a **Microplane,** a **fish spatula,** and a **Y-shaped vegetable peeler.**

Not sweat the small stuff like brands of hot sauce, mayo, or mustard.

Pack all her greens (like spinach), **herbs** (like basil or mint), and **brown sugars into the cup** when measuring.

Go on the interwebs and order some of those **silicone ice cube trays to store the heroes** that make sense in the freezer in individual, easy to access portions.

Use glass over plastic almost always, particularly when heat or extreme cold is involved.

Never let the lack of one ingredient keep her from making a recipe. There's always something in the pantry that can stand in for things that are salty, tart, umami-full, and oniony.

Never blame the recipe if she goes completely rogue and does her own thing. That was her decision and she will live with it.

CHAPTER ONE

LITTLE
Green
Dress

Briny • Herbaceous • Bright • Vinegary

THE HERO THAT SAVED ME

In 2019 my professional life was a vat of turmoil. The mountain of projects I had taken on had slowly distanced me from the day-to-day operations at my restaurants, and my prolonged absence was notable in every part of the business. The restaurants were understaffed, guest counts were down across the board, and morale was at an all-time low. My team members used to feel like they were a part of something. Now that "something" just felt like a job. I had hired a consultant and a chef with pedigree to help figure things out, but somehow that made it worse. I fired people, rehired people, and to save my marriage, decided I could no longer work with my husband. We moved under a tall mountain of debt that caused finger-pointing, infighting, and backstabbing, and I couldn't tell who was doing what. I had abruptly ended our TV show, *A Chef's Life,* and was shooting a new series I had literally fought for but felt compromised by the power dynamics of the work.

All of it was stuff that, on some level, I was doing for other people. I had never wanted to run a restaurant empire, and suddenly I was running one into the ground. Every day I let more and more people down. I felt lost.

I had also gotten myself into a little bit of trouble with this book—a promise I had made but couldn't figure out how to fulfill. All naive and excited, I had agreed to write two books back in 2014 when *Deep Run Roots* found a publisher. Being a writer was all I had ever really dreamed of, and it had taken me two restaurants, a TV show, and plenty of hard experience to finally make it there. In many ways, writing *Deep Run Roots* was easy, a catharsis I had saved up my whole life for. But with this second book I felt that I had written a check I couldn't figure out how to cash, and I floundered. I didn't know what to write about. I had put everything I had and then some into that first book. I worried its success was beginner's luck, that I was a one-hit wonder, that I had told all my stories and written all my recipes. I wanted to give up, return the money to the publisher, and plant a garden instead.

Then, after a couple years of false starts, a lot of hand-wringing and a fair amount of profanity, I threw my hands up and stepped away from it. That separation provided the headspace to see an idea that was embedded in all the half-baked proposals I had written. A huge departure from the time capsule of a place and its food that was my first book, it would be personal, quirky, honest, and practical. It would be about the way I *really* cook rather than the way I thought people *wanted* me to cook. It would be about who I am, and why. Suddenly I spilled over with the stories and recipes that would become *This Will Make It Taste Good.*

My life was a dumpster fire, but somehow writing this book protected me from the fallout.

The trouble was, I am notoriously slow at this writing thing and my deadline had blown past. But I had a heart-to-heart with my editor, Mike, who told me we could still publish the book in 2020 if I was done in five months. I'm sure it was a deadline he thought someone who took years to write her first book would have no chance in hell of meeting. But I love to surprise people. In fact, underestimation is one of the primary fires that fuels me, so I woke up nearly every morning at 5 a.m. to a dark house and a rambunctious cat and wrote my little heart out until my kids roused at 7.

You need to know that I had never, ever, *ever* woken up before my kids on purpose. I am a night person who made her career in restaurants that open at 5 p.m., a person who has been conditioned to work late and sleep in the morning. This book changed that. I tucked myself into bed early because I couldn't wait to crawl into the curve of my couch with my computer the next morning. I felt possessed. No one pushed me to the finish line. Turns out Mike hadn't even told anybody at Little, Brown that I intended to deliver the book. No one but him even knew what it was about. This was a self-imposed sprint, and a force inside pushed me to the finish line.

My life was a dumpster fire, but somehow writing this book protected me from the fallout. Naming my flavor heroes, fleshing out their personalities, shaping their world, and thinking about how they might empower people in their own kitchens gave me newfound purpose. Condiments had become my escape. No, these condiments became my mission.

I wrote about R-Rated Onions first because they seemed like a gateway to understanding my idea for building a pantry of right-hand flavor heroes that make cooking on the quick more dynamic. But for me, caramelized onions are more Ant-Man than Superman. The hero that makes my heart beat fast, the one I would rush in to save from the flames if my house were burning down, is Little Green Dress.

Also affectionately known as LGD, this little number is like chimichurri and salsa verde had a baby in a bed of olives. LGD is condiment, ingredient, texture, acid, herb, oil, and salt all at once. Like the little black dress that's your sure thing, LGD is pretty much perfect for every occasion. I knew if I could get people to make it just once, they'd douse, dollop, and slather LGD on everything. It's a key that opens the door to delicious and makes boring bold, makes simple shine. It's the ultimate trick. It's my favorite. There, I said it.

So I wrote and wrote and much to everybody's surprise, I sort of met my deadline. I finished testing the recipes and writing most of these essays in February 2020 and promised to wrap up the rest in March.

Then, the pandemic. At first we didn't want to believe it was real, but Covid-19 came after everyone—killing tens of thousands of people, confusing the medical world, and igniting political angst. As a nation we were terrified. And like it did to other places all over the country, Covid-19 shuttered my restaurants so fast they looked like crime scenes, where everything is left in mid-sentence and "closed until further notice" signs stood in for yellow tape.

We had been in a similar spot before, when hurricanes shut us down for weeks and a fire closed our doors for months, so I knew the sad truth of what would come next. The restaurants would be bankrupt in days if the measures I took were not major and swift. Suspecting it would last longer than any of the disasters we had endured, and knowing I couldn't make payroll moving forward, I stood in front of my team and furloughed all but ten of my 130 employees. I had no choice, but it still felt like betrayal.

With my unruly restaurant train halted mid-track and its noise stripped away, a lot of things became clear. For several years I had struggled to run two restaurants across the street from each other in a town whose resources couldn't support them both. The economic fallout meant I couldn't do that anymore, so I made the painful decision to permanently close the Boiler Room and put all our resources into Chef and the Farmer. We consolidated inventory, jammed the cow and the pig we had gotten days before in the freezer, and sold back all the booze I didn't think I could drink.

With our skeleton crew of six in Kinston, we stumbled through takeout and curbside pickups for two weeks. But our restaurant model relied on people traveling to dine with us, and our food didn't make much sense in a box. On our last Saturday, we did $600 of business at a restaurant where we often did $11,000. We were losing money, momentum, and our minds. We had to stop and find another way forward.

Fueled by fear, responsibility, and adrenaline, I wrote a menu for a market that would deliver and for family meal kits that spoke to the moment. I reached out to farmers in hopes of distributing their goods. I wanted to feed our furloughed restaurant family. I wanted to feed kids without food because there was no school. I felt pressure to rally for struggling independent restaurants, and I wanted to keep the people I loved safe. But I didn't know how. I felt desperate and confused, like the ball in a pinball machine thrust around a rapidly changing world.

I realized it didn't make sense for me to build a new business around delivery when a majority of our customers pre-Covid had come from far away. How could I ask people to come off unemployment when those benefits were more than I could offer? Why would I put my team in danger in the name of something that might not work, when everything I saw told us all to stay home? Plus, it seemed like a bad idea to merely guess what might be next based on what I saw other people doing. And above all else, I knew I should just be thankful my loved ones were healthy.

I hung on to my habit of waking up before the sun to write, but my mind was far too muddled to make sense of sentences. In those quiet moments with my family asleep and my mind on fire, I turned to Instagram and watched people cook. Everybody but me, it seemed, was in the kitchen trying to make the best of quarantine. Kitchens had become the amusement parks of people's homes. Some were Disneylands of sourdough and stews. Others seemed trapped in a county-fair house of horrors—the only way out, a maze of beans. I so wished the book I was still writing was out in the world. I longed for Little Green Dress, Can-Do Kraut, and Community Organizer to jump in and show people how to make magic kingdoms out of a rickety old roller coaster.

And so it was on one of those quiet, dark mornings snuggled with my cat that I saw a different way out of the mess we were in. In fact, I had laid the groundwork for it during an earlier disaster, Hurricane Florence. We had planned to open a brick-and-mortar bake shop called Handy & Hot. But after the hurricane ruined those plans, we started to sell baked goods online for special occasions. Handy & Hot proved a huge success and frankly represented the only real money the restaurants made that year.

Handy & Hot was our future—a way to share our food with the world when no one could come to our restaurants. But as much joy as pound cakes, s'mores kits, and chocolate pecan chess pies brought our customers, a baked good you eat in a matter of minutes didn't feel right for this long and isolated moment. I wanted to offer something people could spend time with; something they could get to know; something that might make life inside the kitchen more bearable or, for some people, more fun. And I was already writing about just that.

It may come as a surprise that I'm not a particularly spiritual person. Maybe it was too many Sundays as a kid spent on the back pew pondering how long an eternity might feel when one is burning, but I generally take things at face value. From my vantage point, bad things happen. Good things happen. And they happen randomly (although I do believe in karma). Even so, the experience, timing, and gift of this book left me feeling there must be a higher power at work. I found it unbelievable the book I had complained about, stumbled around, and at the last possible moment was possessed to write would light my path forward during the most confusing time in my life.

In the middle of our nation's stay-at-home order, we launched mail-order Handy & Hot quarantine kits with Little Green Dress in the spotlight and Community Organizer with the assist. We had hoped to get orders for 500 kits, but sold twice that in just the first few hours. Two weeks and 110 pounds of mint and parsley later, we released and sold 500 more.

It was the first time in five years that I felt I was really leading my kitchen and my small team with purpose, and I felt grounded, hopeful, full of gratitude, and energized. We made plans to continue. We could release jars of these flavor heroes every month, in the hope of generating some enthusiasm for the book to come, revenue for the restaurant I would eventually reopen, and work for the staff I care so much about. The whole thing felt bigger than me, but not in a train-barreling-down-the-tracks, out-of-control kind of way (I'm well-versed in that sensation). Rather, it made me believe that for the first time in forever I could choose a thoughtful way to move forward rather than simply react to all the pressures around me.

Maybe it's a stretch to suggest that Little Green Dress and this pain-in-the-ass of a book saved my business as well as my sanity, but I don't think so.

Little Green Dress

- This recipe is specific in calling for a certain variety of olive, shallots instead of onion, and a particular hue of vinegar. But know that it is LGD's *equation* that makes it heroic, not its *details*. To make your own variant of LGD, you need fresh, fragrant herbs; something onion-esque; the combined brine power of olives, capers, and anchovy; the juxtaposed acid of both vinegar and citrus; and the fruity fat of a good-quality olive oil. Don't get hung up on the variety of vinegar you don't have or the fact that you've got onion and no shallot. Just follow the equation and taste what happens.

- This is not the place for dried herbs. The parsley and mint must be fresh and fragrant.

- Don't even think about lemon juice from the bottle.

- LGD will keep in your fridge for one month but don't relegate it to your freezer. It doesn't respond well to the lack of attention and its cold environment. Believe it or not, because of its high acid content, it'll be just fine on your counter for about a week.

- Don't let some of the ingredients deter you: I've knowingly fed this to haters of olives and anchovies alike, and everybody wanted more. However, if you are a vegetarian, omit the anchovies and make LGD anyway.

2	medium shallots, peeled
2	cloves garlic, peeled
3	tablespoons red wine vinegar
⅔	cup Castelvetrano olives, pitted
1½	tablespoons capers, rinsed
2	oil-packed anchovy filets
1	bunch fresh flat-leaf parsley (about 1 cup packed)
2	(½-ounce) packages fresh mint (about ½ cup packed)
½	cup tasty extra-virgin olive oil
	Grated zest of 1 lemon
¼	cup fresh lemon juice
1	teaspoon hot sauce
½	teaspoon kosher salt

1 In a small food processor, mince the shallots and the garlic, then stir them in a small bowl with the red wine vinegar. We want them to pickle a bit, so give them all some privacy for about 20 minutes before you add them to the rest of the ingredients.

2 Meanwhile, mince the pitted olives, capers, and anchovies in the food processor. Transfer to a medium bowl. Pick the leaves and smaller stems from the parsley and the leaves from the mint and mince in the food processor; it may take a little while to get them all fully processed. Transfer the herbs to the bowl with the olive mixture.

3 Add the vinegar-shallot-garlic mixture, olive oil, lemon zest and juice, hot sauce, and salt to the bowl with everything else. Stir it all together and let this vinegary puddle of green sit for a minimum of 30 minutes before you bathe in it. LGD will keep for a month in a sealed container in your fridge as long as all the green stuff is submerged in just a bit of olive oil.

MAKES 2 CUPS

1 spoon on baked potatoes

2 dollop on steak, roast chicken, lamb, pork, or seafood

3 add to salads with creamy cheeses

4 serve with scrambled eggs or omelets

5 spoon on top of bowls of soup

6 mash into guacamole or avocado toast

7 mix into chicken, potato, or egg salad

8 serve on deviled eggs or hot dogs

9 simmer with ground meat for tacos

10 spread on top of pizza

11 use as a filling for grilled cheese or quesadillas

12 thin with oil to make a vinaigrette

Jammy Eggs Dressed in Green

makes 2 eggs

There is more than one way to boil an egg, but as a chef you kind of have to pick a way and stand behind it. So that's what I did. I always put an egg from the fridge in water from the tap and brought it up to a boil. Then I let it boil depending on how firm I wanted the yolk to be. But one day I had an "egg-off" with my colleague, Ryan Stancil. We were looking for the very best jammy eggs and the plan was to test his method against mine.

Before we even got into the meat of the competition, Ryan pointed out that different stoves heat water at different rates, so bringing an egg plus the water up to a boil at the same time means your egg starts to cook slowly before it ever boils. He also corrected my concern that cold eggs from the fridge often crack when you drop them into a rapid boil by nestling his eggs near the heat source of the stove while the water heats up. I was impressed. I lost the egg-off and changed my method immediately.

If you're like me and boiled eggs of some degree are a frequent player in your weekday breakfast, then this will improve your mornings immeasurably. It's hard to imagine a boiled egg scarfed down on your way out the door as memorable, but LGD on an egg with a little crunchy salt sure is. If you're serving more than just yourself, go ahead and scale this up.

2 large eggs

1 tablespoon Little Green Dress (page 10)

Flaky sea salt, to taste

① Bring your eggs out of the fridge and set them next to a 2-quart saucepan filled two-thirds of the way with water. Bring the water up to a rapid boil and set an ice bath nearby. Gently drop the eggs in and cook for 6½ minutes. Transfer the eggs to your ice bath and let them rest there for 15 to 30 seconds. You could chill them completely but I like to eat them warm. Peel, slice in half, and top with LGD and flaky salt.

Gas Station Biscuits

makes 8

When I first tried one of these, I texted Baxter Miller, my friend, the photographer of this book, and a fellow LGD disciple, and said, "This biscuit is better than pizza."

Based on an Eastern North Carolina gas station tradition where a knob of hoop cheese is stuffed in the middle of a day-old biscuit and baked again in foil, these biscuits get crispy and the cheese melts around the edges like a lace skirt. I've gilded the lily on something pretty shiny already and stuffed some LGD in there with the cheese. They were so irresistible I had to tuck the leftovers under some raw meat packaging in the trash just so I could step away.

The biscuit itself is the brainchild of my coworker Justise Robbins. They are excellent all on their own. The cheese filling is a modified version of my tomato pie topping and the LGD is a gift from heaven.

2 cups grated Parmigiano Reggiano (use a Microplane)

2 cups shredded Fontina

⅓ cup mayonnaise

½ teaspoon ground black pepper

2½ cups all-purpose flour, plus more to flour your work surface and as needed

1 tablespoon granulated sugar

1 tablespoon kosher salt

2½ teaspoons baking powder

1 teaspoon baking soda

10 tablespoons (1¼ sticks) cold unsalted butter, cut into ½-inch cubes

1½ cups buttermilk

Nonstick cooking spray

⅔ cup Little Green Dress (page 10), drained of all its liquid

1 Preheat your oven to 350°F. Cut eight 6 x 6-inch squares of foil and arrange them on a baking sheet in a single layer (more or less). Each square will hold its own biscuit with the foil folded up around it.

2 In a medium bowl, stir together the cheeses, mayonnaise, and pepper. Set that aside.

3 In a large bowl, whisk together the flour, sugar, salt, baking powder, and baking soda to combine. Using a fork or a pastry blender, cut the butter into the dry mixture until the butter is the size of small peas. Add the buttermilk and stir until the dough comes together.

4 Once the dough is manageable, flour your work surface and turn the dough onto it. Fold the dough in on itself about four times, kneading gently and taking care not to overwork it. Incorporate more flour as necessary to keep the dough from sticking to the table. Roll the dough into a 10-inch square that is ½ inch thick. (Yes, this is thinner than traditional biscuits. Hold your horses and you'll see why.)

5 Using a knife or a pizza cutter, cut the dough into sixteen 2½-inch squares. Spray each of the foil squares on the baking sheet with nonstick spray. Put one biscuit square in the middle of each square of foil. Top each biscuit with a scant 3 tablespoons of the cheese mixture. Top that with about 1 tablespoon drained LGD. Finally, put the additional eight biscuits on top of that. Do not press down or try to crimp the edges. I repeat: *Do not press down and do not crimp the edges!* Instead, lift the sides of the foil up around the biscuits. Each biscuit stack should look like a foil package with an open top. Do not close the packages. (If you do, the biscuits will steam. We want them to brown. I know this looks like a wreck and it may look worse in the oven, but it will work out. Roll with it.)

6 Slide the biscuits onto the middle rack of your oven and bake for 22 to 25 minutes, until they are browned a bit on top. Serve them warm or at room temperature in the foil. But hell, they're probably good ice cold.

Deep Run Summer in a Bowl

Serves 4

Stewed tomatoes plus sweet corn and cucumbers spiked with vinegar send me straight back to my mom's yellow linoleum kitchen table in the heat of an Eastern North Carolina summer. As a kid, my favorite part of this holy trinity of the July garden was lapping up the juice that pooled at the bottom of the plate. Something about the rich and buttery corn milk mingled with the cucumber vinegar and the just-cooked, fresh tomato juice felt like accidental perfection. For me there was never quite enough of it to satisfy.

Now adult Vivian has fixed that by putting it all in a bowl and forcing the three sisters to mingle more. I've also swapped out the sharpness of cucumbers marinated in straight vinegar for cucumbers dressed in the ever-elegant LGD. It's a wardrobe change that makes this bowl of comfort taste all grown up.

1 large English cucumber

1½ teaspoons kosher salt, divided

⅔ cup Little Green Dress (page 10)

3 to 4 medium slicing tomatoes

3 ears of corn (or 2 cups fresh or frozen corn kernels)

2 tablespoons unsalted butter

1 teaspoon granulated sugar

2 teaspoons sherry vinegar

HEADS up

Any ripe tomatoes or corn will work here, but for a next-level experience seek out heirloom tomatoes that haven't been refrigerated and fresh, sweet corn on the cob.

① Begin by splitting your cucumber lengthwise down the middle and scooping out its seeds. Slice the cucumber into thin half-moons and transfer to a medium bowl. Toss with ¼ teaspoon of the salt and the LGD. Let the cukes hang out and make themselves into a crunchy relish while you prepare the tomatoes and corn.

② Bring a large pot of water to a boil and set up an ice bath nearby. Using a paring knife, cut the stem center out of each tomato and make a small X on the bottom. Drop the tomatoes into the boiling water for about 30 seconds. You should see the skin around the X you made start to separate from the flesh. Once that's good and done, transfer the tomatoes to your ice bath.

③ Once the tomatoes have cooled enough to handle, peel away and discard their skin. Slice each tomato through the stem end into eighths, and cut out and discard any white parts from the core. (Do this over a medium saucepan so you don't lose a lot of tomato juice to the carnage.) Drop the tomatoes into said saucepan. Bring the tomatoes to a steady simmer over medium heat. Let them cook, covered, for about 15 minutes.

④ While the tomatoes simmer, cut the corn and all of its magical milk off the cob and add it (or the frozen kernels) to a 10- to 12-inch skillet. Over medium heat, cook the corn for a few minutes, just until it's hot but still crisp and fresh tasting. Then stir in ½ teaspoon of the salt and the butter.

⑤ Season the tomatoes with the remaining ¾ teaspoon salt, the sugar, and vinegar. Spoon the tomatoes into four bowls. Divide the corn and nestle it like gravy into the tomatoes. Crown it all with the cucumber relish and go to town with your spoon.

LGD Goes Ranch

Serves 4

With the strong suggestion of garlicky onion and the whisper of herbs, this creamy puddle of tang is everything we love about ranch dressing, our country's favorite sauce. Drizzle, dip, or douse lettuce, French fries, crudités, chicken fingers, or pizza with this dressing, and say goodbye to Hidden Valley for a bit. Personally, I pretend romaine hearts are chips and that LGD Ranch is their dip. I'm also a big fan of a saltine dipping situation. If you want to go totally wild and do a Vivian's Heroes Collab, add 3 tablespoons of chopped Red Weapons (page 104) and find yourself with a quick and special dip fit for a party.

1 cup mayonnaise
½ cup sour cream
½ cup buttermilk
2 teaspoons granulated sugar
2 teaspoons hot sauce
½ teaspoon kosher salt
½ cup Little Green Dress (page 10)

1 In a medium bowl, whisk all the ingredients together and let them marry for about 30 minutes before the festivities begin. This will keep for up to 2 weeks in a sealed container in your fridge.

Naked Burgers with a Cheese Toupee & Spinach Crown

Serves 4

This is a healthy-ish weeknight dinner for Ben and me when the kids are having real burgers with buns. We are a pig-centric family, so we always have ground pork on hand, but you can use turkey or beef here to great effect.

I love the born-in-an-Applebee's combination of Swiss cheese, mushrooms, and onions on a burger. Add spinach drenched with LGD and you have a sauce of sorts that rounds out a nutritious, satisfying meal.

The onions, charred but still with a raw character, are one of my favorite things to have around. They almost made the cut for one of the flavor heroes in this book, but I decided they're too simple to set apart. Either way, add them to your repertoire. I always make double what I need and am so pleased with myself when I open the fridge and find them there, full of texture and the char of a backyard barbecue.

2   pounds ground pork, turkey, or beef

2½ teaspoons kosher salt, divided

2   teaspoons ground black pepper

1   tablespoon ground cumin

2   tablespoons sour cream

3   tablespoons extra-virgin olive oil, divided

1   red onion, sliced into ½-inch-thick rounds

4   slices Swiss cheese

1   tablespoon unsalted butter

3   garlic cloves, smashed and peeled

4   ounces button or cremini mushrooms, halved (about 2 cups)

5   ounces spinach (about 2 packed cups)

⅔   cup Little Green Dress (page 10)

1   In a medium bowl, combine the ground meat, 1½ teaspoons of the salt, the pepper, cumin, and sour cream. Mix well to combine and set aside as you get everything else ready.

2   Heat 1 tablespoon of the olive oil in a 12-inch skillet till it shimmers. Add the onion slices in a single layer and allow them to char on one side for about 2 minutes. Flip them over and char on the opposite side. Transfer to a plate to cool and season with ½ teaspoon of the salt.

3   Form the meat mixture into four wide flat burgers. In the same skillet you charred your onions, heat 1 tablespoon of the olive oil. Once it's nearly smoking, carefully add the burgers and brown on one side for about 5 minutes. Flip them over, add a slice of Swiss to the top and cook an additional 4 minutes on the opposite side, till cooked through. Transfer the burgers to a plate to rest while you cook the spinach.

4   To that same skillet, add the final tablespoon olive oil, the butter, and the smashed garlic. Once the garlic starts to come alive, add the mushrooms and let them sit and sizzle over medium heat for about 2 minutes. Then stir them around and let them brown on the other side. Season the mushrooms with the remaining ½ teaspoon salt and add the spinach. Let it wilt while stirring. This will take about a minute. Remove the pan from the heat and stir in the LGD.

5   Top your burgers with charred onion slices, then crown with a pyramid of spinach and mushrooms.

Asparagus Bathed in Green Butter

Serves 4

I've watched my family and friends get asparagus wrong for years and I cannot take it anymore. So listen up: Asparagus needs to be cooked at a high heat for a short period of time. End of story. Don't put skinny stalks on a baking sheet and slide them into a 350°F oven for 20 minutes—unless you actually prefer limp, stringy stalks to crisp, green ones. For me, asparagus cooked slow and low is most similar to asparagus in the can and I don't know a soul who gets excited about that.

Even more than roasting or grilling at a high temp, this recipe's method highlights the green, beginning-of-spring taste that's unique to asparagus. A lot of us believe that boiling vegetables is the worst way to cook them, but it's not if you pay attention, set a timer, and think of it more as a blanch than a boil.

I've chosen to puree the LGD here because I like the way the butter combines with the smooth sauce. But if you're not feeling the blender, that's okay: Chunky green butter is fine. Also, if you're serving this as part of a meal, cook the asparagus last. This dish is far better warm, and a re-boil in almost every situation is a bad thing.

¼ cup Little Green Dress (page 10)

1 bunch big thick asparagus, tough ends trimmed away

2 tablespoons unsalted butter, at room temperature

Flaky salt, for finishing

1 Bring a large pot of heavily salted water up to a rolling boil.

2 Puree the LGD until completely smooth in your blender. Transfer to a large bowl and add the room-temp butter.

3 Just before you're ready to eat, drop the asparagus in the boiling water and cook for 1 minute only. Using tongs and taking care to drain off as much water as possible, transfer the asparagus to the bowl holding the butter and LGD.

4 Toss the hot asparagus and watch the butter melt and make a green sauce. Position the asparagus on a platter and pour any remaining green butter over the top. Sprinkle with flaky salt and serve right away.

Cherry Tomato Baked Feta...Surprise!

Serves 4

I've taken to the habit of calling something a "Surprise" when I don't know how to classify it. But if you think about the Mediterranean tradition of dipping bread into seasoned olive oil, then you add cherry tomatoes and feta and then you bake it, you have the gist of what's happening here. Not technically a dip, but perhaps more of a broken spoon-able sauce or spread, LGD stands in for the "seasoned" part of the olive oil and brings more pizzazz with it than dried oregano ever did. Surprise!

While the gateway vehicle for this dip is toast, I love it over grits, pureed cauliflower, couscous, fish, or chicken. I've paired it with swordfish here because swordfish is meaty enough to balance the action—but let's be clear, this recipe is about the Surprise, not its companion.

2   cups cherry or grape tomatoes, halved

6   ounces feta, crumbled

½   cup Little Green Dress (page 10)

2½ teaspoons kosher salt, divided

⅓   cup plus 3 tablespoons extra-virgin olive oil, divided

4   (6-ounce) swordfish fillets, or another meaty fish such as tuna, salmon, or mackerel

⅓   cup pine nuts, toasted

1 Preheat your oven to 375°F. Combine the tomatoes, crumbled feta, LGD, ½ teaspoon of the salt, and the ⅓ cup olive oil in a small baking dish. Slide that onto the middle rack of your oven and bake for 20 minutes, until the cherry tomatoes have shriveled and given up some of their juice to the mixture, while you prepare the fish.

2 With the surprise in the oven, heat the remaining 3 tablespoons olive oil until shimmering in a 12-inch heavy-bottomed ovenproof skillet. Season the fish on both sides with the remaining 2 teaspoons salt and gently place them in the oil to sear. Cook on that first side for about 3 minutes or until nicely browned. Flip the fish over, transfer the skillet to the oven, and bake for 5 to 6 minutes more, till it is opaque throughout and warm in the center.

3 Take the fish and the Surprise out of the oven. To plate, divide the Surprise over the fish and sprinkle with the pine nuts. Serve warm.

Tuna Salad Snack Crackers

Serves 4

This is what I want for lunch: There's a cracker, which makes it feel somehow lighter than a sandwich. There's a little something green that also happens to be rich. And there's tuna salad, which from my experience is only ever eaten midday. Think about it. Have you ever craved tuna fish first thing after brushing your teeth in the morning? Or have you stirred together canned Chicken of the Sea with mayo in lieu of popcorn when watching a movie? Probably not. But if you were to consider tuna salad for breakfast or an evening snack, this lighter, vinegar- and brine-driven riff would be the right choice.

10 to 12 ounces tuna packed in water

½ cup finely chopped celery

1 teaspoon kosher salt, divided

½ cup Little Green Dress (page 10)

2 tablespoons mayonnaise

1 large or 2 small avocados, halved, pitted, and peeled

Juice of 1 lemon

8 Wasa crackers

① Drain the water off the tuna and transfer the tuna to a medium bowl. Stir in the celery, ½ teaspoon of the salt, the LGD, and mayonnaise. Make sure it's well incorporated and set aside.

② Cut the avocado into thin slices. Squeeze the lemon over the avocado and season with the remaining ½ teaspoon salt. Divide the avocado slices among the crackers and spoon the tuna overtop. Serve soon.

HEADS up

Either you know what Wasa crackers are and you're wondering why the heck I would suggest them, or you're a Wasa virgin who has yet to experience these healthy, crisp cardboard-ish crackers. I don't enjoy them with everything and certainly not on their own, but when I want something crunchy and substantial to balance punchy toppings like my tuna salad with avocado, I find them the perfect vehicle.

Roast Chicken Toast

Serves 4

To all the toast I've cooked before—I'm sorry you don't hold a candle to this guy.

Basically a piece of bread transformed into a crouton under roasting chicken legs, the bread itself is squishy and rich with chicken schmaltz in some spots and astonishingly crisp for the same reason in others. It's stupid easy to do, makes use of not-fresh bread, and is a revelation to eat. I seriously can't understand why we haven't been doing it for centuries. So while I'm probably not the first person to roast chicken over bread, I want to be the one who takes the technique mainstream.

After the chicken roasts, pull apart its meat and toss it with copious dollops of LGD and a big handful of arugula before piling it back on that happy place I call chicken toast. It is best warm, so if you don't want to eat it right away, reheat the pulled chicken and the toast in your oven when you're ready and toss it with the LGD and arugula just before serving.

4	chicken leg quarters
2½	teaspoons kosher salt, divided
1	teaspoon ground black pepper
1	loaf sourdough, ciabatta, or other sturdy, rustic-style bread
2	tablespoons extra-virgin olive oil
⅔	cup Little Green Dress (page 10)
1	teaspoon hot sauce
4	ounces (about 2 cups packed) arugula

❶ Preheat your oven to 400°F. Season the chicken legs on all sides with 2 teaspoons of the salt and the pepper.

❷ Slice the loaf of bread in half, separating the top from the bottom. Trim the raised dome from the top portion so you have two flat, roughly 1- to 1½-inch-thick slices of bread. Cut each of those pieces into two to create four bread pillows for your chicken. Put the bread pillows on a baking sheet, crust side down.

❸ Place a chicken leg on top of each bread pillow and trim around the bread to roughly fit the chicken. Drizzle the olive oil over top. Slide that baking sheet onto the middle rack of your oven and roast for 50 minutes, or until the skin is crispy and the internal temperature is 165°F.

❹ Pull the pan out and transfer the chicken to a rack or a plate. Slide the chicken toast back into the oven to keep it warm, but turn the oven off and open the door a bit to allow some heat to escape. Once the chicken is cool enough to handle, pull it apart and toss with the remaining ½ teaspoon salt, the LGD, hot sauce, and arugula. I include at least some of the skin in the toss, but that's a choice you can make to suit your taste.

❺ Pull the toast out of the oven and pile the chicken salad on top of each piece. Grab a knife, fork, and sturdy napkin, and get at it.

Mussels Will Work for You

Serves 4

My plan for this book was only to offer recipes with ingredients I could find in my local Walmart. Not out of love for Walmart, but because I want you to be empowered by these recipes, not discouraged by what you can't find because of where you live. *But*...I made a few exceptions, one of them for mussels. Here's why:

- While mussels are not readily available in my little town, they are by no means hard to find or expensive.

- They come generally clean and ready to cook.

- Because they open up when they die, it's easy to see, even before you buy them, if they're past their prime.

- They keep longer in the fridge than many things that emerge from the sea, so you don't have to make them the same day you buy them (see the Heads Up).

- From start to finish, they take all of 5 minutes to cook and are a true one-pot meal.

- Merely by opening up under the pressure of heat, they give us both sustenance and a sauce that screams, "Get some bread and sop me up, stat!"

- They suggest a measure of sophistication and skill in a cook because they're something we most often eat in restaurants.

- Trust me when I say it: Mussels are hard to screw up.

3 to 4 pounds mussels

2 tablespoons extra-virgin olive oil

3 cloves garlic, thinly sliced

½ teaspoon red pepper flakes

½ cup white wine

1 cup water

½ cup Little Green Dress (page 10)

2 tablespoons unsalted butter

Good crusty toast, for sopping with

① Begin by rinsing your mussels under cool water in a colander. Pick through and make sure they are closed or that they do close when you suggest it with your fingers. Throw away any mussels that remain open—those are the bad ones.

② In a Dutch oven or large sauté pan with a lid, bring the olive oil, garlic, and pepper flakes up to a sizzle over medium-high heat. Add the mussels and toss to coat in the oil. Add the white wine, then the water. Put the lid on and let it come up to a boil.

③ After 2 minutes, remove the lid and give the mussels a stir. At this point, you can see what kind of progress they're making. Some may have started to open and if so, put the lid on and let them cook an additional 2 minutes, or more as necessary. If they take longer, they take longer.

④ Once about 90 percent of your mussels have opened up, remove the pan from the heat and toss them carefully with the LGD and butter. The rest should open up with the residual heat. If they don't, throw those suckers away. Serve in bowls with lots of toast for sopping.

 HEADS up You'll want to cook your mussels within a few days of bringing them home, but until then, store them in a bowl in your fridge with a damp towel draped over top. They are alive and may spit out a little water, so the bowl prevents a mess and the towel keeps them moist.

CHAPTER TWO

R-RATED Onions

Rich • Deep • Soft • Meaty • Sweet

You think you know them. You may even think you make them. But most of you do not.

The term "caramelized onions" means about as much nowadays as the label "farm to table." There's something really moving about the true meaning of the words, but the way we most readily interpret both terms is not that.

A lot of recipes say, "Let the onions cook until caramelized, about 10 minutes," or, "Cook 1 sliced onion for about 10 minutes, until golden brown and caramelized." It may seem like I'm pointing fingers at how we got to a place where caramelized onions are a fraction as good as what they once were, but I'm not. I told people to "cook onions until caramelized, about 10 minutes" at least twenty-five times in *Deep Run Roots*, so the finger points back at me as much as anybody else.

As for attempting to properly caramelize one lone onion, well that's just not possible without a tiny, tiny little pan poised on a working dollhouse-size burner. Show me that and we'll talk.

What I meant by those instructions, and what I think most recipe writers mean, is "cook the onions as long as you're willing and make sure they are brown in spots and not crunchy because that's all I suspect you have time for."

But like all true transformations, onions require more than 10 minutes over medium-high heat to fully develop. The process, the slow push from blonde to nutty brown, moves in stages. Onions' maturation from PG to rated-R requires patience and a watchful eye. It's not difficult, but it's not a cinch. That's why I suggest you make a big batch at once—as big as you can manage—so you have fully developed R-Rated Onions waiting when you're in need of grown-up flavor but are short on time.

Manipulated in the best kind of way by steam heat, then dry heat over a longer period of time than I'm typically keen to require in a multi-part recipe, caramelized onions are a leisurely labor of love that loves you back. Like a perfect stock or just the right amount of MSG, onions cooked low and slow until their sugars deepen and their flavor shape-shifts lend a hard-to-quantify but easy-to-appreciate dimension to food. In their most well-known role as the foundation for French onion soup, they define the rustic, unforgettable flavor of a broth that launched the soup sections of a thousand menus. And in less scene-stealing appearances, caramelized onions show us that a simple ingredient coddled a certain way can give a flimsy dish a sultry backbone, or make a one-note meal all grown-up. ➤

R-Rated Onions

HERE'S WHAT'S IMPORTANT

- Do *not* shrink the recipe. It won't work if you start with a dinky mound of onions. You need girth to produce the steam that will initially soften them, and you need the insulation provided by their bulk to prevent them from burning before they can soften up. Trust me. One cup of onions will not do.

- The pan you use is crucial. A flimsy and light cheap aluminum thing will encourage burnage, and traditional nonstick surfaces don't promote the stick-and-stir environment you need. And contrary to conventional wisdom, more surface area is not advantageous here, so don't bring out your 24-inch stew pot in hopes it will make things happen faster. In short, choose something of an appropriate size with a heavy bottom and a tight-fitting lid. A 10- to 12-inch cast-iron skillet or Dutch oven is ideal, but a nice-quality stainless-steel pan with high sides works too.

- I divide the fruits of my labor into half-cup portions and store any extra in the freezer. Silicone ice cube trays meant for giant cocktail cubes make great storage vessels as well. But you may want to keep those for emergency Manhattans. You do you.

- R-Rated Onions will keep in the fridge for a week and in the freezer for 3 months.

4 to 5 large or 6 to 8 medium yellow or white onions

1 tablespoon olive or vegetable oil

1 teaspoon kosher salt

1 Peel your onions and cut them in half through their stem ends—*longways,* if you will. Slice them thinly with the grain, following the line from root to stem rather than cutting the onion across its belly. This is actually important because slicing it the other way makes the path to silky onions a longer one.

2 Once your onions are sliced, heat your skillet over medium-high heat and add the oil, then the onions and the salt. Let the onions sizzle for a couple minutes. Stir with a wooden spoon or a heatproof spatula and watch as they wilt for about 3 more minutes. At this point, reduce the heat to medium low. Put a lid on and step away for a few minutes. Give the onions a stir every now and then. You don't have to stand over it like risotto, but don't go for a walk around the block either. Caramelized bits will accumulate at the bottom and sides of the pan, and that's good. Just scrape them up and stir them in. A little color building as you go is okay, but don't rush to brown them. The point is to cook the onions gently, coaxing them through stages of raw, wilted, sweaty, soft, light brown, and finally deeply caramelized.

3 About 45 minutes in, remove the lid for the last time. They should be a light caramel color. Now, with the lid off, you will need to watch more closely and stir more frequently. At some point you may find that despite your best efforts some of the caramelized bits, verging on burnt, cling to the pan and threaten overall onion ruin. Do not fret! Just add a ½ cup or so of water and use its energy to help scrape up the stubborn but tasty film. Let the water cook out of course. When you're smiling over a soft, creamy, fragrant pile of mahogany onions, you're done.

MAKES 2 CUPS

1
add to scrambled eggs, quiche, and frittatas

2
toss with sautéed green beans and lemon

3
stir into hummus—or any dip, really

4
top toast you've smeared with creamy cheese

5
simmer into soups, stews, and braises

6
top baked potatoes, along with Parm and olive oil

7
add a little to just about any pasta dish

8
top a burger or tuck inside a grilled cheese

9
use as a base for pizza toppings

10
stir into a pot of beans

Pinch Me, Frenchie

serves 6 to 8

Because you can get a recipe for French onion soup anywhere, I made a point to not include one in this book. Still, I cannot deny its appeal. The thing is that with every bowl of French onion I've ever slurped, what I enjoy most is the little crouton at the top soaked with sweet, rich broth and lacquered with broiled cheese.

So in lieu of the soup itself, I give you a Bundt pan full of oniony bread. Monkey bread, also known as a pinch-me loaf, is often a sweet pull-apart treat where small balls of dough are coated in butter, cinnamon, and sugar then proofed and finally baked together. It comes out of the oven and everybody gathers 'round to pinch off gooey morsels from the group. Pinch Me, Frenchie is just that, except the plump little yeast rolls are rolled in R-Rated Onions, butter, and cheese. It's not dessert, but it could be.

I've chosen to bake this in a Bundt pan because monkey bread is a communal, get-all-the-fingers-in-there kind of thing. But you could do this in a couple muffin tins to give your pinchers individual servings to work with. Just decrease the baking time by about 7 minutes if you go that route.

2	teaspoons instant dry yeast
1½	cups warm water
2	tablespoons extra-virgin olive oil
3½	cups all-purpose flour
2	teaspoons kosher salt
1	cup R-Rated Onions (page 38)

¾	cup (1½ sticks) unsalted butter, melted
1	tablespoon picked thyme leaves
1	cup grated Parmigiano Reggiano (use a Microplane)
2	cups shredded Fontina, provolone, or Gouda
	Nonstick cooking spray

1 In a large bowl or in a standing mixer fitted with the dough hook, mix the yeast and warm water and let it sit for 5 minutes. Add the olive oil, flour, and salt. Mix with your hands or the hook until the dough comes together and is homogenous and elastic, about 3 minutes.

2 Coat the inside of a large bowl with cooking spray and dump the dough into it. Cover with a towel and put it in a sunny window or a generally warm spot in your kitchen. Let it rest and rise for 1 hour, or until doubled in size.

3 While the dough proofs, mix the R-Rated Onions in a bowl with the melted butter and thyme. In another bowl, stir together the cheeses.

4 Once the dough is twice as big as it was, flour your hands and punch that dough back down where it belongs. Spray the inside of a Bundt pan with the cooking spray. Pinch off a ½-inch round of dough and roll between your hands to make it a little more round. Then roll it in the butter onions, followed by the cheese. Lay that down in the bottom of your Bundt pan and start doing the same thing with the rest of the dough.

5 When you have one layer of dough balls down, sprinkle about one-third of the remaining cheese and one-third of the remaining butter onions over the top. Then pinch, roll, double-douse and place the remaining balls over top. If you end up with extra cheese or extra butter onions, distribute those on top of the whole monkey.

6 Cover the Bundt pan with a towel and let the dough rise another 15 minutes. Meanwhile, preheat the oven to 350°F.

7 Transfer the Bundt pan to the middle rack of your oven and bake for 30 to 35 minutes, until nicely browned on top. Bring Pinch Me, Frenchie out of the oven and let it sit for 10 to 15 minutes before you even think about turning it out of its pan. The cheese needs to cool and firm up a bit in order for the loaf to hold together.

ATTENTION I don't feel comfortable telling you to use canned buttermilk biscuit dough, but if you chose two 8-ounce containers of such a product from your grocer's refrigeration case, and cut those biscuits into quarters, it would work. But I make homemade dough every time...I swear.

Sloppy Joe Shirred Eggs with Spinach

Serves 4

Years ago, eggs baked in marinara sauce rendered me speechless at a restaurant called Bar Pitti in Manhattan's West Village. Ever since, I've been shirring eggs (a more seductive term for baking or broiling whole eggs out of their shell) in all the saucy stuff I have on hand. This version builds on a turkey sloppy joe ragout I make for my kids. I swap out the sugar in standard sloppy joes for carrot and caramelized onion, and nestle each egg on a mound of garlic-forward wilted spinach. A perfect bite of this reminds me of one of my guilty pleasures—a sausage, spinach, and cheese omelet covered in ketchup. The great news is that you can use one pan from start to finish here. That alone should encourage you to make it.

If you want, double the sloppy joe portion of the recipe and serve it between buns with melted sharp cheddar and kraut (page 68) for an adult riff on an American classic.

1 medium carrot, top removed and cut into about 6 pieces

1 (14.5-ounce) can diced tomatoes, or 2 scant cups roughly chopped fresh tomatoes

2 tablespoons extra-virgin olive oil, divided

3 garlic cloves, minced

8 ounces fresh spinach (4 cups packed)

3 teaspoons kosher salt, divided

1 pound ground turkey

2 teaspoons ground cumin

1 teaspoon smoked paprika

½ teaspoon ground black pepper

½ cup R-Rated Onions (page 38)

2 tablespoons red wine vinegar

4 large eggs

Parmigiano Reggiano, for serving (optional)

1 Preheat your oven to 400°F. Combine the carrot, tomatoes plus their juice, and 1 cup water in a blender. Blitz till it's as smooth as your blender allows.

2 In an ovenproof 12-inch sauté pan or skillet set over medium heat, cook 1 tablespoon of the olive oil and the minced garlic. Watch for the garlic to start sizzling, then stir in the spinach and ½ teaspoon of the salt. Continue stirring for a minute, until all the spinach is wilted. Remove it from the pan and set aside.

3 Add the final tablespoon olive oil to the pan, raise the heat to medium, and add the turkey plus 1 teaspoon salt. Using a wooden spoon or spatula, break the turkey up into small morsels as it browns. When you have browned turkey, add the cumin, paprika, and black pepper. Stir to incorporate, toasting the spices for about 30 seconds.

4 Add the carrot-tomato mixture, the R-Rated Onions, vinegar, and ½ teaspoon salt. Let this cook for about 15 minutes, uncovered, stirring occasionally. You may need to lower the heat to prevent Joe from sticking or splattering. When the ragout is done it will be thick and juicy. If it seems too dry, stir in a little water. Taste the ragout for seasoning and adjust as you like.

5 Turn the heat off and make four indentions in the ragout. Divide the spinach and put equal amounts in each indentation. Top each section of spinach with a cracked egg. Sprinkle the eggs with the remaining 1 teaspoon salt.

6 Slide the skillet onto the middle rack of your preheated oven. Bake for 10 to 12 minutes, until the whites are set and the yolks are slightly runny.

7 To serve, scatter ribbons of Parmigiano Reggiano or another hard cheese over the top. If bread is your thing, this is great with toast.

PEOPLE PLEASER

I'm the youngest of four girls. By the youngest, I mean I'm nine years younger than the sister closest to my age. I was an accident—an accident of such great scale that my mom called for a family vote to determine whether or not I would be born.

Leraine, who was fifteen at the time, voted "yes" to me. She loved to cook, wanted to be a farmer like my dad, and had a hankering to play mommy. The first born, Leraine was supposed to be a boy. Currie, who was thirteen at the time, had her sights set on boarding school. She voted "no" to the addition of a needy, squirming bundle of baby and warned it would mean dividing the inheritance four ways instead of three. Named after my dad's dad, her birth certificate reads Tharon Currin Howard. She is classic "middle child with a devastating boy name." At nine, Johna enjoyed being the baby and thought she would always inhabit that role. Named after my dad (John plus an "a"), Johna voted "no" for obvious reasons. Her name probably gives it away, but Johna was supposed to be a boy, too. Since the tally was two to one, dad held tremendous power. He could tie the vote or render me a stop on the Howard family story tour. Dad voted "yes." You can probably guess why.

After the vote and the fortuitous decision to choose me, my family's church, Bethel Baptist, went straight to praying. Mom's concern around pregnancy wasn't selfish. At thirty-eight years old in the 1970s, hers would have been a high-risk pregnancy no matter what. But she had been sick with rheumatoid arthritis for years, and a cocktail of high-powered medications made her life bearable. Tempting fate with a new baby seemed risky, so Bethel Baptist prayed. They prayed Mom would go into remission. They prayed I'd be born alive. They prayed I'd have all my parts and nothing extra. Dad prayed I'd arrive with a penis.

I was born on March 8, 1978. I was not a boy, but I appeared to be normal and that was a relief. Maybe I had absorbed the mixed sentiments around my birth in utero or maybe I learned them out in the open air, but for as long as I can remember, the drive to please the people around me has watered the root of much that I do.

From the start, I had some work to do. After all the prayers and the worrying, I should have at least come out blazing with an emergency C-section or a water-break at the grocery store. But no. It was all normal. And with no one other than Leraine turning cartwheels over the idea of a new female Howard, I took early measures to make sure everybody was glad I showed up.

As a toddler I dressed up like Nicky from *The Young and the Restless* and stripped for tips like she did. My family clapped and howled with pleasure as I slung my tiara across the living room energized by their delight. When in third grade I realized the little stories I wrote brought my teacher and then my parents joy, I wrote more stories and dropped them around the house in hopes that an irritable sister or a fatigued parent might find them and find pleasure in my creativity. I won the citizenship award in elementary school and the service award in junior high. I was the teacher's pet and everybody's friend. Eventually stripping for laughs morphed into kind-of-good comedic dancing, and in boarding school I performed regularly during morning chapel to get people pumped for the day. I was an entertaining, joke-dropping, good listener who based my worth on other people's smiles. I still am.

But in the last few years I've learned a lot about myself. With the small dose of celebrity brought on by *A Chef's Life,* people started to look to me to make them feel a certain way. I no longer just moved through the world guided by my own desire to please. Now people actively sought me out to *be* pleased. Fans made pilgrimages from all over to eat at Chef and the Farmer with the hope I would stop by their table. When I did and they squealed and sometimes even cried, my heart ached for all the people who made the same trip with the same hope but didn't get that moment. People with cancer, young children with dreams to be "just like me," and viewers who swore the sound of my voice put them at ease sought me out like balm for a wound. The pressure and responsibility of all that, and the reality that I wasn't able to give everybody what they wanted, was too much.

My DNA code reads "please people, seek their approval...and when you can't, avoid them." So when I couldn't please everybody that's what I did. I hid. I stopped interacting with guests. The thought of being in the dining room during service gave me a stomachache. I even recharted the drive home from my office so I wouldn't have to drive past Chef and the Farmer and see how many people I would disappoint on any given night. The cycle of needing to disengage and the guilt that followed was nasty. I felt empty, unworthy, and really freaking lonely.

As it turns out a break was necessary. I had offered up little pieces of myself to people for too long. I worried if I didn't touch everybody, give them the experience they had hoped for, it would all go

"My DNA code reads 'please people, seek their approval...and when you can't, avoid them.'"

away because that's where I saw my worth. But at the end of it I wondered who I was and where I had gone. My hunger to please had starved me.

Now, at the age of forty-two, I finally understand that my love of both cooking and writing are paths that allow me to give people pleasure without wearing myself out. Neither craft requires me to strap on my show-pony saddle to gain approval or smiles. They are both solitary, meditative, therapeutic practices that don't deplete while I do the thing my DNA tells me to do. It's a complicated thing to be born with something to prove, but I'm finally grateful I get to prove I can make people smile.

People Pleaser Party Dip

Makes 2 cups

We've done a lot of special events upstairs at Chef and the Farmer, and for years I fought that reality hard, calling upstairs parties the bane of my existence. Parties were a big burden on top of an already hectic nightly service, and I was annoyed by the distraction events caused our cooks. But we did the numbers and learned that upstairs parties were absolutely necessary for a profitable bottom line. I stopped resisting and started pushing to make them work for the kitchen as well as the balance sheet.

This dip, made with the deeply caramelized onions we always have on hand, was one of the pieces that made upstairs parties less of a headache and more a spoke in the wheel that makes the restaurant go 'round. It's inspired by the dip made with that French onion seasoning packet many of us grew up eating, but it's lighter and somehow more addictive with the addition of a bit of balsamic vinegar and Worcestershire. Creamy, cool, and simple, it's better the next day—which is a plus whether you're planning a party at home or because it's your job.

⅔ cup <u>R-Rated Onions</u> (page 38)

3 garlic cloves, grated on a Microplane

2 tablespoons good balsamic vinegar

1 teaspoon Worcestershire sauce

4 ounces (half an 8-ounce package) cream cheese, at room temperature

½ cup sour cream

½ cup mayonnaise

1 teaspoon kosher salt

1 teaspoon hot sauce

Chopped fresh chives, for garnish

Potato chips, for dipping

❶ In a small saucepan or skillet, cook the R-Rated Onions, garlic, vinegar, and Worcestershire for a few minutes over medium heat until the onions have absorbed the liquid and the pan is nearly dry.

❷ Meanwhile, in a mixer fitted with the paddle attachment, combine the cream cheese, sour cream, mayo, salt, and hot sauce. Paddle on medium until you have a homogeneous, lump-free mixture.

❸ Once the onions have cooled slightly, add them and any residual liquid from the pan to the mixer. Paddle that for about a minute so the flavors get acquainted. Transfer to a serving vessel and chill a minimum of 30 minutes, but preferably overnight, before serving. Crown with chopped chives and serve with your favorite potato chip.

Tomato "Pie" for Dough Dummies

Makes 6 individual "pies"

I'm a little bit famous for my tomato pie, and with its luxurious but tart basil-scented filling, I kind of understand why. What's not to love? I'll tell you what...the act of making, rolling out, and blind-baking a pie crust. I've addressed that here by flipping the pie on its head and using a slice of tomato as a "crust."

This shortcut to the satisfying combination of tomato, cheese, and pornographic onions bound by mayonnaise and heat takes the dough trouble out of the pie and swaps it for crumbled buttery crackers. As many of us already know, Ritz crackers are a fast track to happy.

6   (1- to 1½-inch-thick) slices of tomato

2   teaspoons unsalted butter

3   cloves garlic, grated on a Microplane

4   ounces fresh spinach (about 2 cups packed)

1¾   teaspoons kosher salt, divided

¼   teaspoon red pepper flakes

½   cup R-Rated Onions (page 38)

⅓   cup mayonnaise

⅓   cup shredded Fontina

⅓   cup grated Parmigiano Reggiano (use a Microplane)

20 to 25 fresh basil leaves (about ⅔ cup packed)

½   teaspoon ground black pepper

14   Ritz-style crackers, roughly crushed

❶ Preheat your oven to 350°F. Lay the tomato slices on a baking sheet, leaving about an inch of space between them.

❷ In a 10-inch skillet, melt the butter with the grated garlic over medium-low heat. Add the spinach and season with ¼ teaspoon of the salt and the pepper flakes. Wilt the spinach and stir in the R-Rated Onions. Remove from heat.

❸ In a medium bowl, stir together the mayo, Fontina, Parm, ½ teaspoon salt, and the basil leaves. Add the spinach-onion mixture and combine thoroughly.

❹ Just before you're ready to bake, season the tomatoes with the remaining 1 teaspoon salt and the black pepper. Then fold the crushed Ritz into the spinach onion topping. Divide the mixture among the six tomato slices, giving each thick slice a creamy, crunchy, punchy crown.

❺ Slide the baking sheet onto the lower rack of your oven and bake for 10 minutes. Move the baking sheet up to the middle rack and bake for an additional 15 minutes. The topping should be browned and your kitchen should smell like a pizza parlor. Serve as soon as you can.

Cheaters Only BBQ Pork

Serves 4 to 6

I come from Eastern North Carolina, the world's epicenter for pork barbecue (not up for debate 'cause this is my book). Still, I've never cooked a whole hog at home and I frown at the prospect of fiddling with the temperature of a grill for long periods of time just to achieve the perfect piece of smoked butt. That kind of thing is really for barbecue enthusiasts and I consider myself more of a connoisseur of other people's efforts. So when I want the flavor of smoke, vinegar, and pig, I turn to the oven and my bag of tricks.

Smoked paprika, cayenne, time, vinegar, and a coating of caramelized onions lend this roast a lot of the qualities you'll find in legit ENC-style BBQ. The onions themselves go from sweet and deep to charred and earthy and are what sets this apart from just another slow-roasted pork butt. As with true barbecue, the sum is far greater than its parts.

1 (3- to 4-pound) bone-in pork picnic or Boston butt

1½ tablespoons kosher salt

1½ tablespoons smoked paprika

1 tablespoon cayenne

1 tablespoon ground black pepper

½ cup R-Rated Onions (page 38)

½ cup apple cider vinegar

❶ Preheat your oven to 350°F. Rinse and dry the pork butt with paper towels. Season all sides with the salt, paprika, cayenne, and black pepper. Then, as if the pork is your face and the R-Rated Onions are a mud mask, slather all sides of the pork roast with an even layer of the onions.

❷ Carefully place the pork butt, fat cap facing up, in a Dutch oven just large enough to hold it. Pour the cider vinegar around it, taking care not to wash off the onions. Cover with a tight fitting lid or a double layer of foil. Slide the pot onto the middle rack of your oven and bake.

❸ After 3 hours, remove the lid and roast another 30 minutes uncovered. The onions on top will crisp up, even char a bit, and that's what you want. The bitterness that comes with the char will balance the sweetness of the onions and give the impression of burnt ends in proper barbecue.

❹ Allow the pork to rest for about 15 minutes, then skim some of the rendered fat off the vinegary juice that has pooled at the bottom of the pan. Roughly chop, pull, or slice the falling-apart-tender roast and toss it around with the vinegar sauce. Serve warm in tacos, on a sandwich, or with something crunchy and bright in the spirit of slaw.

Here's to Eggplant

Serves 4

I often wish tomatoes were as prolific as eggplant, but I often wish my legs were long and my butt were smaller, so here's to purple vegetables everywhere!

Really my favorite way to prepare eggplant is grilled. Something about the dry, harsh direct heat of the grill uncovers an almost meaty quality in an otherwise subtle vegetable. But even with the aid of smoke and char, eggplant needs to be coaxed into stardom with assertive flavors. Lemon, sweet onions, and briny olives do that, and feta, a cheese with fat, acid, funk and a generous dose of salt, marries them all into a broken vinaigrette that makes sense.

If you can't get behind eggplant, and I know some of you can't, try this vinaigrette tossed with other grilled vegetables or leftover chicken. Or think of it as sauce and spoon it on grilled fish, lamb, or beef.

¼ cup R-Rated Onions (page 38)

½ cup crumbled feta plus 1 tablespoon feta brine, if you've got it

½ cup pitted kalamata or picholine olives, quartered, plus 1 tablespoon olive brine

2 teaspoons fresh thyme leaves (or 1 teaspoon dried thyme)

2 teaspoons fresh oregano leaves (or 1 teaspoon dried oregano)

Grated zest and juice of 3 lemons (about ¼ cup juice)

2 tablespoons red wine vinegar

2 to 3 garlic cloves, grated on a Microplane

1½ teaspoons kosher salt, divided

½ teaspoon ground black pepper

½ cup plus 2 tablespoons nice extra-virgin olive oil, divided

2 medium globe eggplants

½ teaspoon red pepper flakes

1 Roughly chop the R-Rated Onions and transfer to a medium bowl. Add the feta and its brine, the olives and their brine, the thyme, oregano, lemon zest and juice, vinegar, garlic, ½ teaspoon of the salt, and the black pepper. Agitate the mixture with a whisk or a fork like it really matters, 'cause it does. Then whisk in ½ cup of the olive oil. Set the vinaigrette aside to mellow while you grill the eggplant.

2 Halve the eggplant lengthwise, then cut each half into 6 wedges. Preheat your grill or grill pan till it's screaming hot. Toss the eggplant with the remaining 2 tablespoons olive oil, but resist seasoning them with salt at this point. *Resist seasoning them with salt at this point.* Using tongs, position the eggplant on the grill so each piece has a little room to breathe. We want them to char, not steam, and they need room to do that. Cook the eggplant, resisting the urge to move them even a hair, for about 3 minutes on the first side. Flip, revealing what are hopefully impressive grill marks on the first side, and again force yourself to leave the second side where it lands for another 2 to 3 minutes.

3 Pluck the eggplant from the grill and transfer to a rack to cool. Not everyone has a cooling rack and that's not a deal breaker. Just make sure you don't pile your hot eggplant slices on top of each other or they will continue cooking and you'll end up with mushy, soggy eggplant. Season them on all sides while still hot with the remaining 1 teaspoon salt and the pepper flakes.

4 Divide the vinaigrette among four plates. Position the eggplant on top of the vinaigrette. This step is important because tossing the eggplant with the vinaigrette muddies the grilled nuance and texture you've gone to lots of trouble to preserve, so why ruin it now?

Steaks Dripping in Blue Cheese-Onion Butter

Serves 4, with more compound butter than you'll need... depending on your butter tolerance

I admit it. I love steak. I know a lot of people do, but my desire for big slabs of red meat is not a longing I share freely, the way I might tout my affection for beets nowadays. But if you're with me in this steak affinity, even if it's only because you're "anemic" or "depleted," you'll be hard-pressed to find an easier, more satisfying way to enjoy a lean cut of beef than what I'm suggesting here. If filet mignon is not on your shopping list, choose a different cut without a lot of fat. Hanger steak or strip steak, yes. Rib eye or chuck steak, probably not.

Compound butter on its own is a marvelous way to encapsulate flavor till you're ready to fat-drench a dish with it. I hope you'll come up with your own combinations, but keep in mind that, for me at least, it's not about the butter. The butter is the glue that turns the flavorful components you choose into an easy-to-apply sauce. And this compound butter, with its blue cheese funk and fat, its sweet deep onions, and its measured tang of sherry vinegar, demonstrates that better than any formula I can conjure.

BLUE CHEESE-ONION COMPOUND BUTTER

- ½ cup R-Rated Onions (page 38)
- 2 tablespoons sherry vinegar
- ¼ cup (½ stick) unsalted butter, at room temperature
- ½ cup ripe, moist, funky blue cheese like Stilton, Gorgonzola, or Maytag
- ½ teaspoon kosher salt
- 1 teaspoon coarsely ground black pepper

STEAKS

- 4 (6- to 8-ounce) beef tenderloin steaks, often called filet mignon
- 2 teaspoons kosher salt
- 1 tablespoon vegetable oil

1 **Make the Butter:** In a medium bowl, or ideally in a mixer fitted with the paddle attachment, combine the R-Rated Onions with the sherry vinegar and stir to make a homogenous mixture. (Adding the vinegar first will help the butter accept the vinegar.) Add the room temperature butter, blue cheese, salt, and black pepper and stir or paddle till it all comes together.

2 Lay out a 14 x 14-inch piece of parchment paper or aluminum foil and use a spatula to transfer the compound butter to the center of the sheet. Roll up the bottom of the paper and use your hands to spread the butter and form a round log about 2 inches thick. Twist the ends like a Tootsie Roll wrapper, and fold them under the log or tie them off with string or rubber bands. Put the butter in the fridge to firm up. You'll need four 1-inch-thick slices of the log for the steaks. Store the rest in the freezer for steaks and baked potatoes of your future. It will keep for 6 months just like that.

3 **Cook the Steaks:** Bring the steaks out of the fridge 30 minutes before you're ready to cook them and season them all over with the salt. Preheat your oven to 400°F.

4 Heat a 12-inch heavy-bottomed, ovenproof skillet over medium-high heat and add the vegetable oil. When it is a hair from smoking, add the steaks, lower the heat a smidge, and sear those suckers on one side for about 3 minutes.

5 Flip the steaks and slide the skillet onto the middle rack of your oven. Let them roast for about 8 minutes for medium rare (120°F on an instant-read thermometer). Pull the skillet out of the oven, place over medium heat, and roll the sides of the filets around in the pan briefly so they brown a bit.

6 Transfer the steaks to the plates you're going to eat them on to rest and plop the pats of butter on top. As they rest, the butter will melt a bit, basting the beef. Feel free to use that hot skillet with all those browned beefy bits on the bottom to quickly pan-roast some asparagus to accompany your steaks.

Make It Today, Slurp It Tomorrow Vegetable Soup

Serves 4

Even though I purposely omitted a recipe for French onion soup in this book, I do want you to consider using the power of caramelized onions to build the base of a hearty, deeply distinct, quick-to-make vegetable soup on the fly. No stock or bouillon required. Instead I use Parmigiano Reggiano rinds, saved from many a night of grating cheese, and caramelized mushrooms to balance the sweet, rich notes of the onions. The umami funk of the cheese rind and the earthy backbone offered up by the mushrooms will make you think there's meat hiding somewhere in your bowl. It's a trick used by vegetarians for years, and it works.

Use any vegetable or legume you like to give the soup heft. I particularly enjoy a mix of spicy greens like mustard, turnip, or arugula with tomatoes and lentils for a balanced bowl of satisfaction. I know people always say this or that is better the next day, but this soup really improves through the cooling and reheating process, so don't hate on it if you choose to ignore its name.

ATTENTION

Never throw away the rind from a hard cheese like Parmigiano Reggiano, Pecorino Romano, or aged Gouda again! Aside from the fact you've already paid for it, when simmered in a liquid for at least 30 minutes, the rind from hard cheese builds flavor and provides backbone to a broth or sauce that might otherwise taste wimpy. Just store the rinds in a plastic bag in your freezer until you need to add oomph to something simmered. Then pluck the rind out once the dish is done.

8 ounces (2½ cups) thinly sliced button or cremini mushrooms

1 tablespoon extra-virgin olive oil or unsalted butter

2 teaspoons kosher salt, divided

6 cloves garlic, sliced

1 teaspoon ground black pepper

½ cup R-Rated Onions (page 38)

2 x 4-inch piece Parmigiano Reggiano or other hard salty cheese rind

1 cup fresh or canned diced tomatoes

4 cups packed greens of your choice

1½ cups cooked beans or legumes (page 181)

Additional Parm for grating on top

Chopped fresh herbs (like rosemary, thyme, or sage), for serving (optional)

Croutons, for serving (optional but highly recommended)

1 In a 4- to 6-quart Dutch oven over medium-high heat, brown the mushrooms in the olive oil or butter. Once they are nicely caramelized, add ½ teaspoon of the salt and stir. Add the garlic and black pepper and cook until you begin to smell both. Stir in the R-Rated Onions, cheese rind, tomatoes, remaining 1½ teaspoons salt, and 8 cups water.

2 Put a lid on it and bring the broth to a boil. Lower the heat and cook, still covered, at a strong simmer for 30 minutes. At this point, add your greens, beans, wings (just kidding), or whatever you choose to make the soup suit your tastes. Just before serving, fish out the cheese rind and throw in chopped herbs for dimension and aroma. Then please feel free to top each bowl with croutons and grated cheese for additional pleasure...or combine those ideas and grab a fistful of Cheez-Its or your favorite snack cracker.

ATTENTION While you could leave them out of this recipe, the garlic bread crumbs are a great way to add texture to lots of simple pasta or bean dishes. I make a bit more than I need and keep them on hand, sealed in a container, for up to a week, for use on the fly. You should too.

Anchovy Gateway Spaghetti

Serves 4

Some people slam on the brakes when they hear a recipe has anchovies in it, and that bothers the bejesus out of me. Anchovies bring a singular saltiness to dishes—they're not a fishy fish I'm asking you to slurp whole. If you consider all the things we love that build on a foundation of that tiny fish, like Worcestershire sauce and Caesar dressing, maybe we change the anchovy narrative in this flounder-fillet-loving country.

This spaghetti is an easy drive into Anchovyland because the briny notes of the fish are set against the sweet silkiness of R-Rated Onions. It's yin and yang spaghetti-style. I promise.

GARLIC BREAD CRUMBS

- 2 tablespoons extra-virgin olive oil
- 3 cloves garlic, finely chopped
- ½ cup panko bread crumbs
- ¼ teaspoon kosher salt

ANCHOVY PASTA

- 10 ounces dried spaghetti
- 4 anchovy fillets packed in oil, or 1 tablespoon anchovy paste
- ½ cup R-Rated Onions (page 38)
- 3 tablespoons unsalted butter, divided

- 1 tablespoon extra-virgin olive oil
- ¼ teaspoon red pepper flakes
- ⅔ cup grated Parmigiano Reggiano (use a Microplane)
- 2 tablespoons fresh lemon juice
- ½ teaspoon finely chopped fresh rosemary

Kosher salt to finish (optional, depending on the saltiness of your pasta water and how much pasta water you end up using)

1 Toast the Bread Crumbs: In a 10- to 12-inch skillet, heat the olive oil and garlic gently until the garlic starts to sizzle. Add the bread crumbs and salt and toast, stirring frequently for a few minutes. Once the bread crumbs are brown and crisp, transfer them to a paper towel–lined plate to cool.

2 Make the Pasta: It's very important to have all your ingredients prepped and ready when you gear up to put this pasta together, because if you don't move fast and the spaghetti sits in the half-finished sauce while you grate cheese or squeeze lemons, it will dry up and turn into sludge. So be ready.

3 Boil the spaghetti in plenty of salted water until it's cooked but still toothsome. Trust that the spaghetti will continue to soften as you incorporate it with the sauce, so drain the noodles just before their texture is to your liking. But before you drain it, dip a mug in and draw out about 1½ cups of the pasta cooking water. Set the noodles and the starch-filled water next to your range so they are easy to reach.

4 Finely chop the anchovies if you're using fillets and run your knife through your R-Rated Onions just to make them a little smaller and more sauce friendly. When you have all your ingredients prepped and within arm's reach, combine the chopped anchovies, onions, 1 tablespoon of the butter, the olive oil, and pepper flakes in a 12-inch skillet over medium heat. Cook until the anchovies sort of dissolve in the fat and all the ingredients come together as one.

5 Add the cooked spaghetti, about ⅔ cup pasta water, and about ½ cup of the grated cheese. Using tongs, work everything together allowing the water to cook out and creating a silky sheen on the spaghetti. To finish, add the remaining 2 tablespoons butter, the lemon juice, remaining cheese, and rosemary. If you need to add additional pasta water to make things creamy again, by all means go for it. Taste and add a little salt if you need it.

6 Serve immediately smattered with the garlic bread crumbs.

Once-a-Week Roasted Chicken with Sweet Onion Cauliflower Puree

Serves 4

I'm not sure how we got here, but a lot of us would no more roast a whole chicken than barbecue a whole pig. I have some theories behind our collective fear of cooking an entire bird. Mostly I think chefs and TV cooks have made too big a deal of the process—brining, trussing, stuffing, and larding little birds beyond the point of weeknight do-ability. I also believe too many mouthfuls of dry turkey taint our belief we can successfully and easily roast a whole bird.

But roasting a chicken in the oven is one of the most effortless means to get dinner on the table. And when that chicken roasts on top of something like cauliflower steaks, basting the white florets in a comforting warm poultry bath, you have an entire supper in a single skillet. I blend the cauliflower with milk and mount it with R-Rated Onions to create the comforting illusion of gravy with the healthful qualities of cauliflower. Yes, I know I'm sneaky. It's one of my finest qualities.

1	(3- to 4-pound) whole chicken
1	head cauliflower
2	tablespoons extra-virgin olive oil
2½	teaspoons kosher salt, divided
1	teaspoon ground black pepper
1	lemon, halved
1	cup milk, plus up to a cup more as necessary
½	cup R-Rated Onions (page 38)
2	tablespoons unsalted butter

❶ If time allows, bring your chicken to room temperature for 30 minutes to 1 hour before you cook. Preheat your oven to 475°F.

❷ Slice the cauliflower into 2-inch-thick "steaks" and nestle them in a single layer in an ovenproof 12-inch skillet. Drizzle the olive oil over the cauliflower steaks. Season the chicken inside and out with 1½ teaspoons of the salt and the black pepper. Stuff the halved lemon into its cavity and set the bird on top of the cauliflower.

❸ Slide the skillet onto the middle rack of your preheated oven and roast for 50 minutes. If your chicken is larger than 3½ pounds, roast it 5 minutes more per each additional half pound. You're looking for an internal temp, taken between the joint of the thigh and breast, of 165°F.

❹ Take the skillet out of the oven, set the chicken on a platter to rest, and pluck the lemon halves from its cavity. Squeeze the juice from the lemon into a blender and add the cauliflower, any collected juices from the skillet, and the milk. Blend until totally smooth. Your puree should be the consistency of loose mashed potatoes, so you may need additional milk depending on how big your head of cauliflower was.

❺ Add the onions to the skillet and stir them around over medium heat, loosening any bits of chicken-ness stuck to the bottom of the pan. Add the cauliflower puree, the remaining 1 teaspoon salt, and the butter. Heat through and serve alongside the chicken.

CHAPTER THREE

Can-Do Kraut

Salty • Funky • Crunchy • Bright • Bracing

I'm well aware

that a lot of you don't look at kraut and see yourselves in it. You don't know how to use it and the thought of making it lies far beyond what you see as the borders of possibility. You think of it as fringe food. Funky, mystical, and only an apt companion for a hot dog or corned beef, it's not an item you deem essential in your kitchen. But I'm here today on this page to tell you that you are wrong. You can make it. You can cook with it. You can and should eat it. Kraut can change your life.

Blindly believe me when I say that sauerkraut is the most misunderstood, vastly undervalued ingredient you're missing when you make dinner. Its bright, probiotic, clean crunch will make rich things more craveable and light things more exciting. If you're not using it to your advantage on a regular, you're missing out. Big time.

Please don't perceive my kraut diatribe as cheffy judgment from above. Not that long ago, I was one of you. I saw bags and jars of translucent white kraut in the deli meat section of the supermarket and wondered who spent money on that stuff. I thought it was stinky, processed weirdness meant for someone other than me. If I wanted something crunchy and hard to identify, I'd call on pickle relish. If I wanted a proper hot dog dressed in all the condiments, I'd go to a hot dog shop.

Then, as luck would have it, professional kitchen trends forced me to look closer at the ancient art of fermentation and I fell in love with the transformative qualities of kraut and the oddly easy process of making it.

In its simplest form, kraut is fermented cabbage. Like country ham, kimchi, and pickles of all kinds, the tradition of kraut grew out of a need to preserve food before there was refrigeration. Today we eat it because it adds a distinct dimension to our plates. I'm crazy for its crisp texture, its thirst-quenching bite, and its ability to taste at once neutral and earthy.

The other thing about kraut is that it's flush with probiotics that are good for your gut and your immune system. If I feel a cold encroaching, I eat fistfuls of kraut in lieu of drinking sugar-packed cups of orange juice. When I have my daily afternoon slump, if there's kraut nearby I choose it over coffee, 'cause kraut doesn't keep me up at night. Just call me Popeye and kraut my spinach.

By now, after I've spent so long extolling its virtues, you'd have to be dense or think I'm insane not to want the magical fairy that is kraut in your kitchen. Still, you may be on the fence about making it yourself. You may think you can buy it at the grocery store or the farmers' market to the same effect, and to some degree you can. It's just that the quality of store-bought kraut runs the gamut between great and awful, so your ability to make these recipes the best they can be with kraut you bought is a crapshoot. If that's not enough, here are four reasons to make kraut magic yourself:

1. It takes about 20 minutes of actual work for a slow kitchen prepper to turn one cabbage and one cucumber into a half gallon of kraut.

2. Kraut from the grocery store or farmers' market is expensive, but a half gallon of kraut you make yourself costs about $4.

3. Contrary to popular belief, you don't need special equipment to wield kraut magic. A knife, a clean nonreactive container, a dish towel, and a rudimentary weight is all that's required...plus about a week of inactive wait time.

4. To ferment something in your home kitchen is to give yourself unprecedented pride and confidence in your domestic abilities. ➜

Can-Do Kraut

- People make kraut with all sorts of sturdy things like radishes, green tomatoes, apples, and beets. And I'm a fan. I'm also a fan of adding chiles, herbs like dill and mint, or spices like coriander and celery seed. But for the purposes of my everyday kitchen, I keep my kraut basic, using only cabbage and cucumber, so I can make decisions about flavor on the fly. We all know you can add ingredients later, but once that dill is in there you can't take it away.

- Fermentation takes time. The prep here is only about 20 minutes, but for the cabbage and cucumber to transform into kraut, it'll take at least a week.

- I recommend pickling salt because it produces a clear pristine brine while kosher and table salts have a tendency to make the liquid surrounding your kraut cloudy. But if pickling salt is elusive to you, and kosher's all you've got, go with it. It'll taste just as good. I don't get down with table salt ever, so I can't really recommend it.

- Heating kraut kills the probiotic qualities we worship it for, so whenever possible, eat it cold or at room temperature. Or eat a handful of it that way while you bake the rest with macaroni and beef.

- Once fermented, kraut will keep in your fridge for 6 months and possibly even longer, but if you haven't eaten it over the course of a half-year you should probably offer its space up to something else.

1 head green cabbage
1 English cucumber
4 teaspoons pickling or kosher salt

1 Using a knife or the shredding attachment of your food processor, slice the cabbage and cucumber as thin as you can manage. Thicker slices will work too but they will take more massaging and more time to ferment. Don't peel the cucumber and don't remove the seeds. Feel free to remove the core from the cabbage but take care to use its outer leaves as the dark green color will make pretty kraut.

2 Transfer the vegetables to a large bowl and add the salt. Now put your back into it and rub the cabbage, cucumber, and salt together with a deep-tissue massage in mind. Once the vegetables are sufficiently bruised and about two-thirds of their original volume, let them hang out for about 15 minutes. They should deepen slightly in color and start to weep.

3 Meanwhile, fetch and clean a glass, ceramic, or hard plastic container to house your kraut. Mason jars work well because of their shape, lack of exposed surface area, and handy lids, but just about any solid, deepish vessel will do. You'll also need a weight, as well as something to cover your kraut with that will allow it to breath as it ferments. Weights need only to be clean and heavy enough to push the solids below the liquid as the kraut ferments. I've used plates, small jars filled with water, and actual glass weights purchased from the interwebs to great effect. As for the cover, you can secure a clean dish towel or piece of cheesecloth

MAKES 2 QUARTS OR ½ GALLON

around the rim of your container with a rubber band. But if you want to make your kitchen a kraut factory, I recommend the silicone lids with air-escape nipples designed to make you a fermentation boss.

4 Once you have your soldiers in place and the cabbage-cucumber mixture is starting to get juicy, cram everything into your vessel. When I say cram, I really mean it. Force more kraut inside than you thought possible. You can use a pestle, the back of a wooden spoon, or the handle of a rolling pin to do so. This recipe looks like it makes a ton, but with proper cramming it should fit into two 1-quart jars or one ½-gallon container.

5 Once all the vegetables are snug inside, pour any lingering liquid overtop, weigh it all down to keep the cabbage submerged under the liquid, and cover with your towel, cheesecloth, or breathable nipple lid. I've used a number of things to ensure my kraut stays submerged in the brine. Actual paper weights work great. Plates with something heavy-ish on top work too, if the vessel is wide enough. Or use a small jar filled with a salt solution that is 1 cup filtered water to 1 teaspoon salt. (In case the jar leaks, you don't want it to dilute your kraut brine.)

6 Put your magical fairy in waiting somewhere that's roughly 70 degrees and out of direct sunlight, but not out of your line of sight. It's important you keep an eye on it as it ferments. First, you will enjoy watching the process. Second, the transformation will produce a brine, and that brine may overflow its vessel as science takes hold and bubbles ensue. This is not a big deal. Just wipe it up and move on, making sure that after about 24 hours, the kraut is always submerged in its brine. If for some reason your kraut doesn't produce enough brine to be submerged, use the same ratio suggested above of salt to filtered water, and pour that over the dry kraut to submerge.

7 Over the course of the fermentation process you may see a film develop on top. Just skim it off and move on. You may smell something a little funky. That's normal. All these phenomena are parts of the fermentation process, so don't fret. After about a week, start tasting your kraut. If you like the way it tastes, it's ready to eat. After 2 weeks, this magical fairy has likely done all it will do and you should put a real lid on it and transfer it to your fridge, where it will keep for close to forever.

1 eat by the forkful

2 pile on a hot dog, hamburger, or sandwich

3 use the brine in place of vinegar or citrus

4 stir into egg, potato, tuna, or chicken salad

5 mix with corn and tomatoes for a quick relish

6 make quick snack crackers with summer sausage and mustard

7 toss into a cabbage or carrot slaw

8 blend into soups that taste flat

9 munch on as a hangover cure

10 dollop on top of hard-boiled eggs

11 serve with grilled meats as condiment and contrast

12 use in a dirty martini instead of olive juice

Picklesicles

makes as many as you want

On any given Saturday between 1985 and 1988, adolescent Vivian was on roller skates at the Galaxy of Sports in Kinston, North Carolina. Sweat teemed on her upper lip, Michael Jackson's *Thriller* pumped through the speakers, and she licked a picklesicle as she skated through the neon strobe lights that streaked the social hub of tweens in Lenoir County.

The Galaxy, as it was ironically called, was a frugal establishment that took to freezing the left-over brine from the giant, other-worldly dill pickles that sat next to the cash register in the roller rink's snack bar. They opened every Saturday with just a few picklesicles for the taking, and I reserved mine for 90 cents before I ever laced up a skate.

Today I re-create the experience, minus the skates and Michael Jackson, for my own kids using the leftover brine from homemade kraut. Hear me when I say that a picklesicle is just about the most thirst-quenching thing you can imagine on a hot summer day. It may sound like a gimmick driven by nostalgia and silliness, but there's actual science that says kraut juice is the sugar-free, probiotic-rich answer to Gatorade.

Brine from Can-Do Kraut (page 68), or any pickle brine

① Just like at the Galaxy, kraut juice at my house is in limited supply. As I work through a jar of kraut, I take shots of its brine or stir it last minute into dishes that need a little pick-me-up, so there's never quite enough at the bottom of the jar to go around.

② So if you want to make picklesicles, plan ahead and ladle enough brine off the top for a couple treats before you get to the business of using your kraut. Fortunately though, because it's tart and salty, a little goes a long way. I use small silicone ring-pop molds, but you could just as easily rely on an ice-cube tray fitted with wooden popsicle sticks or sturdy paper straws. Just pour the brine in and freeze it.

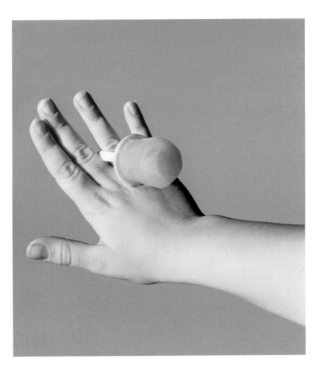

Breakfast of Compromisers

serves 2 (or 1, depending on the person)

Breakfast is a tough one for me. It's the meal that sets the tone for the day so I really want to be healthy about it, but if I ate my actual desires I'd have an everything bagel slathered with cream cheese or a cheddar-stuffed biscuit seven days a week. Unfortunately those carb-crazy pleasures leave me with a hangover I didn't properly earn, so I've devised a compromise.

A three-egg omelet stuffed with Swiss cheese, poppy seeds, and kraut strikes a lot of the chords I crave in the morning and never makes me feel like a failure straight out of the gate. Gaining texture and health from the kraut, quirk and whimsy from Mr. Poppy, protein and comfort via the eggs, and satisfaction granted by cheese, this breakfast gives me the morning gumption to move through my day like the clever champion I so deeply desire to be.

3 large eggs	2 to 3 slices Swiss cheese or ⅓ cup shredded
¼ cup milk	½ cup Can-Do Kraut (page 68), drained
½ teaspoon kosher salt	
¼ teaspoon hot sauce	1 tablespoon poppy seeds
1 tablespoon extra-virgin olive oil	

❶ In a small bowl, whisk the eggs, milk, salt, and hot sauce together until you've got a homogenous yellow puddle. Set that aside.

❷ Heat a 10-inch nonstick skillet over medium heat and add the olive oil. Once the oil starts to shimmer the tiniest bit, pour in your egg mixture. Lower the heat and lay or sprinkle the Swiss over one half of the egg bed. Top the cheese with a sheet of kraut and a sprinkle of poppy.

❸ Let the omelet cook undisturbed for about 3 minutes. You'll see the egg start to firm up around the edges while it stays soupy in the middle. Swirl the pan around a bit to force some of that egg soup to the edges.

❹ Once it's firmed up enough that you think you can fold it over on itself, go for it. I like a big spatula for this daunting and sometimes unsuccessful task. Once it's folded over, you'll notice the bottom is brown. This is not a proper French colorless thing. This omelet is American, and a brown bottom is expected.

❺ Let the remaining egg, cheese, and kraut soup seep out around the edges to firm up. After about a minute, slide the giant compromise onto a plate and pursue your day.

Avocado Toast on Its Coronation Day

serves 2

I consider myself a bit of a nonconformist, and for that reason it pains me a little to exalt the many splendors of avocado toast, the dish of the decade. But rule breaker or not, I'm no fool. Avocado toast is freaking good. With austere simplicity swirled around the notion that it's at once decadent and healthy, it's new-world deep on a level only millennials fully understand. I'm not a millennial, but I do love to eat, so I'm here to lift avocado toast to new heights even as her power confounds me.

Kraut brings to avocado toast a texture that complements, even spotlights, the green creamy nature of the world's most sought-after tree fruit. Kraut doles out extra acid and salt that laser-focuses avocado's subtle pleasant flavor. And kraut, with its buzzword-friendly probiotic bacteria, makes avocado toast even more healthy and, if it were possible, even more trendy. All hail avocado toast! She's finally got her crown.

2½ tablespoons extra-virgin olive oil

2 slices substantial bread of your choosing

1 large or 2 small ripe avocados, halved, pitted, and flesh scooped

Juice of ½ lime or lemon

1 teaspoon flaky salt

½ to ⅔ cup Can-Do Kraut (page 68)

A few squirts of hot sauce (optional)

1 In a 10-inch skillet, heat the olive oil over medium heat till it shimmers. Add the bread and toast it till it's nicely browned and crisp on the first side. Flip the bread over and brown the opposite side. You may need a bit more oil to get it just right, but that's ultimately up to you.

2 Transfer your toast to a plate or cutting board and go about preparing the avocado. I like to slice and fan out avocado for my toast. Neatly sliced with all her shades of green on display, avocado is elegant as all queens should be. If I want mashed avocado I make guacamole, but this nuance is also up to you.

3 So, slice and fan out (or whatever) the avocado, then season with the lemon or lime and the flaky salt. Place the avocado on top of your toast and crown it all with kraut. Squirt it with hot sauce, if you like. You can certainly eat this with your hands, but a knife and fork makes the experience a dainty one.

Krautcakes with Fried Apples & Dijon

makes 6 cakes

Sometimes a recipe starts with a dish and sometimes it starts with a name. In this case the name came first and the dish followed. My thought was that if Americans celebrated pancakes made of bland stuff like flour, eggs, and milk while a cornerstone of Japanese comfort food rested on *okonomiyaki,* a pancake made from plain old cabbage, then a name like "krautcake" must suggest something special.

Just like all the other things kraut lends texture, acid, and excitement to, these flat brown pancakes are more than meets the eye. Soft in places, crunchy in others, they act as a foil for other characters, coaxing out the subtle sweetness of fried apples and the sharp edge of Dijon. In short, the cakes, the apples, and the mustard balance and bring out the best in each other. And even though the name came before the dish, my krautcakes deserve a spot in our savory pancake canon.

1 large egg	3 tablespoons unsalted butter, divided
3 tablespoons buttermilk	2 teaspoons minced fresh ginger
¼ cup plus 2 tablespoons all-purpose flour	2 medium crisp apples, cored and sliced (about 2 cups)
½ teaspoon baking powder	2 tablespoons light brown sugar
1½ teaspoons kosher salt, divided	2 tablespoons fresh lemon juice
2 cups Can-Do Kraut (page 68), drained	⅓ cup whole-grain Dijon mustard

① Preheat your oven to 250°F. In a medium bowl, whisk the egg and buttermilk. In another smaller bowl, stir together the flour, baking powder, and 1 teaspoon of the salt. Whisk the dry ingredients into the wet and let that sit for about 10 minutes. Just before cooking your pancakes, stir in the kraut.

② Melt 1 tablespoon of the butter in a 10- to 12-inch skillet over medium heat. Once the butter foams and sizzles a bit, spoon about three ¼-cup mounds of pancake batter over the bottom of the skillet to form your krautcakes. Cook them on the first side for about 3 minutes, until they are nicely browned. Then flip them and cook on the opposite side another 3 minutes. Transfer the cooked pancakes to the warm oven while you cook the remaining batter in another tablespoon butter. Once all the krautcakes are nestled in the oven, go about frying the apples.

③ Wipe out your skillet and add the remaining 1 tablespoon butter and the ginger. Let that melt, sizzle, and pop over medium heat for just a bit, then throw in the apples and add the sugar and remaining ½ teaspoon salt. Cook, shaking the pan occasionally, for about 3 minutes, until the sugar and butter form a glaze on the apples. Stir in the lemon juice and you're done.

④ To eat, spread Dijon over the top of each cake. Spoon some apples on top of that and dig in.

Chicken Dinner for Pregnant People

Serves 4

Being pregnant was the most bizarre experience of my life. I was carrying twins, so perhaps my experience was heightened, but as a pregnant person I was at once tortured and empowered.

Tortured because I was constantly hungry, yet the thought of food and every food-related smell made me want to vomit. I craved baked potatoes, chicken sandwiches with extra pickles from Chick-fil-A, and milkshakes from Hardee's—and that's all.

I felt empowered like a waddling dictator, because about 3 months in I realized pregnant people and their desires carry real weight. For the first time in my life I ordered my husband around with entitled authority. I used the word "fetch" sans apology and my pointer finger became my most important appendage.

This recipe of kraut stewed in the juice of roasting chicken served over baked potatoes is what dinner looked like in my house during that time. It's an oddly delicious memory, and one I often re-create—without the dictatorial dynamics, of course.

1	(3- to 4-pound) whole chicken, spatchcocked (see instructions on page 195)	Small bunch fresh rosemary
3	teaspoons kosher salt, divided	Small bunch fresh thyme
2	teaspoons ground black pepper	2½ tablespoons extra-virgin olive oil, divided
4	cups Can-Do Kraut (page 68), drained	4 small baking potatoes
		1 tablespoon unsalted butter

1 Preheat your oven to 450°F and position yourself in a good spot in your kitchen for giving directions. Have your without-child partner bring the chicken out of the fridge about 30 minutes before you plan to have them cook it.

2 Watch as they season both sides of the spatchcocked bird with 2 teaspoons of the salt and the pepper. Show them how to spoon the kraut over the bottom of a rimmed baking sheet, taking care to nestle the herbs on top of the kraut. Have them position the chicken, skin side up, overtop those herbs. Lend a loving hand and drizzle your chicken with ½ tablespoon of the olive oil.

3 Meanwhile, demonstrate the appropriate way to bake a potato by rubbing the outside of one potato with ½ tablespoon olive oil and ¼ teaspoon salt. Let them do the rest while you fix yourself a fizzy beverage with lots of ice. Have them put the olive oil– and salt-rubbed potatoes on a baking dish and slide that dish onto the bottom rack of your oven.

4 Point to the skillet holding the kraut and the chicken and tell them it goes on the rack above the potatoes. Set your timer for 45 minutes. Release your partner for a bit. Grab your fizzy beverage and go to another room so the aroma from roasting chicken doesn't make you nauseous.

5 After 45 minutes, fetch your partner and tell them to pull everything out of the oven and transfer the chicken to a cutting board to rest. (They should look for an internal temp, taken between the joint of the thigh and breast, of 165°F.) While they stir the butter into the poultry-rich kraut jus, refill your fizzy beverage. Tell them although the former you would have preferred a leg and thigh, the pregnant you would like a breast—and that you'll be making your nest on the couch while they split the potatoes, top them with the kraut sauce, and carve the chicken.

Bloody & Pickled Marys

makes 1 quart

Bloody Marys are how we day-drink, how we tailgate, and how we attempt to cure a hangover. Often home to skewers of olives, spears of celery, and a bevy of pickled vegetables, a Bloody Mary can be both a meal in a glass and a means to a buzz. This one teems with kraut brine and the probiotics and electrolytes the brine brings with it, so drinking a Bloody & Pickled does more to prevent or cure a hangover than hair of the dog alone ever did. If you forgo the vodka and add a handful of Cheez-Its alongside, you'll have one of my favorite 4pm snacks.

2½ cups tomato juice

1½ cups vodka

⅔ cup brine from Can-Do Kraut (page 68)

¼ cup fresh lemon juice

1 tablespoon prepared horseradish

1 tablespoon Worcestershire sauce

2 teaspoons celery salt, plus more to rim glasses

1 teaspoon hot sauce

1 teaspoon ground black pepper

1 Whisk together all the ingredients and chill for a few hours, ideally, before serving over ice. I like to rim my glasses with additional celery salt, but that's up to you.

Macaroni Hot Dish

makes one 9 x 14-inch casserole

This is how I get my kids to eat kraut. Macaroni and ground beef baked with cheese is actually the way I get them to eat a number of things I like to hide inside its bubbly decadence. I'm not sure if the good outweighs the bad when I sneak healthy green stuff into fatty, decadent stuff, but that's what I do and I have no plans to stop. Just call me Mary Poppins and listen to me sing "a spoonful of cheddar makes the vegetables go down!"

From an entirely adult perspective, though, the kraut makes this casserole-style dinner more enjoyable to eat. It gives a dish that's otherwise one-note comfort the crunchy relief of barely cooked cabbage and acid that makes me crave another bite. There's broccoli, too, but its subtle flavor fades in the face of all the cheese and is really just part of my nutrition strategy.

1. Preheat your oven to 350°F. In a 12-inch skillet over medium heat, brown the ground meat in the olive oil. As it browns, season it with 1 teaspoon of the salt, the cumin, garlic powder, and black pepper.

2. Using a slotted spoon, transfer the beef to a plate. Leave the fat in the skillet and add the onions, plus ½ teaspoon of the salt. Add another teaspoon of oil if the pan is dry. Sauté the onions for a couple of minutes so they soften, then stir in the reserved beef, the broccoli, and remaining ½ teaspoon salt. Add 1 cup water and continue cooking until the water has cooked out and you have a homogenous, aromatic meaty mix, about 10 minutes.

3. Transfer the meat mix to a large bowl and stir in the cooked macaroni, half of the melting cheese, half of the Parm, the kraut, milk, and sour cream. Pour all of this into a 9 x 14-inch casserole dish and top with the remaining melting cheese and Parm. Slide the dish onto the middle rack of your oven and bake for 45 minutes. The top will brown in spots, the sides will be bubbly, and your kitchen will smell like delicious dinner.

1 pound lean ground beef, pork, or turkey	2 cups finely chopped broccoli
2 teaspoons extra-virgin olive oil, plus more if needed	3 cups cooked macaroni (from about 4 ounces dry)
2 teaspoons kosher salt, divided	2½ cups shredded melting cheese of your choice, divided
2 teaspoons ground cumin	1 cup grated Parmigiano Reggiano (use a Microplane), divided
2 teaspoons garlic powder	3 cups Can-Do Kraut (page 68), drained
1 teaspoon ground black pepper	2 cups milk
2 medium onions, diced	½ cup sour cream

Hippie Burritos

makes 2 big burritos

These days everybody wants to put their lunch in a bowl. Grain bowls, smoothie bowls, burrito bowls, poke bowls—they're everywhere and I suppose they're fine. But I argue that when you take stuff out of its original vessel in the name of filling up a bowl, you end up with more food and wacky proportions that force texture and flavor out of balance.

So yes, we're swimming against the current here with lentils stuffed in a flour tortilla. But I promise when you reach the other side of the stream, this burrito's combination of creamy, crunchy, earthy, and sweet smooshed together inside a tortilla will eat the way a burrito is meant to.

This is a great way to repurpose leftover lentils or beans of any kind. And although I'm partial to the combination of kraut and apple for the salsa, you can swap in a number of things like tomatoes, corn, watermelon, beets, or radishes and find yourself with a tasty salsa that's a welcome addition to just about any dish in need of something bright and fresh.

1. In a medium bowl, combine the kraut, apple, red onion, mint, parsley, lemon juice, hot sauce, honey, and salt. Let those ingredients mingle into a salsa while you prepare everything else.

2. In a 10-inch skillet, fry the kielbasa until it's heated through and a little crispy. Take that out of the pan and reheat your lentils in the same skillet. If they need it, season them with additional salt. Then stir in the olive oil.

3. I like to heat my tortillas before filling them, but this is totally optional. If you have a gas range, put the tortilla directly on the flame. Once it's charred in a few places, flip it over and do the same on the opposite side.

4. To fill your burritos, divide the warm lentils in half and spread them over the middle of the two tortillas. Top the lentils with the cheese, followed by the kielbasa. Put the sour cream over that and finish with the salsa. Fold those puppies up burrito style and get at it.

½ cup Can-Do Kraut (page 68), drained, plus 2 tablespoons kraut brine

½ cup diced crisp apple

½ small red onion, sliced very thin

2 tablespoons chopped fresh mint

2 tablespoons chopped fresh parsley

2 tablespoons fresh lemon juice

1 teaspoon hot sauce

1 teaspoon honey

½ teaspoon kosher salt, plus more to taste

1 cup (8 to 10 ounces) diced kielbasa

2 cups cooked lentils (page 181)

1 tablespoon extra-virgin olive oil

2 large flour tortillas or other wraps of your choice

½ cup shredded sharp cheddar

½ cup sour cream

SWEET POTATO CHOWDER THAT SATISFIES

Balance is such a loaded word. On the one hand I angle for it in every dish—a little something salty set against something sweet, or a squirt of bright on top of something mild. Balanced bites are the delicious harmonies that make our mouths come back for more. Then there's the other balance. A distribution of weight between work and family, rest and play. This kind of balance evokes a Zen attitude, a clear purpose, a tidy home, well-behaved kids, a peaceful mind, a full heart.

I've been asked the question a thousand times. Usually posed to successful women with children, "How do you balance it all?" is the zinger the moderator saves for the end of a public inquisition. It draws a heart around the meat and muscle of the interview. If answered appropriately, you sound feminine and warm, sharp and relatable.

Of course I want to be tied to all those virtues, so for a long time I played along. I knew what the answer should be and I did what I could to back my experiences into it. "Oh, you know, balance is something I'm trying to find. I work a whole lot, but when I'm home I'm really engaged, really present." Or, "You know, sleep and exercise really help me find my center when things get crazy. Sleep is the key that unlocks balance for me." And this one is my favorite—I could actually see people in the audience calling B.S. on me when I said, "You know, I don't get caught up in trying to balance my days or even my weeks. I look for balance over the course of a year. If the fall is super busy, I plan for a more tranquil winter or spring, a season to set me straight."

I got tired of my giant, fluffy, untruth of an answer. My life and work had been the subject of a televised docuseries. I had written a really long book. I was the mom of twins and wife to my business partner. I was at the helm of three restaurant kitchens. I was the cheerleader for a depressed region. I was doing everything imaginable to be relevant on a national level from the most unlikely of places. None of that spells "balance." What it spells is "hold on tight and pray nothing falls apart or falls away."

I was sick of the questions about achieving balance. I was confused by the expectation. I wanted to know if they would be asking the same question if I were a man.

It's not to say things were mayhem around here. My life just didn't represent the type of balance we learned about when moms stayed home and dads went to work—the days when the school of thought suggested you couldn't be a good mom and be ambitious. But actually, it's often that ambitious thing, the wild, all-consuming, risky drive I've got going on, that brings out the best in me and makes me a brighter light for my children.

So, no, I don't pursue balance. Balance is boring. I seek satisfaction instead, and I find it most often in the challenges I face, in the work of meeting them, and in the unexpected lessons learned when I try to do something hard.

Back when I dropped canned answers to the canned questions around balance, I wrote a recipe for sweet potato chowder with bacon and sour cream. It was a candidate for *Deep Run Roots,* but I ended up cutting it because it was too measured, too predictable. Frankly, it was boring... and balanced. This time around, with satisfaction as my goal, I've added something unexpected, an ingredient that challenges the notion that chowders can only be creamy and rich.

Kraut's salty edge makes the feminine sweet potato her best self. Kraut adds texture to an otherwise soft slurp from a spoon and it brings tension with acid that pulls everything forward. Kraut renders this chowder a satisfying one. It's the ingredient that makes you want more. And isn't that the goal?

"I was sick of the questions about achieving balance. I was confused by the expectation. I wanted to know if they would be asking the same question if I were a man."

Sweet Potato, Kraut & Bacon Chowder

Serves 6 (2 cups each)

The brand of comfort that clam chowder blankets me with is transportive and transformational. I've never been to Cape Cod, Maine, or any of the rocky seaside places New England clam chowder calls to mind, but a bowl of warm and welcoming chowder takes me to a wharf somewhere north of here. I'm wearing an oversized sweater. I'm in a simple restaurant on the second floor. I'm watching the fishing boats come in as I blow on my steaming spoon full of soup. I digress...

The kraut here stands in for clams' salty edge and the sweet potatoes answer my long-standing desire to balance the briny notes of chowder with the sweet ones from yams. And the bacon is bacon. It makes sense at the wharf, with kraut, with sweet potatoes—or anywhere you place it, really.

12 ounces bacon, cut into bite-size 1-inch squares

2 leeks, light green and white parts only, sliced into ½-inch rounds

3 stalks, celery, sliced (1 cup)

2 tablespoons minced fresh ginger

4 garlic cloves, sliced thin

1 teaspoon kosher salt

½ teaspoon red pepper flakes

2 pounds sweet potatoes, peeled and cut into 1-inch cubes (6 cups)

1 pound white potatoes, peeled and cut into 1-inch cubes (3 cups)

3 cups Can-Do Kraut (page 68), drained

8 cups chicken broth

2 cups heavy cream

2 cups milk

1 In a 6-quart Dutch oven over medium heat, render the bacon until crispy or until it's the way you enjoy it on top of soup. Take the bacon out of the pan and save it to scatter on top of each bowl of soup, but leave the bacon fat behind.

2 Add the leeks, celery, ginger, garlic, salt, and pepper flakes to the pan. Sweat that over medium heat for about 5 minutes.

3 Add the sweet potatoes, white potatoes, kraut, chicken broth, cream, and milk. Cover and bring all of this up to a hard simmer. Cook for about 30 minutes, or until the potatoes are beginning to fall apart. Uncover and simmer for another 10 minutes.

4 Working in batches, put the soup in a blender or food processor and carefully blend till smooth. Add it back to the pot and stir to incorporate. If you don't feel like breaking out your blender or you're happy with the consistency of the soup as is, use a potato masher or a ladle to encourage the potatoes to break up.

5 Serve warm with lots of bacon on top.

Steak Salad Kind of Gal

serves 2

I still remember my first steak salad. It was 1998 and I was in Charleston for the summer, working as a waitress and generally having a marvelous time. My friends and I went to dinner at a place we knew accepted our fake IDs and I ordered a Long Island Iced Tea and the steak salad special. My experience told me steak went with baked potatoes but there was usually a salad bar nearby so I thought I'd give the restaurant's ingenuity a try and have my salad with my steak.

When it arrived I was a little confused that there was no potato to speak of, but I didn't want to draw attention to myself and my other underage companions, so I went about the business of eating a steak on top of salad. That business changed my approach to salad and the way I looked at steak from there on out. The acid in the dressing and the light quality of the salad's ingredients highlighted the steak and made a piece of meat I had always thought was perfect taste even better. I was a changed twenty-year-old.

½ cup Can-Do Kraut (page 68), drained, plus ¼ cup kraut brine

1 cup crumbled blue cheese, divided

½ cup extra-virgin olive oil, divided

¼ cup red wine vinegar

1 tablespoon honey

1 teaspoon ground black pepper

½ red onion, sliced into ½-inch-thick rounds

1 cup cherry tomatoes

2 teaspoons kosher salt, divided

8 to 10 ounces strip, flank, or skirt steak

3 cups packed arugula; or 1 head romaine lettuce, chopped

1 In a medium bowl, whisk together the kraut, its brine, ½ cup of the blue cheese, ⅓ cup of the olive oil, the vinegar, honey, and black pepper. Set the dressing aside while you prepare the rest of the components.

2 In a 12-inch skillet, heat 1 tablespoon olive oil on high till shimmering. Add the onion slices in a single layer so they have the opportunity to char on one side for a few minutes. If you have room in your skillet, you can add the tomatoes while the onions char. If not, char the onions on both sides, then take them out of the pan and blister the tomatoes. Once the onions are nice and burned up and the tomatoes have burst their skins, season them with ½ teaspoon salt and set them aside while you cook the steak.

3 Season the beef with 1 teaspoon salt and add the remaining olive oil (a scant 2 tablespoons) to your already flaming-hot skillet. Sear the steak on the first side for about 3 minutes, then flip and sear on the opposite side. I'm looking for a medium rare, and this period of time should do the trick. If you want your steak cooked more, give it more time in the pan. Transfer the steak to a plate to rest for about 3 minutes before you slice it.

4 After the steak has rested, slice it and toss with the arugula or lettuce, blistered tomatoes, charred red onion, remaining ½ cup blue cheese, remaining ½ teaspoon salt, and the dressing. Divide the salad between two bowls and serve.

Beets Meet Reuben

serves 4

When we think of sauerkraut, we think of a Reuben sandwich. The combination of corned beef, Russian dressing, kraut, Swiss cheese, and rye bread is an American classic that requires both a napkin and nap.

I try to provide recipes that Google does not, and I don't skew toward dishes that bring me guilt or force me to lie down in the wake of eating them, so you won't find a true Reuben here. Instead, I pay homage to the iconic sandwich in salad form minus the meat.

Like apples, beets are an ingredient people often pair with and sometimes make kraut out of. Also like apples, I like the way beets taste in kraut's company. The earthy, meaty nature of one of my favorite roots also plays an apt companion for creamy Russian dressing and caraway-spiced rye bread, so for today pretend beets are corned beef and say hi to this reimagined Reuben.

4   medium beets

3   tablespoons extra-virgin olive oil, divided

2   teaspoons kosher salt, divided

2   tablespoons sherry or red wine vinegar

1   teaspoon granulated sugar

½   cup Can-Do Kraut (page 68), drained, plus ¼ cup kraut brine

½   cup mayonnaise

2   tablespoons ketchup

2   teaspoons Worcestershire sauce

1   tablespoon prepared horseradish

½   teaspoon ground black pepper

4   slices rye bread

① Preheat your oven to 350°F. Give your beets a rinse and put them in a casserole dish with about ¼ inch of water. Drizzle them with 1 tablespoon of the olive oil and sprinkle with ½ teaspoon of the salt. Cover the dish with foil and slide it into your oven for about 1 hour. Check to see if the beets are done by sliding a knife into their centers. If the beets offer little resistance, you're good. If you've got to work to get the knife in there, let them bake a bit longer.

② Once they've cooled enough for you to handle them, use a paper towel or four to peel the skins away. This should be fairly easy and oddly satisfying. While the beets are still warm, slice them into ½-inch-thick rounds and toss those rounds in a medium bowl with the vinegar, 1 teaspoon salt, and the sugar.

③ To make the dressing, combine the kraut, its brine, the mayo, ketchup, Worcestershire, horseradish, remaining ½ teaspoon salt, and the black pepper in another small bowl.

④ All of the above can be done several days in advance, but just before you get ready to eat, drizzle the rye bread with the remaining 2 tablespoons olive oil and give it a good toast in a skillet. Cut or crumble the rye toast into small croutons.

⑤ Spread a little of the Russian-ish dressing on the bottom of your plate and shingle the beets and more dressing overtop. Dot with lots more dressing, sprinkle with the rye croutons, and eat with your hands or with a knife and fork.

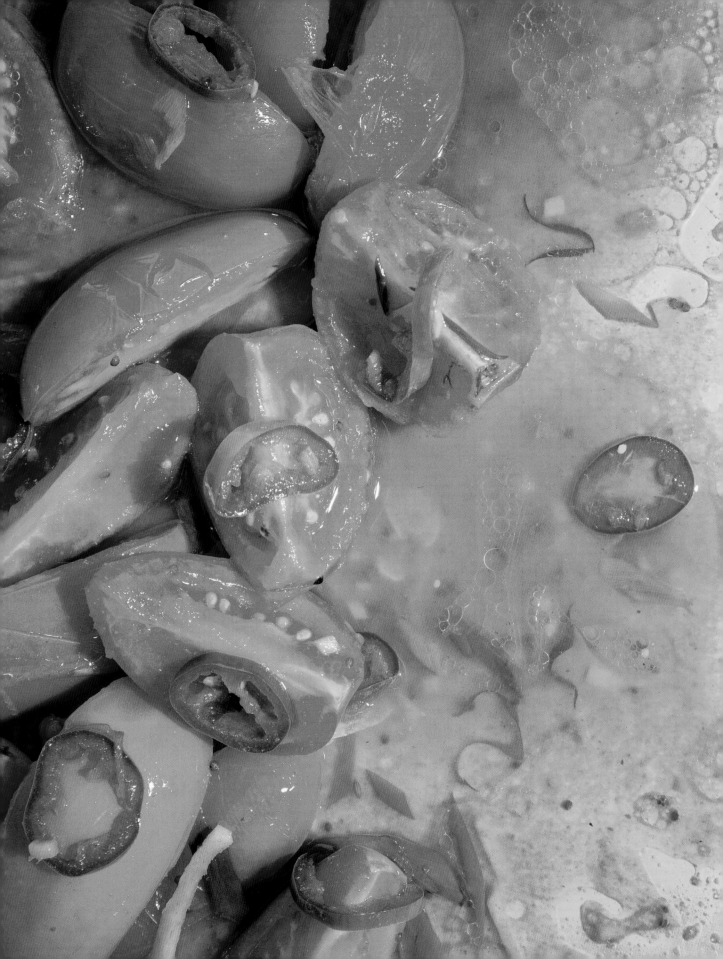

CHAPTER FOUR

Red

WEAPONS

Approachably Spicy • **Uplifting & Acidic** • **Fresh** • **Vegetal**

Full disclosure, this is not my recipe.

I lifted these spicy pickled tomatoes from Ben and Karen Barker's book *Not Afraid of Flavor: Recipes from Magnolia Grill* more than a decade ago. I've tweaked them over the years both to suit the specific needs of my kitchen and because I hate being a copycat, but the recipe you see here, the one I can hardly cook without, is more or less theirs. I say "more or less" not only because the recipe has evolved under my watch, but because the Barkers credit another book with the recipe that encouraged them, like me, to make spicy pickled tomatoes a cornerstone of their kitchen. Thanks for the permission.

My Red Weapons start with tomatoes. I suggest firm plum tomatoes (like Roma), but really you can use any tomato you have. They get quartered or halved, depending on their size, and nestled in a heatproof container. Then you heat a brine of vinegar, sugar, oil, and lots of aromatics and pour it over top. The tomatoes need to sit a bit to transform, but that's really it.

After a day or two you'll find yourself with not one, but four distinct ingredients whose versatility will force you to find a permanent space in your fridge to house them. Those four are the pickled tomatoes themselves, the jalapeños, the pickling liquid, and the oil that floats to the top.

First I'll start with the tomato part of the arsenal. So many recipes using tomatoes require them to be peeled, which calls for boiling water, an ice bath, a knife, and ultimately a mess. The beauty here is that you leave the skin on so the tomatoes hold their shape as they absorb the spicy, sweet, assertive brine in which you've doused them. And because the Red Weapons end up as seasoning rather than substance, it's no effort to peel a few skins away before you drop them into a sauce, salad, or stew to power their punch. At the restaurant we call them "spicy toms." It's not an incredibly accurate description because they're not really that spicy and the title calls to mind canvas shoes of a benevolent nature. Still, in a kitchen where the menu changes all the time, it says a lot that we've given them a nickname. Think of them as approachable hot sauce with body and a world will open up to you where salads are brighter, tartares espouse more dimension, dressings move with more focused direction, and sauces stick lighter landings.

Next let's talk about the jalapeños. By-products of loading your Red Weapons with spice, the sliced jalapeños happen to pickle in the process. They lose some of their green luster and firm pepper texture, but they emerge mellow yet tart and are, for lack of a better way to say it, a great thing to have around. My husband, Ben, always wants things spicier and for a long time I bought pickled jalapeños in a can to scratch that itch. Then I had an "aha" or a "duh" moment (depending on how you look at it) and realized I had pickled jalapeños floating in my Red Weapons all along. When we make tacos, Ben plucks a few slices out and tailors his taco to his taste. When he makes omelets or avocado toast, he does the same. The jalapeño part of Red Weapons will work for any recipe that calls for pickled or fresh jalapeños. Don't forget they're in there!

I look at the third and fourth offspring of Red Weapons a little like fraternal twins. They have the same parents and they developed in the same womb at the same time, but they have different DNA and are more like siblings than carbon copies of each other. Twin A is the liquid

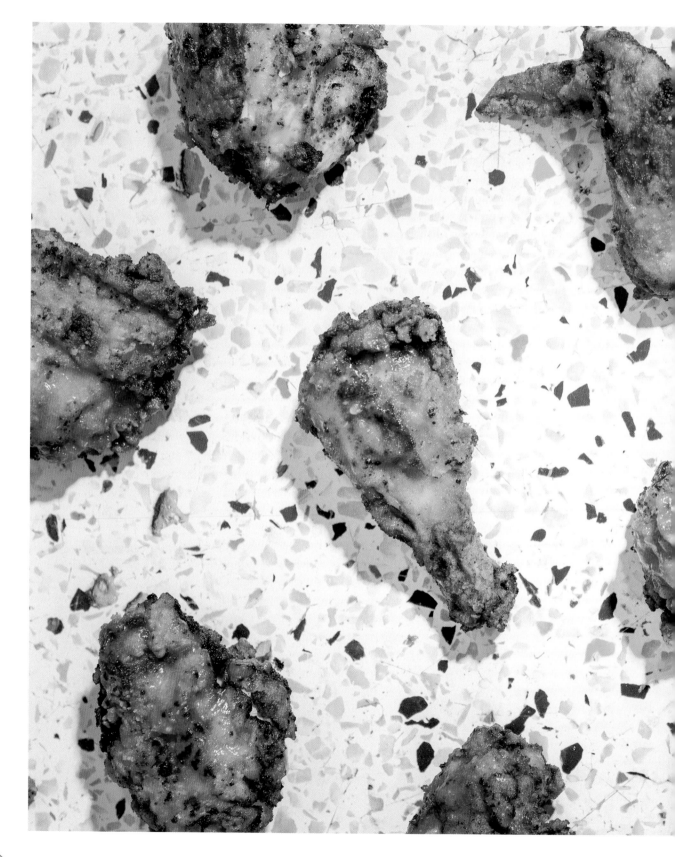

that leeches off the tomatoes nurtured with the vinegar, sugar, and seasonings that give the weapons their power. She is briny, watery, spicy, and bright. She's born with baggage like a Pisces, but it's scallions, garlic, and whole spices that Twin A totes around. At times you appreciate her chunky complexity. Other times you can strain it out. Either way, Twin A acts like a less lip-puckering lemon juice packed with hidden flavors. She lifts up and thins out sauces and soups and defines dressings and marinades with her layered character.

Twin B is the oil that distinguishes Red Weapons from traditional vinegar pickles, making them rounder and more versatile, the way a mom grows more nimble with both a boy and a girl to mother. In his DNA, Twin B has heat from the jalapeños, lemony notes from the coriander, and an aromatic personality from the scallions and garlic. He wants to be drizzled on crudos, dipped into with bread, whisked into vinaigrettes, and stirred into marinades. He's elusive and hard to separate from his twin at room temperature, but when refrigerated he rises to the top and is a cinch to scoop away for a play date.

The Barkers, and their influential book, first gave me Red Weapons. Now I've pointed out four tricks in their bag. If you're not motivated to pack this kind of heat, I can't save you. ❧

Red Weapons

HERE'S WHAT'S IMPORTANT

- This process is so easy it barely warrants directions: You make a flavorful liquid full of aromatics and pour it over tomatoes to pickle them. The most important step, however, is the one where you wait. The tomatoes must sit in their brine for a minimum of 3 days before they mature into the weapons I promise. After that they'll keep in your fridge for 3 months.

- Don't get caught up in the details here. I call for plum tomatoes because I like their firmness and availability, but any tomato will do. In fact, if you find yourself in a fortunate place where you have a bounty of cherry or slicing tomatoes, this is a quick and painless way to preserve them.

- I've provided a guide to make a relatively small batch because of that little detail we call refrigerator space, but this is incredibly easy to double, even triple.

- Don't freak out about the measurements on aromatics and spices. If you're short a little ginger, turmeric, or a jalapeño or two, don't put aside the recipe.

- Red Weapons will keep in your fridge for 3 months but they don't like the freezer and emerge from its depths mushy and weird. If you make too much and your fridge offers too little, consider canning them in a hot water bath just after you pour the hot brine over top. Those will keep unopened till the end of time.

HEADS up

Once the tomatoes have spent a few days in the fridge you'll notice *Twin B*, the olive oil component, rises to the top and creates a "lid" over *Twin A*, the pickling liquid, and the tomatoes and other solid stuff. This act of science makes the weapons and their offspring easy to separate from one another, but it's definitely not a pretty process. You will likely find yourself with a hand in a jar or a puddle on the counter, but who really cares? Just know all of the extraction and separation will be easier if your Red Weapon family is cold.

2 pounds plum tomatoes, cut into quarters lengthwise	1½ tablespoons ground cumin
1 bunch scallions, sliced thin	1 tablespoon plus 1 teaspoon kosher salt
5 jalapeños, sliced into thin rings	1½ teaspoons cayenne
3 tablespoons minced fresh ginger	1½ teaspoons turmeric
3 tablespoons minced garlic	½ cup unseasoned rice wine vinegar
1½ tablespoons yellow or brown mustard seeds	¾ cup white wine vinegar
	¾ cup packed light brown sugar
	1½ cups extra-virgin olive oil

MAKES 2 QUARTS

① Put your tomatoes in a large, wide, heatproof bowl that is plenty large enough to hold all the ingredients. I like to assemble and start to "pickle" my weapons there on the counter, letting their flavors marry as they cool down. Then, once they're mixed together and have reached room temperature, I transfer them to smaller containers suitable for the fridge. (This recipe is sized to just barely fit into two quart-size mason jars, but you may have a little extra. While you can try to pull it all together directly in the jars, that might just be a big mess waiting to happen.)

② In a large saucepan or Dutch oven, bring all the ingredients except for the tomatoes and the olive oil to a boil over medium heat. Let it boil for 1 minute. Then add the olive oil and bring back to a boil. Immediately pour over the tomatoes in the big bowl, pressing them down to make sure they are submerged.

③ Let the tomatoes and the liquid cool to room temperature without the aid of an ice bath or anything to speed the process along. If you've got room in your fridge, the big bowl can go in there. But if the weapons sit out at room temperature overnight, that's totally fine. The more slowly they cool down, the more quickly they will pickle. Once they've cooled, transfer the weapons to jars and refrigerate for a minimum of 3 days or up to 3 months.

1
on every egg everywhere

2
thrown into braising liquids or soups

3
mashed into guacamole or on top of avocado toast

4
with plain cream cheese on a bagel

5
as a base for cocktail sauce

6
mixed into just-cooked rice or beans

7
as a sauce or marinade for grain, legume, or pasta salads

8
tossed or reheated with leftover chicken or pork

9
as a marinade for ceviche or a dressing for crudos

10
chopped with fresh herbs for salsa

11
blended with mayo for a dipping sauce

12
stirred into potato, chicken, shrimp, or tuna salad

Give the Gift of Pickled Shrimp

makes 1 pound

When I wrote my first book I vowed that if I ever got a tattoo it would be of the word "hors d'oeuvre." I couldn't spell the word, and my attempts didn't even get me close enough to trigger spell check, so over and over in an effort to keep moving I tried to swap "hors d'oeuvre" out for "snack" or "appetizer." Unsatisfied with the substitutions, I always toggled back to the Internet to hunt down the spelling because "snack" and "appetizer" just don't mean the same things as "hors d'oeuvre." Pimento cheese crackers and popcorn are snacks. Potato skins, salad, and crab cakes are appetizers. Pickled shrimp are hors d'oeuvres.

Shrimp cooked then marinated in a flavorful acidic liquid and served at room temperature with toothpicks embody the temperament and spirit of the word. Resolutely Southern, pickled shrimp are somehow elegant without being fussy. They are a small, interesting conversation-worthy mingle food that aims to whet your appetite rather than fill you up. Unfortunately, though, most of my attempts at pickled shrimp have been pretty bad. Either cooked too long or marinated in a liquid that lacked balance, I was never compelled to search out the spelling of hors d'oeuvres and record the recipe for the pickled shrimp of my past.

But with Red Weapons, it's a new day in hors d'oeuvre land. These pickled shrimp are tender, sweet, spicy, and bright. Effortless to make, they're cooked in Twin B, marinated in Twin A, and tossed with a little of the tomato Red Weapon and a lot of herbs. Yes, they're an hors d'oeuvre, but I most often eat them in salads or in burritos.

1 pound shrimp (21/25), peeled and deveined

¼ cup plus generous 1 tablespoon <u>Red Weapon oil</u> (Twin B, page 104), divided

½ cup <u>Red Weapon pickling liquid</u> (Twin A, page 104)

1 teaspoon kosher salt

⅓ cup chopped <u>Red Weapons</u> (page 104)

4 scallions, sliced thin

½ cup packed picked fresh parsley leaves

¼ cup packed fresh cilantro stems, finely chopped

¼ cup packed fresh mint leaves, roughly torn

❶ In a 12-inch skillet, combine the shrimp and the ¼ cup Twin B oil over medium heat and cook, stirring often, until the shrimp are just cooked through. This will take about 4 minutes from start to finish.

❷ Use a slotted spoon to transfer the shrimp to a medium bowl. (Discard the oil in the skillet). While the shrimp are still warm, stir in the generous tablespoon Twin B oil, the Twin A liquid, and the salt.

❸ Once the shrimp have cooled completely, stir in the chopped Red Weapons, scallions, parsley, and cilantro. Refrigerate until you're ready to serve. The shrimp will need a minimum of 3 hours in the marinade to pickle, but will be best if they can sit in the fridge overnight where they will keep for about a week.

❹ Just before you put them out as an hors d'oeuvre, toss the shrimp with the mint. You could do this sooner, but the mint will brown and nobody wants that.

Where's My Medal Grits & Chicken

serves 4

In grit circles I'm pretty much a baller. For five years, grits were the star of an entire section on my menu, the focus of episodes of *A Chef's Life,* and the center of multiple recipes in my first cookbook. I've made grits in double boilers, rice cookers, Instant Pots, and regular old saucepans. At some point along the way it dawned on me that I've never seen anyone, myself included, cook grits from raw in the oven.

Lots of people bake already-cooked grits with cheese and eggs and other creamy stuff to make something like a casserole, but never raw grits with liquid straight in the common kitchen hot box. The thought must be that grits require some measure of stirring to latch onto and absorb liquid, but if that were the case then several of the methods above wouldn't work either. So I did what ballers do. I pushed the limits of what we believed possible and cooked grits under chicken thighs with Red Weapons and sautéed leeks in the oven.

The result is a pan of grits that feel lighter and fluffier than their counterparts stirred on the stove toward starch. They emerge more buoyant and balanced by the pickle and heat pumped in by Red Weapons as they slow-cook. And like everything lucky enough to sit under chicken as it renders, the grits trap the bird's true flavor with more depth than what we can normally offer via broth or bouillon. Best of all is that grits and chicken cooked this way leave you with an entire dinner to eat, and only one pot to wash.

4   bone-in skin-on chicken thighs

1   tablespoon kosher salt, divided

2   tablespoons extra-virgin olive oil

1   leek, white and light green parts, sliced into ½-inch rounds

3   garlic cloves, thinly sliced

1   cup uncooked stone-ground grits

1   cup roughly chopped Red Weapons (page 104)

½   cup Red Weapon pickling liquid (Twin A, page 104)

2   cups milk

❶ Preheat your oven to 375°F. Season the chicken thighs with 2 teaspoons of the salt. In a 12-inch ovenproof skillet or braiser, heat the oil over medium heat. Brown the chicken skin side down, until nicely caramelized. Take the chicken out of the pan and set aside.

❷ Lower the heat slightly and add the leeks, garlic, and ½ teaspoon salt to the pan. Sauté for 2 to 3 minutes, until the leeks have softened and picked up all the browned bits from the bottom of the pan. Stir in the grits, the chopped Red Weapons, Twin A, milk, remaining ½ teaspoon salt, and 1½ cups water. Make sure everything is mixed together in a homogenous way and that nothing is stuck on the bottom of the pan.

❸ Nestle the thighs on top of the grit mixture. They will sink a bit because the grits are watery at this point, but as long as the browned chicken skin peeks out, all is good. Slide the skillet onto the center rack of your oven and bake for 40 minutes, until an instant-read thermometer hits 165°F.

❹ Bring the skillet out and allow everything to cool for about 5 minutes before serving. If you're feeling extra, this would be great dotted with a little Herbdacious (page 206).

Does Not Disappoint Breakfast Casserole

serves 4 to 6

The breakfast casserole genre frustrates me. On the one hand, what's not to love? All the things that make breakfast feel traditionally American—eggs, meat, cheese, bread—get tossed together and baked in a streamlined, easy-Sunday-morning, one-dish-to-wash kind of way. Plus, breakfast casseroles are ideal for entertaining because you can assemble them the night before and bake them the next morning while you shove your family's mess in a closet before your guests arrive.

But more often than not, I'm let down by the breakfast casseroles I encounter. They seem lazy rather than convenient. The ingredients, although clearly baked as one, somehow taste distinct and confused at the same time. They're like a bedroom with a bed, dresser, side table, and chair that needs a rug to tie the room together.

In my version of the breakfast casserole, Red Weapons are that rug. They bring juiciness that mingles with milk and egg to create a near-hollandaise effect. And they provide acid where you wouldn't think it belongs. It's that bright surprise, that acidic pucker, that pulls you back for another bite and makes my take on this genre one that does not disappoint.

1 pound breakfast-style sausage, loose or removed from its casing

10 ounces (about 5 cups packed) fresh spinach

1½ teaspoons kosher salt, divided

4 cups diced crusty bread, such as baguettes, sourdough, or ciabatta

10 ounces sharp cheddar cheese, grated or (my preference) cut into ¼-inch cubes

½ cup diced roasted red bell peppers

6 large eggs, whisked

1 cup milk

½ cup heavy cream

1 cup roughly chopped Red Weapons (page 104)

1 Preheat your oven to 350°F. In a 12-inch ovenproof skillet, brown the sausage over medium heat. You want hunks of moist sausage suspended in the finished dish, so take care not to overcook or over-crumble it this go-round. Scoop the sausage out of the skillet and transfer to a bowl large enough to hold all the ingredients. Go about wilting the spinach with ½ teaspoon of the salt in the same skillet. Squeeze as much liquid out of the spinach as you can without much trouble and transfer to the bowl with the sausage. Add the bread, cheese, and roasted red peppers.

2 In a smaller bowl, whisk the eggs, milk, cream, and remaining 1 teaspoon salt till homogenous. Stir the Red Weapons into the egg mixture, then pour that into the big bowl with the sausage and other stuff. Stir it up and dump everything back into the skillet.

3 At this point you could refrigerate the breakfast casserole overnight or you can go right to the business of baking it. Either way, whenever you're ready, slide the skillet onto the middle rack of your oven and bake for 1 hour, until the top is crisp and browned in spots.

Red Devils

makes 12

Deviled eggs are sacred to me. My mom carried our loaded 24-count Tupperware deviled egg case to every baby shower, graduation party, engagement celebration, and covered-dish lunch we attended. But so did everybody else. At an event for forty people there would be ten trays of deviled eggs, and I learned early on that not all deviled eggs are created equal. I liked my mom's and that was about it. Other people put too many things in their filling. Pickles and pimentos, olives and red stuff dusted on top turned me off. I liked my deviled eggs austere, tart, smooth, and yellow. I was a purist.

I feel the same way today, especially since the pickle-flecked, olive-topped deviled eggs of my adolescent nightmares have been replaced with creative monstrosities on restaurant menus that tout everything from pimento cheese to asparagus puree as apt additions to the filling. The discovery and celebration of Southern food has not been good to the deviled egg. So it's with great trepidation that I offer up a deviled egg recipe that's outside the lines of what my mom made. But here I am and here are my Red Devils.

The reason I risk it all for this recipe is because Red Weapons actually improve my deviled eggs. They bring vinegar, sugar, and spice—all things whipped into the traditional ones my mom made—but they also add dimension and a fluffy lightness that's downright remarkable. Believe me: My deviled egg reverence is deep. I would never do anything to tarnish the legacy of the South's most quintessential hors d'oeuvre.

1. Put the eggs in a saucepan, add enough water to cover them by 1 inch, and bring up to a boil over high heat. Set up an ice bath nearby. Let the eggs boil for 8 minutes, then transfer to the ice bath to cool. There are a lot of nuances around the way people cook eggs. I'm willing to consider and respect our differences as stewards of our kitchens (just read the story attached to the second recipe in this book, page 13), but I will not bend when it comes to the role of the ice bath here. Rapid cooling of your eggs is essential to prevent the gray death cloak that surrounds yolks that have been left to cool on their own time.

2. Peel the eggs and slice them through their equator. This is not the traditional way we would typically halve an egg for deviling, but when I go outside the lines, I go all the way. Scoop out the yolks and pass them through a sieve, or put them in the bowl of a food processor and pulse. There's more than one way to devil an egg and I'm okay with any of them. Either way, you want to get them pretty smooth before you add anything else.

3. Next add the room-temperature butter and work it into the yolks. When those two are married as one, it's safe to stir or process in the mayo, Twin A liquid, Red Weapons, and salt. Taste for seasoning. You may want more salt or a pinch of sugar. I'll give you that. Deviled eggs are personal.

4. Discard or eat for protein the four least-desirable egg white halves. Cut a tiny flat foot on the bottom of the ones you will stuff. This will help the non-traditional egg chariot stand up.

5. Wait to fill your eggs just before serving or the filling will form a skin. Use a piping bag or a spoon to overstuff each white and garnish with the nuggets of Red Weapon ginger, jalapeño, and tomatoes.

8 large eggs

2 tablespoons unsalted butter, at room temperature

2 tablespoons mayonnaise

1 tablespoon Red Weapon pickling liquid (Twin A, page 104)

¼ cup roughly chopped Red Weapons (page 104)

¼ teaspoon kosher salt
Snipped fresh chives, for garnish

Do Try This at Home Tartare

serves 4

There are things we order in restaurants that we would never consider making at home, and oddly enough it's the raw things, the things that require the least work, that we dodge in our own kitchens but clamor to eat when we're out. We're more than willing to attempt to properly brown and braise short ribs, but we're scared to death to chop and dress a tartare made of fish or meat.

One takes a fair amount of skill, a good ventilation system, and several hours to get right. The other requires a cutting board, a fresh piece of protein, some oil, and some acid. So why are we so scared? I think one fear lingers behind the curtain of the wonderful wizard of raw: the protein itself. We worry we don't have enough sense to select a proper piece of meat or fish to safely serve raw. We think somehow that people who work in restaurants possess a keener sense for raw meat. We are wrong. Here's why:

- We *think* we don't know what kinds of things make a good tartare, but I promise that you know more than you think you do, so lean into that. Don't use poultry or pork. The experts do that kind of stuff in Japan. Let's leave that to them.

- If you're a tartare beginner, choose fish you've seen in tartares or on sashimi menus before, like flounder, tuna, and salmon. Don't, for the love of God, turn tilapia or anything raised in a tank in Indonesia into tartare. You know better than that.

- Beef and lamb are A+ choices for tartare, but make sure you choose a lean, tender cut. Raw fat and sinew are enemies of a good tartare, so avoid cuts like a nicely marbled rib eye or anything with connective tissue. I like tenderloin, sirloin, and top round from both beef and lamb.

- I know you're concerned you won't know if it's fresh enough. Chances are if you're worried about that, you're already able to identify something fresh. If the piece of protein smells good, if it's dry rather than tacky or slimy, and if it's the color you identify with fresh versions of itself, it's most definitely fresh enough for a delicious tartare. Go to a grocery store, fish market, or butcher shop you trust and buy the best quality they have. It also never hurts to ask questions or tell the person at the counter what you're doing. They know what they're selling, how fresh it is, and whether or not there's a chance you're gonna come back disappointed.

Now that you're armed with confidence around knowledge you already had, here's why you should exercise it. Meat, especially quality meat, is expensive. Eating meat costs our wallets and our planet more than any other food we consume. When you eat tartare, you're still eating meat but you eat less of it. The fact that it's raw gives us pause and we consider it and consume it differently. When you chop fish, beef, or lamb for tartare by hand, dress it with garnishes, and savor the finished dish on something crisp, you celebrate that protein the way that costly foods should be celebrated.

I know this will sound strange, but at your next party make tartare for people to share. It will be the chips and dip of your next affair. You'll likely turn someone on to something new, you'll look like a kitchen boss, and everyone will crowd around protein on a pedestal—exactly where it should be.

8	ounces lean, tender, fresh fish, beef, or lamb	
½	teaspoon kosher salt	
1	tablespoon <u>Red Weapon pickling liquid</u> (Twin A, page 104)	
1	tablespoon <u>Red Weapon oil</u> (Twin B, page 104)	
¼	cup roughly chopped <u>Red Weapons</u> (page 104)	

1	tablespoon tasty extra-virgin olive oil
1	tablespoon capers, rinsed and roughly chopped
½	teaspoon Dijon mustard
3	tablespoons chopped fresh parsley
2	tablespoons chopped fresh mint
	Your favorite snack chips, for serving

1 Put your protein in the freezer for about 15 minutes. This will make it much easier to cut. Once it's firmed up a bit, slice it into thin strips, then cut across those strips to make tiny cubes.

2 Just before you want to serve the tartare, put the meat in a bowl and sprinkle in the salt. Stir that around to make sure the meat itself is seasoned. Then stir in the Twin A, Twin B, Red Weapons, olive oil, capers, Dijon, parsley, and mint. Mound the tartare on a platter and surround it with chips. Serve immediately—or wait and watch sadly as the acid in the dressing cooks your protein.

Fried Chicken Finally

serves 4

I have avoided the fried chicken crusades. We don't serve it in our restaurants and I have never developed a Fried Chicken by Vivian manifesto because I never had anything to add to the already-crowded crispy bird narrative. But now I do. I morphed the spunk of Nashville hot chicken with the pucker of Chick-fil-A's pickle brine and softened both with the spirit of McDonald's nuggets dunked in honey. I'm ready to weigh in.

I have always had strong beliefs on the subject. I don't like a whole lot of batter or breading. That prevents me from tasting the skin, and really, chicken for me is all about the skin. I appreciate what buttermilk does for the bird and believe that that marriage is one of the most brilliant unions in Southern cooking. I like breasts cut in half so there's more surface area to fry. I prefer chicken shallow-fried in a skillet rather than deep-fried in a vat. And I like both hot sauce and honey, sweet and heat. All these beliefs manifest in this recipe.

1 (3- to 4-pound) chicken, cut into pieces	⅓ cup Red Weapon oil (Twin B, page 104)
3 teaspoons kosher salt, divided	1½ cups all-purpose flour
⅔ cup buttermilk	½ cup Red Weapons (page 104)
⅔ cup Red Weapon pickling liquid (Twin A, page 104), divided	⅓ cup honey
	Peanut or other vegetable oil, for frying

1 If your chicken breasts are not cut in half through their thickest part, go ahead and do that. Then put the chicken in a bowl and toss it with 1½ teaspoons of the salt. Combine the buttermilk, ⅓ cup of the Twin A liquid, and the Twin B oil. Pour that over the chicken and massage it a little to get everything coated. Leave this out at room temperature for 2 hours if you plan on frying soon. Otherwise, cover and refrigerate for as long as overnight.

2 Mix the flour with the remaining 1½ teaspoons salt in a shallow bowl and get ready to dredge the chicken. To do this, make sure you shake off any excess liquid, then roll the chicken around in the flour. Transfer the pieces of chicken to a rack positioned on a baking sheet and put it in the fridge for 1 hour. This step helps crisp things up and prevents the breading from flaking away while it fries.

3 At some point while everything marinates, put the Red Weapons, honey, and remaining ⅓ cup Twin A liquid in a blender and let her rip. Set the Red Weapon honey aside.

4 Bring the chicken out of the fridge 30 minutes before you want to fry it. Fill a 12-inch skillet halfway up the sides with the vegetable oil of your choice and heat it over medium heat. Most recipes call for thermometers here, but I've watched a lot of people shallow-fry chicken and never seen a thermometer. Nevertheless, you can look for oil that is 350°F before you fry and maintain a temp of 325 to 350°F throughout the sizzle. If you're a thermometer renegade, drop a bit of flour into the oil to see how it responds. If it sizzles and comes to life immediately, the oil is ready.

5 Using tongs, lay the chicken in the oil, skin side down. The pieces should not touch one another but they can be quite close. Like the flour, the chicken should start to sizzle immediately. If it doesn't, take the chicken out and let the oil heat a bit more.

6 Once all the chicken is in the skillet, cover and let it cook on one side for about 3 minutes. Remove the lid, flip the chicken, and put the lid on once more for 3 minutes. After 6 total minutes covered, remove the lid and flip the chicken. Continue cooking and flipping, uncovered, for another 12 to 15 minutes. The wings and legs will likely take a little less time than the breasts and thighs. You're looking for "fried chicken brown" skin and an internal temperature of 165°F. When you find it, pluck the chicken out of the skillet and drain on paper towels.

7 Once all the chicken is done and everybody is drained, drizzle the Red Weapon honey overtop and serve. This is good hot, but like the best fried chicken it's also great cold.

DINNER FOR A LEGEND

Genetically, John Currin Howard is where I get a lot of things. My blue eyes, full lips, olive skin, and penchant for storytelling are all chromosomes I'm happy to share with him. I also inherited his fidgety nature. We both pick at our hands, doodle to avoid prolonged eye contact with others, and manipulate anything bendable and within arms' reach to soften the exposure of what it is we're supposed to be focused on. I've got his body type too. Rather, I've got his mom's body—all of it—from deep wrinkly knuckles to legs so substantial we call them trunks. I've never been called a waif. Nope. My physique is decidedly Dad's.

If nature gave me Dad's build, then nurture passed on a few of his qualities too. First, we share an obsession with and deep respect for work. Farming is Dad's work. It's also his hobby, his escape, and the source of all his excuses. I'm not talking about someone who responds to emails just before bed. I'm talking about a man who sulks on Christmas because our culture requires a day off. His idea of a vacation is flying to some flat swath of the U.S. with no good restaurants, renting the cheapest car available, and driving hundreds of miles a day looking at farmland.

His other passion, or perhaps obsession, is eating, and it's easy to argue I wouldn't be in this line of work if I didn't share his affinity. Notice, though, I didn't say Dad's obsession is food. That's a difference between us, I think. The act of eating or not eating is what motivates him, not the desire to wallow in memorable tastes or textures. He's more impulse than epicure, more knee-jerk than gastronome. On more than one occasion I've stumbled upon Dad as he scarfed down cold cans of Vienna sausages, chicken noodle soup, and

baked beans in the middle of the night. Hovering over our kitchen table, surrounded by hastily opened cans full of preservatives, and clad only in tighty-whitey underwear, Dad did not look like the picture of someone who relished the pleasures of delicious food. No. Slurping up cold forcemeat at 1 am is high-intensity exercise in a serious relationship with eating.

Like everything Dad does, his eating habits long-jump from one end of a spectrum to the other. His favorite saying on the subject—"If you ain't losing, you're gaining"—is a clear window into his approach. Until I was well into my thirties, Dad was either on a hardcore diet or a binge. In his own words, he's lost and gained more than a thousand pounds in his adult life. From Optifast, SlimFast, Weight Watchers, Atkins, and South Beach to a lot of lesser-known regimens in between, Dad was the master of the fad diet. He took Fen-Phen, Alli, and caffeine pills of all kinds and when the diet stopped working and his weight hit a plateau, he ate a raw Irish potato and swore something about that terrible experience knocked off a few pounds.

Rather late in life Dad was forced to reevaluate his lifestyle. In 2007, in the wake of some gnarly family drama and a series of difficult years farming, Dad's weight ballooned to a number he still won't share and he developed what I call diabetes and what he calls "a little bit of sugar." The doctor gave him two choices. He could take medicine to treat his "sugar" or he could "diet" and exercise. Dad had always hated the idea of taking medicine to control something he could control himself...except of course if it was a short-term solution like a diet pill. So he chose the latter. All of us expected another starvation style, short-term diet coupled with a complete disregard for exercise. That would make sense. He had never taken to movement for movement's sake and we'd never seen him make measured changes in the way he ate. But at age sixty-seven, he surprised us.

It started with the exercise. Dad didn't know how to go about it and he sure as hell wasn't gonna ask one of his children, a personal trainer, or even his doctor for advice. Instead, he took to exercising in secret.

Rural legend has it that Dad woke up at 4am and walked around the pond next to his house wearing only his tighty-whitey underwear and work boots. Four times around the pond was 2.38 miles. By then, the sun was coming up, Dad was the type of hungry only exercise makes you, and it was clearly time to put on some clothes.

I never saw the near-naked pond-walking spectacle, but I heard the rumors and about the time those rumors started to make noise, Dad moved his walking up the road to his office. There, ever practical and precise, Dad determined how many laps up and down the long hall equaled 2.38 miles and he set about walking it out every morning at 4am in his underwear. To keep track of his laps, Dad filled his hand with coins and dropped a coin on the floor by the water fountain each time he completed a lap. When his hand was empty, he had done his exercise for the day.

The walking ritual became a source of pride for Dad and he approached it with resolute discipline. He talked about his coin strategy and how many miles he'd walked to date with anybody who would listen, much like he used to brag about the liquid diet he was on and how many pounds that liquid had shed. He swore if he missed a day of walking he'd fall off the wagon and stop forever. So when he traveled and couldn't get to the office, he doubled his mileage before his trip or walked up and down the hall of his hotel fully aware that an unsuspecting guest might see him in his tighty-whitey / work-boot workout attire.

Even more of a surprise was the way Dad approached the "diet" portion of his prescription. Instead of short-term starvation, he leaned into

actual moderation...kind of. Dad cut everything white out of his diet. No white potatoes, no white rice, nothing with sugar, no pasta, and no bread. He was obsessive about it, and you didn't share a meal with John Howard without hearing a sermon around what he did and did not eat.

The pounds didn't fall off like they had when Dad starved himself and broke his fasts with raw potatoes, but he lost weight over time and seemed to enjoy himself while doing it. Dad's pride in his new obsession caught my attention. I had always related to his struggles around weight, but I was never able to fast or binge with any success. I actually loved food. I didn't find satisfaction in merely filling up. I felt full when I ate something that was delicious and what I understood about Dad's new way of eating was that there were a lot of things in his diet I adored.

Never a sweets person, I could do without dessert (most of the time). I loved sandwiches but really what I loved about them was what's inside. I liked potatoes, but they were something I rarely ate because I knew they liked to linger on my thighs. I loved pasta, but I craved sauce more. So in my thirties, much to my surprise, I started eating a lot like, and cooking a lot for, my dad. It's not a formal thing or a way of eating and cooking I project through a megaphone. It's just something I do. I make food that for the most part leans deep into color. I'm not saying you'll never find me with a french fry in hand or that I never put a little sugar in a sauce, but when I mow down a white bread tomato sandwich or use potato to thicken a soup, I do it with reverence for the big picture. I want to make our most recent obsession a sustainable one.

This dish is the picture of a perfect meal for the legendary John Howard. For starters, there's nothing white anywhere. It requires a knife and a fork—which imply dinner will be hearty. I've hidden carrots and spinach in the sauce, so it's packed with vegetables you don't see. There's sausage, which makes me think of Dad and his affinity for Viennas in the can. And it's something everybody at the table will enjoy even with nary a white potato or piece of bread in sight.

Sunday Sauce over Roasted Broccoli

serves 4

1 pound hot or sweet Italian sausage, removed from its casing

4 tablespoons extra-virgin olive oil, divided

1 medium yellow onion, halved and roughly chopped

5 garlic cloves, peeled

4 ounces (about 2 cups packed) fresh spinach

1 medium carrot, roughly chopped

1 cup Red Weapons (page 104)

1 cup Red Weapon pickling liquid (Twin A, page 104)

1 (14.5-ounce) can diced tomatoes with their juice

2 teaspoons kosher salt, divided

2 large heads broccoli

½ cup grated Parmigiano Reggiano (use a Microplane), plus more to sprinkle on top

1 Preheat your oven to 375°F. In a Dutch oven or braiser fitted with a lid, brown the sausage in 1 tablespoon of the olive oil over medium-high heat. As it browns, break it up a bit with a wooden spoon or spatula.

2 Combine the onion, garlic, spinach, carrot, Red Weapons, Twin A liquid, canned tomatoes, and 1 teaspoon salt in a blender. Let it rip until the mixture is smooth. Carefully pour that into the pan with the browned sausage and lower the heat to medium. Bring it up to a simmer and cover with the lid. Let it cook for 30 to 40 minutes, stirring occasionally, until the color shifts slightly to become a rust-colored sauce.

3 As the sauce simmers, cut the broccoli heads in half vertically so you have four large pieces. Toss them with the remaining 3 tablespoons olive oil and the remaining 1 teaspoon salt. Put them on a baking sheet and roast on the middle rack of your oven for 30 minutes, until the broccoli is tender-crisp and parts of the florets are browned.

4 Once the broccoli is roasted, stir the cheese into the sauce. Serve the sauce underneath the broccoli like mashed potatoes under a steak. Sprinkle with additional Parm if you and yours so desire.

Red Weapon Greens on Mozzarella Toast

serves 4

This is a kick in the butt to find the green leaves in your fridge and inject them with excitement. I'm always on the hunt for something green to round out the rich and balance the brown on our plates. In my house that's often spinach. I buy it every time I go to the store. We use it in smoothies. I puree it into sauces. I fold it into omelets. I sauté it with garlic. It's utilitarian and fairly boring.

Half the time I hide spinach's mildly flavored leaves in anything blendable so my kids eat something green without knowing it. And other times bribe them to eat the least exciting thing on the plate. But I'm done with all that (at least for the purposes of this headnote). Let's highlight the green stuff. Stewed briefly with Red Weapons then perched on top of mozzarella toast, greens shine like pepperoni on a pizza. I've chosen dino kale as my model because she's my current green crush. I like that she cooks quickly and her dark green leaves suggest heft and intense nutrition, but use any green you got...even spinach.

On top of toast, this is the centerpiece of a meal, but you could forego the bread bed and serve the stewed greens alongside anything that's a match for their charisma.

1 Preheat your broiler to medium or set your oven to 450°F. In a 12-inch skillet, heat 1½ tablespoons of the olive oil over medium heat till it shimmers. Add the bread slices and brown them on the first side. This should take 2 minutes. Turn the toast over and season the browned sides with ¼ teaspoon of the salt. Add the remaining olive oil to the pan if it's dry and brown the other sides. Transfer the toast to a baking sheet.

2 In the same skillet or in a Dutch oven set over medium heat, melt 1 tablespoon of the butter. Add the greens, Red Weapons, Twin A liquid, and remaining ½ teaspoon salt. If your skillet has a lid, use it. If not, use the baking sheet that holds the toast to help the greens along by building up a bit of steam. Cook, covered, until the greens are wilted down and just about where you want them. Depending on the greens you choose and the degree of doneness you prefer, this could take anywhere from 5 to 20 minutes. If you need to add a little water to keep the stew action happening, please do but make sure that liquid cooks out before you serve your greens.

3 Put the mozzarella on the toast and slide that onto the top rack of your oven to melt. Stir the remaining 1 tablespoon butter and the Parm into the greens. Once the mozzarella is nicely melted, divide the greens overtop and serve with a knife and fork.

Up to 3 tablespoons extra-virgin olive oil	½ cup roughly chopped Red Weapons (page 104)
4 (1-inch-thick) slices of rustic, sturdy bread such as ciabatta or sourdough	¼ cup Red Weapon pickling liquid (Twin A, page 104)
¾ teaspoon kosher salt, divided	6 ounces mozzarella cheese, cut into 4 slices
2 tablespoons unsalted butter, divided	3 tablespoons grated Parmigiano Reggiano (use a Microplane)
Just over a pound of dino kale, large stems removed, roughly chopped	

One Vinaigrette & Two Creamy Dressings Walk into a Salad Bar

makes 2 cups each

Red Weapons scream "make salad dressing with me." And since I abhor store-bought dressings for their synthetic taste and odd mouthfeel, Red's ability to be both vinaigrette and a means to enliven creamy dressings is an attribute I admire. But beware. Because the Red Weapon family is assertive, they don't play well with all the salads out there.

Consider the vinaigrette to dress meaty things like tuna or chicken salad or as a drizzle on grain or breakfast bowls rather than a sheath for delicate tossed lettuce. I also find its sweet heat an ideal sauce for sautéed fish or roasted vegetables. Blended with avocado, Red Weapons make a pillowy dressing that tastes like a rendezvous with guacamole and salsa. Thin it out a bit with Twin A liquid and you've got an addictive puddle that's a perfect perch for chopped salads of any kind. Keep it thick and call it dip for vegetables or chips. Whisked with the things that generally make dressings creamy, the Red Weapon family pushes Ranch out of the way and begs to cascade down a wedge of iceberg or a grilled heart of romaine.

The below recipes are just suggestions. You can swap in herbs or assertive cheeses to tailor the dressings to your whim. Herbdacious (page 206) or Little Green Dress (page 10) would make an apt addition to any of the three. Have fun playing dress-up and never buy the bottled stuff again.

① RED VINAIGRETTE

- ½ cup Red Weapon oil (Twin B, page 104)
- ¼ cup Red Weapon pickling liquid (Twin A, page 104)
- ¼ cup chopped Red Weapons (page 104)
- 1 tablespoon red wine vinegar
- ½ teaspoon kosher salt

In a medium bowl, whisk together all the ingredients. Taste and adjust the acid level with additional red wine vinegar or more Twin A liquid. This is a broken dressing rather than one that's emulsified in a blender, so it will require some whisking or shaking just before using.

Makes about 1 cup

② PINK & DREAMY DRESSING

- 1 cup Red Weapons (page 104)
- 2 tablespoons Red Weapon pickling liquid (Twin A, page 104)
- 1 cup mayonnaise
- ½ cup sour cream
- ¼ cup buttermilk
- ¼ teaspoon kosher salt

Use the blender to whiz everything into a super-smooth dressing, or whisk it for something less refined and a bit chunky. Consider adding crumbled feta or blue cheese for an even more distinct and assertive take.

Makes about 3 cups

③ FEISTY CREAMYCADO DRESSING

- ½ cup Red Weapons (page 104)
- ½ cup Red Weapon pickling liquid (Twin A, page 104)
- 1 small ripe avocado, halved, pitted, peeled, and flesh scooped
- 2 tablespoons Red Weapon oil (Twin B, page 104)
- 2 tablespoons fresh lime or lemon juice
- ½ teaspoon kosher salt

Put all the ingredients in the blender and process until smooth. As mentioned above, Herbdacious (page 206) makes a great addition here, but also consider blending in a handful of cilantro, mint, tarragon, or whole leaves of basil.

Makes about 1½ cups

Relish Me This Grilled Vegetables

makes 4 cups

During the summer I'm a grilling fool. On Sunday nights I'll barbecue chickens and use the excuse of a hot grill to put marks and char on the high volume of vegetables that find their way to my kitchen from May to August. Corn on the cob, flat meaty Roma beans, candy-sweet onions, colorful peppers, loads of eggplant, and pounds of squash get tossed in oil and transformed by the unique heat of the grill. I didn't start doing this with meal prep in mind, but my Sunday evening exploits with fire produced so many charred smoky slices of eggplant, wedges of squash, and rings of onion that meal prep Vivian style was born.

I can't leave well enough alone, and while grilled vegetables seasoned with salt and brightened by lemon juice are more than "well enough," meal prep for me meant taking them farther. Diced up and marinated with Red Weapon and her Twins, leftover grilled vegetables of any kind become a relish to remember. Serve it with fish, spoon it on top of hummus, toss it with grains like farro or quinoa, make it the filling for tacos. Don't walk. Run to this relish. Her possibilities and the pleasures she provides are endless.

3 cups diced grilled vegetables

½ cup roughly chopped Red Weapons (page 104)

½ cup Red Weapon liquid (Twin A, page 104)

⅓ cup Red Weapon oil (Twin B, page 104)

½ teaspoon kosher salt

Fresh herbs like basil, mint, thyme, tarragon, cilantro, or chervil, if you like

❶ As simple as it seems, combine the vegetables, the Red Weapons, Twin A liquid, Twin B oil, and salt in a bowl and let it marinate for a minimum of 15 minutes before serving. If you choose to include herbs other than parsley, incorporate them just before you plan to eat. Otherwise the acid in the marinade will turn them brown.

❷ Relish Me This will keep for a week in your fridge, but it will evolve and intensify in flavor over time. Like everything that's not meant to be eaten ice cold, I let this warm up to room temperature before I eat it.

HEADS up

While any number of vegetables will work, I like to include grilled onion of some kind, whether it's a spring scallion or a sweet Vidalia. The onion gives some background to the relish and I miss it when it's not there. I also try to include a crunchy vegetable or two for a pop of texture. Kernels of corn cut off the cob or sugar snap or snow peas add this to great effect.

K&W Made Me Do It Skillet Cornbread

makes one 10- to 12-inch skillet of cornbread

I'm not sure what it says about me that I've chosen to immortalize K&W Cafeteria in this book, but the fact is I experienced a lot of firsts in K&W's carpeted dining room—my first baked spaghetti, my first congealed salad, and my first argument with Grandma Hill all happened over the restaurant's melamine trays. Grandma took issue with K&W's cornbread. She said cornbread didn't have "stuff" in it. And cornbread wasn't fluffy like the pale, flour-filled, jalapeño-spotted square on my tray. Grandma said what I had was corn cake and corn cake was wrong. I shrugged and said, "I like corn cake."

This cornbread with a lot of stuff in it is inspired by those trips to K&W and fueled by my affinity for breaking the rules. I do not agree with Grandma in its nomenclature as corn cake. It has no eggs and no sugar. It's cornbread with stuff in it, and that stuff makes it taste good.

ATTENTION You can use either a 10- or 12-inch cast-iron skillet to bake this. The 10-inch will result in a thicker finished product. The 12-inch will bake something much thinner, something more like a giant cornbread cookie. Grandma would choose the 10-inch. I'd go with the 12.

½ cup all-purpose flour

½ cup cornmeal

1½ teaspoons baking powder

¾ teaspoon kosher salt

1 cup buttermilk

½ cup roughly chopped <u>Red Weapons</u> (page 104)

⅓ cup <u>Red Weapon jalapeños</u> (page 104)

⅓ cup grated white cheddar

5 tablespoons <u>Red Weapon oil</u> (Twin B, page 104) or melted butter, divided

❶ Preheat your oven to 350°F and slide the cast-iron skillet you plan to use in there as it heats.

❷ In a bowl large enough to hold all the ingredients, stir together everything except 2 tablespoons of the Twin B or butter. It will be a lumpy mess given all the stuff in it, but that's what we're going for. Once the oven is heated, add the remaining 2 tablespoons Twin B or butter to the screaming hot skillet and swirl it around to cover the bottom and sides. Pour the cornbread batter in and slide the skillet onto the middle rack of your oven. Bake for 25 to 30 minutes, until it becomes a ldeep brown around the edges and a lighter, golden brown on top.

❸ Serve warm or at room temperature, and if you want to really get at Grandma, crown your slice with a dollop of sour cream.

CHAPTER FIVE

Citrus Shrine

Focused • Floral • Briny • Elegant

There are only a few things I can't possibly cook without.

Sure, I appreciate ingredients like flaky salt and fruity olive oil that refine and elevate the food I cook. And there are magic fairy ingredients like Parmigiano Reggiano and bacon fat that I turn to over and over for a specific quality that only they offer up. But my list of true ride-or-die ingredients is small. On it is citrus—perhaps the only ingredient I truly worship.

When I say citrus, I mean lemons, limes, oranges, and all the varieties that live within those distinctions. I squeeze citrus juice to punctuate, point, and elevate. I Microplane citrus skin to accentuate or reinforce citrus's presence in things. But despite its singular importance to me, citrus usually lives in the background. It's part of the chorus that supports the star's role. It may have a solo from time to time, but citrus rarely ever takes center stage.

But preserved citrus is citrus transformed. After weeks submerged in an acidic salty brine, lemons, limes, and oranges emerge as the distilled, meaty, supple essence of their sunny attributes. Their skin becomes the prize and their pulp, the place where the juice once lived, takes a backseat. Preserved citrus is citrus ready for its closeup.

Citrus Shrine's origin story begins in North Africa, where lemons have been preserved for centuries. Their influence on that culture's cuisine can't be overstated. If Italy is Parmigiano Reggiano and prosciutto, if Japan is miso and wasabi, and if the American South is collard greens and cornbread, then Morocco is preserved lemon and olives.

I've preserved lemons as long as I've worked in restaurant kitchens. It's one of those things budget-conscious, strategic chefs do because it's an easy way to transform an ingredient you already have. Plus, preserved lemons hold a definitive spot in world cuisine. So making them a part of our repertoire was a no brainer. The idea to preserve oranges and limes came a little later when I realized lemon, with her fragrant rind, bitter white pith, and tart pulp, was really no different from her citrus sisters. And the idea to cram all three types of citrus in a single jar to preserve together grew out of my desire to have multiple expressions of compact sunshine in my kitchen at home.

Citrus Shrine is easy to make, impossible to screw up, versatile beyond belief, and basically never goes bad. If you make it today, I bet you'll soon decide your kitchen needs it forever. ➜

Citrus Shrine

HERE'S WHAT'S IMPORTANT

- I call for run-of-the-mill citrus here, but you can use anything that strikes you. Meyer lemons, Cara Cara or blood oranges, key limes, grapefruit—you name it. As long as it's citrus and in good condition, you can preserve it.

- There's more than one way to preserve citrus in salt. Sometimes the citrus is sliced. Sometimes people add spices or oil. If that's what you do, keep doing it. The below method is just a suggestion. As you take citrus out and make room inside the jar, you can add leftover lemon, lime, or orange slices to the brine to marinate. Or, once the preserved citrus is ready, you can take it out of its brine and transfer to another container. Store that container in the fridge and use the leftover brine to start a new batch of citrus in a freshly sterilized jar.

3 to 5 lemons
3 to 5 limes
3 to 5 oranges
Roughly ⅔ cup kosher salt, plus more as necessary

Juice of roughly 2 lemons (don't even think about using that stuff in a bottle)

1 Begin by sterilizing the jar or jars you want to use. I like to use a half-gallon mason jar for this because you can't really fit three types of citrus into quart jars in a worthwhile way, but if wide-mouth quart jars are all you have then go for it. I find the easiest way to sterilize a jar is to run it through your dishwasher, but you could also steam it for about 10 minutes.

2 Wash your citrus and peel off any annoying stickers. Slice an X from the top down to within ½ inch of the bottom. The idea is to almost cut the citrus into quarters but to leave it attached at its stem end.

3 Rub the inside of the exposed flesh liberally with salt, then reshape the fruit. Put about ¼ cup salt in the bottom of your jar, if using a half-gallon. If using quart jars, divide that salt between the two. Then go about the business of cramming your citrus into your jar. When I say cram, I mean cram. Imagine your kitchen is the circus. This jar is the clown car. The lemons, limes, and oranges are the clowns, and you are the ringmaster. Now cram the clowns in.

4 Put a layer of lemons in and sprinkle 2 to 3 tablespoons salt on top of that layer. Use the back of a clean wooden spoon to bruise them inside the jar, which will also work to squeeze out some of their juice.

5 Follow with a layer of oranges. If your oranges are large, you may have to cut them in half; it's okay if a layer ends up being just one orange. Sprinkle that layer with salt and bruise it up.

MAKES ½ GALLON

⑥ Now for the limes. Do the same as the lemons and oranges, and continue to alternate citrus until your clown car is full. When I say "full" I mean there may be a clown head or rear-end that peeks up into the neck of the jar. That's okay. As long as you can screw the lid on securely and it doesn't buckle, your clowns should be fine.

⑦ Finish with a layer of salt and pour in the lemon juice. If you've properly crammed and bruised your citrus, it may take a minute or two for the juice to seep down and through the tiny avenues that exist between your lemons, limes, and oranges, but be patient because the salty lemon juice is what will do the pickling here and we need it to be everywhere. When you're done, the lemon juice should cover everything, but if a small piece of citrus rind pokes through that's okay, everything will soften and shrink over the next few days and it will end up submerged.

⑧ Leave the sealed jar in a cool, visible spot out of the sun in your kitchen for 4 weeks. From time to time, turn the jar over and let it sit on its lid for a day or so.

⑨ When the citrus is ready it will have deepened in color just a bit and the skin should feel supple and soft. If that's not the case, give it more time. Once the citrus meets the criteria, it's ready to use.

⑩ Store the finished shrine in the fridge or keep it on your counter. If you see weird, white lacy stuff around the citrus, that's fine, just rinse it off before using it. Your Citrus Shrine will keep for a year at this point.

How to Use the Stuff

Once the citrus is preserved, there are two parts you can use (the rind and pulp) and one you will always remove (the salty brine). **The rind** is the most colorful, soft, sexy part. It's employed in every recipe that calls for preserved citrus. Separated from the pith, it can be used "raw," but it blooms and comes to life when it meets heat. It's pretty versatile and should be something you consider in just about everything you cook that calls for citrus.

The pulp, or the place where the juice once lived, is sometimes used "raw" but is most often roughly chopped and thrown into stews, syrups, or sautés to add a singular salty, sunny funk only it can provide. When you get ready to make something that calls on citrus juice as a cooking liquid, strap on your thinking cap, chop up some preserved pulp, reduce the amount of salt the recipe calls for by a bit, and throw in preserved pulp. Don't forego the juice the recipe suggests. Instead, just revel in the fact that the preserved pulp will add a layer of citrus personality to the finished dish you never thought possible.

Some more tips for using preserved citrus:

- Always, always, always rinse the entire orange, lemon, or lime inside and out before you do anything else with it. It's slimy and salty and will appreciate the bath before it meets your knife.

- Cut through the bottom that's holding it together. This will separate the citrus into four quarters. Some of my recipes will call for a quarter, two quarters, or three quarters of preserved citrus. This is sometimes an easier measurement because a tablespoon of thinly sliced, unwieldy rind is kind of a hard thing to measure.

- Cut the pulp away, doing your best to leave the white pith with the rind at this point. The science that happened during preservation should make this easier than it would have been with fresh citrus. If the recipe calls for preserved pulp, this section is what it's talking about. Just remove the seeds and roughly chop what's left.

- To mine the rind, lay a quarter of a citrus peel whose pulp has been removed on the cutting board white pith facing up. Use a sharp knife (but not a serrated one) to cut as much of the pith away as possible. The pith is bitter and adding it to stuff will make you wonder why you trust my taste. Once you've cut away as much as you think possible, cut a little bit more. What you're left with should be shiny, soft, smooth, and supple. This is the stuff of transformation and you made it. Now go mix yourself the margarita on page 155.

- If you separate more rind or pulp than you need for a recipe, put what you don't use in a container or back in the brine and slide that in the fridge until you need it. Just rinse all parts again before you use them.

Citrus Shrine will keep for a year in its jar right on the counter, but for some reason, maybe too many run-ins with the health inspector at the restaurant, I tend to keep it in my fridge.

1
braise with
olives and any
kind of meat

2
whiz into salsa,
pesto, or salad
dressing

3
stir into any sauce
you finish with that
particular citrus

4
fold into
savory or sweet
doughs

5
throw onto
roasted vegetables
or meats

6
fold into tuna,
chicken, or pasta
salad

7
sprinkle on baked
potatoes with
butter and Parm

8
blend with butter
and use as an
overnight marinade
for chicken

9
stir into herbs to
make a relish for
grilled meats or
vegetables

10
add to grain
salads and
pilafs

11
toss with
pasta, garlic, and
olive oil

Fish in a Bag

serves 4

At first impression, food cooked in parchment seemed to me like a cheffy gimmick designed for drama at the table. Then I tried the technique and learned its power. You see, in a restaurant situation it's important to have some dishes that don't require time in a pan or on a grill to cook. Dishes where the work is done ahead of time—meaning it's prepped hours before, then thrown in the oven when ordered—free up cooks' hands and coveted heat sources and make the kitchen more efficient.

It's also just a really great way to cook fish because the pouch forces the fish to steam to the tune of whatever you tuck in there. You end up with moist fish, flavorful sides, and a light sauce all trapped in a bag. This frontloaded way of approaching dinner resonates at home too. And whether it's just your family or a dinner party, the shared experience of cutting open the bag and inhaling its fragrant steam is remarkable.

I use quinoa here because I'm always trying to make quinoa taste good (and I succeeded this time), plus spinach because it's mild and cooks quickly. But you could get wildly creative with your bag. If it's grains, make sure they're already cooked and if it's vegetables, make sure it will cook to your liking in the minutes it takes to bake your fish.

⅓ cup tahini

3 tablespoons fresh lemon juice, divided

1 tablespoon honey

1 clove garlic, grated on a Microplane

2½ teaspoons kosher salt, divided

¼ cup ice water

1 cup fresh orange juice, divided

2 cups cooked quinoa

8 ounces (4 cups packed) fresh spinach

4 tablespoons thin strips Citrus Shrine preserved lemon rind (page 140, white pith removed), divided

4 (6-ounce) pieces flounder

1 teaspoon cayenne

2 tablespoons extra-virgin olive oil

1 tablespoon chopped fresh parsley

1 tablespoon chopped fresh mint

1. Preheat your oven to 500°F. In a small bowl, whisk together the tahini, 2 tablespoons of the lemon juice, the honey, garlic, and ½ teaspoon of the salt. You'll notice the tahini seizes up with the addition of the lemon. To make it silky and loose again, add the ice water and whisk. Finally, whisk in ⅓ cup of the orange juice. The sauce should be quite loose, like pancake batter.

2. Cut four 12 x 8-inch rectangles of parchment paper and lay them out on two baking sheets. In a large bowl, toss together the quinoa, spinach, 2 tablespoons of the Citrus Shrine lemon rind, and ½ teaspoon salt. Divide that mixture by four and spoon each quarter of it onto the middle of your parchment squares. Season the fish on both sides with the remaining 1½ teaspoons salt and the cayenne. Lay the fish on top of the quinoa mixture and spoon the tahini sauce over top.

3. Fold up the sides of each sheet of parchment and staple the ends to make an open-top pyramid-shaped pouch. Pour the remaining ⅔ cup orange juice into the pouches, taking care not to pour off the seasonings on top of the fish. Finish by drizzling each piece of fish with the oil. Staple the pouches closed and accept that they may not look like the origami masterpieces you had hoped for.

4. If you can, consolidate the pouches onto one baking sheet and slide that onto the middle rack of your oven. Bake for 12 to 15 minutes. While the fish bakes, make an herb relish by tossing the remaining 2 tablespoons Citrus Shrine lemon rind in a small bowl with the remaining 1 tablespoon lemon juice, the parsley, and mint.

5. When the fish comes out of the oven, the pouches should be browned in spots and give the perception of lots of activity happening inside. Carefully place each pouch on a plate and travel to the table with it, scissors and lemon wedge in hand. Once everyone is seated and at attention, cut open the pouches, savor the aromatic steam bath opening ceremony for your dinner, and sprinkle the Citrus Shrine herb relish over top.

Autumn's Crunch Factor Slaw

serves 6

It's hard to get excited about slaw. The word itself reads as a sloppy afterthought. But this hyper-crunchy, bright, fresh cast of colors makes me want to rename the genre. Orange Citrus Shrine and pickled ginger are the sharp notes that pull the more muted ones from shy sweet potatoes and subtle beets as the juice from shredded apples bathes everything in a fall glow. And lots and lots of fresh mint turn this salad-slaw mashup into a veritable palate cleanser.

Yes, this tastes like fall and calls on ingredients we associate with the season, but apples, beets, and sweet potatoes are omnipresent and of good quality all year long in the grocery store. So when you're asked to bring slaw to the picnic, choose this no matter the season and you'll become the slaw provider moving forward.

If you'd like to turn this slaw into a bona fide lunch, season some avocado with salt and lemon juice and spoon this, the crunchiest thing you can imagine, on top of that, the creamy thing the whole world seems to love, and there you have it—lunch.

1 You're going to have to shred a lot of vegetables here. I don't bring out kitchen gadgets unless they save a lot of time because I hate washing dishes, so the fact I am suggesting you use the shredding blade of your food processor should tell you something about the time it saves. But if you don't have a food processor, strap on your knife or employ a mandoline and cut the apples, sweet potatoes, and beets into thin strips.

2 Because of the red-bleed potential beets promise, start with the apples and follow up with the sweet potato. Combine them in a large bowl and go about shredding (or chopping) the beets. Once the beets have been cut, put them in a separate bowl and rinse and drain. Do this four or five times. This may sound like a lot of work, but it will wash away a lot of the red dye that will otherwise make your slaw all one unappetizing color. Once you've rinsed your beets, add them to the other shredded vegetables, along with the scallions, pickled ginger, and ½ teaspoon of the salt, and toss to combine.

3 To make the dressing, whisk together the Citrus Shrine rind, mayo, sour cream, sugar, vinegar, and remaining ½ teaspoon salt. Pour the dressing over the shredded vegetables and let everything mingle together in the fridge for at least 30 minutes.

4 Just before serving, stir in most of the mint. Save a little for the top as garnish.

4	small crisp apples, cut from their cores
1	medium sweet potato, peeled
2	medium beets, peeled
4	scallions, sliced thin
¼	cup pickled ginger, drained
1	teaspoon kosher salt, divided

2	tablespoons minced Citrus Shrine preserved orange rind (page 140, white pith removed)
½	cup mayonnaise
¼	cup sour cream
1	tablespoon granulated sugar
2	tablespoons cider vinegar
	As much fresh mint as you can muster to pick, but no less than ½ cup

HEADS up

I've gone to great lengths (and to Walmart a lot) to make sure you can buy just about everything in this book just about everywhere. I'm also adamant you only buy things you will use over and over again when you cook. Pickled ginger is one of those things, and believe it or not, it lives in the "international" aisle of Supercenters everywhere. It's got all the things—texture, acid, sweetness, and a palate-cleansing spice. Put it on your shopping list and don't forget to use its brine to lend lift to sauces or a distinct punch to vinaigrettes.

Shrimp Cocktail I Can Get Behind

serves 8

I've never quite understood our blind love of shrimp cocktail. Far too often the shrimp squeak against your teeth like bland rubber, the cocktail-sauce part of things tastes metallic and tired, and if you're lucky enough to get some tartar sauce, it feels like mayo's stepsister.

The thing is, we keep coming back to this steakhouse classic because our bellies know that somewhere in there, if treated the right way, there's something really good. The other thing, and the reason I fuss with shrimp cocktail at all, is that it's just about the perfect party food. Here's why:

- Cocktail sauce and tartar sauce are better the next day, and the shrimp need to chill properly, so it all benefits from being prepared in advance.

- You don't have to fret about keeping it warm while the party goes on.

- You can plainly see what shrimp cocktail is and people know what to do with it, so no surprise food allergies emerge and nobody feels unsophisticated in its presence.

- Shrimp are seafood and seafood isn't cheap, so even if you serve beans and bread the rest of the night your guests will deem you a generous host.

- It's gluten free. There's one in every bunch.

- It's fun to eat, needs no knife or utensil to speak of, and the size of a shrimp doesn't encourage a double-dip.

- We've all had lots of bad shrimp cocktail, so if you do it better than most, your party guests will take note. And this is better than most.

 HEADS up Although there are very big shrimp available for the cocktailing, I prefer 21/25s. That means there are between 21 and 25 shrimp in a pound. Any bigger and I think shrimp's flavor and texture starts to suffer.

If you don't have LGD on hand, you can substitute 2 tablespoons chopped mint, 2 tablespoons chopped parsley, 1 tablespoon rinsed and chopped capers, 2 garlic cloves grated on a Microplane, and 1 tablespoon red wine vinegar.

PRESERVED LEMON OIL
- ¼ cup tasty extra-virgin olive oil
- 3 tablespoons finely minced Citrus Shrine preserved lemon rind (page 140, white pith removed)

COCKTAIL SAUCE
- 2 cups ketchup
- ¼ cup finely chopped Citrus Shrine preserved lemon pulp (page 140)
- 3 tablespoons fresh lemon juice
- 2 tablespoons prepared horseradish
- 2 tablespoons Worcestershire sauce

TARTAR SAUCE
- 1½ cups mayonnaise
- ⅓ cup Little Green Dress (page 10)
- ½ cup minced dill pickle
- 1 tablespoon fresh lemon juice

SHRIMP
- 2 pounds 21/25 shell-on shrimp
- ½ cup kosher salt
- ½ cup granulated sugar
- 6 cups warm water

① **Make the Preserved Lemon Oil:** Gently heat the olive oil and Citrus Shrine rind just until the lemon begins to sizzle. Then take off the heat and set aside. This is what you will dress your shrimp in after it's cooked.

② **Make the Cocktail Sauce:** Stir together the ketchup, Citrus Shrine pulp, lemon juice, horseradish, and Worcestershire.

3 **Make the Tartar Sauce:** Combine the mayo, LGD, minced pickle, and lemon juice.

4 **Brine and Cook the Shrimp:** Use kitchen shears to cut through the shell along the shrimps' curved backs. This will open up and expose the intestinal tract. Wipe that away with a paper towel. Once you've eviscerated all your shrimp, dissolve the salt and sugar in the warm water. Pour that over your shrimp in a large bowl and let them soak in the brine for 30 minutes.

5 Bring a large pot of salted water to a boil. Often I season the water with lots of sliced lemons, vinegar, onion, smashed garlic, and herbs. This is totally optional and an added bonus, so use the aromatics you have on hand, and don't stress out about this part.

6 When your water is at a rapid boil, take the shrimp out of their brine and drop half of them into the pot. Stir the shrimp around and watch as they begin to turn pink. Let them cook for no more than 2 minutes. After 60 seconds, I lift a shrimp out and cut through its thickest part. If it's nearly opaque, I start taking them out of the water with a slotted spoon.

7 Spread the cooked shrimp on a rimmed baking sheet. Slide that into your fridge or freezer. Go about cooking and cooling the remainder of your shrimp the same way. A lot of people cool their shrimp down by shocking them in an ice bath. While I'm a huge fan of ice baths in other circumstances, I don't use them for shrimp. I think the "shock" of it changes the texture of the shrimp and if by chance your cooking water was flavored in any way, the ice bath would wash that flavor away. Still, it's very important to cool the shrimp down quickly, so don't skip the baking sheet/fridge step.

8 Once your shrimp have cooled, peel them, leaving the tails intact. Toss the shrimp with the preserved lemon oil. Serve the shrimp cold with the cocktail and tartar sauces.

Chicken Wangs!!

serves 4

Citrus Shrine is certainly at home hovering behind the scenes. She adds depth to dishes and makes the background a brighter, more interesting place to be. But in my mind, to really appreciate Citrus Shrine's personality, she's got to be the star. And nothing highlights her sunny, assertive self like the gnaw, lick, and smack act of eating a chicken wing.

Chicken wings just make me happy. Eating with my hands while I build little piles of cartilage and bone evidence feels like a party and requires the kind of outside-the-lines, bad-manners behavior only baby back ribs can touch. Both finger foods make more sense with a Wet-Nap than a fork, and we all need a little Wet-Nap in our lives. Am I right?

10 to 12 whole chicken wings, cut into drumettes and wingettes (20 to 24 pieces)

2 teaspoons kosher salt

1 tablespoon extra-virgin olive oil

⅓ cup thin strips mixed Citrus Shrine preserved citrus rind (page 140, white pith removed)

1 cup honey

⅓ cup cider vinegar

1 tablespoon soy sauce

8 garlic cloves, sliced thin

1 teaspoon red pepper flakes

1 Preheat your oven to 400°F. Season the wings with the salt and spread them out on two baking sheets. Drizzle the wings with the olive oil and slide the baking sheets into your oven. Roast for 15 minutes. Then rotate the baking sheets between the racks and roast another 15 minutes, until they are golden brown and crispy.

2 Meanwhile, combine the Citrus Shrine strips, honey, vinegar, soy sauce, garlic, and pepper flakes in a saucepan and bring up to a simmer over medium heat. Cook for about 10 minutes. The sauce will thicken and little and grow slightly darker, but keep an eye on it. It will continue to thicken as it cools, so don't take it too far. Glaze is what you want. Garlic caramel is not.

3 After the wings have cooked for 30 minutes total, bring them out of the oven, pour off the rendered chicken fat, and combine the wings on one baking sheet. Pour the glaze overtop and stir the wings around to coat them with the glaze. Slide the baking sheet onto the top rack of the oven and roast for an additional 5 minutes, until the glaze has become sticky. Bring the wings out, stir them up again, and once they've cooled enough to handle, gather round the sheet pan with handfuls of Wet-Naps and have a party.

 HEADS up

If the meal requires more decorum than a bib allows, simmer the spicy glaze of candied garlic and citrus in the name of giving life to pork tenderloin, roasted vegetables, fish, or a whole bird of any feather. This glaze is a fun thing to have around and will keep in your fridge for weeks.

New Leaf Pilaf

serves 4

Near the end of my five years living in New York, I was the butcher at a café called the New Leaf on the grounds of the Cloisters museum. I remember a lot about this short, sort of odd and strenuous job of mine in upper, upper Manhattan, but the memory I come back to in my own kitchen is of the beans and rice a Dominican prep cook made nearly every day for family meal.

I watched the short man with a mischievous smile slide the hotel pan in the oven—basic looking black beans surrounded by uncooked rice and liquid. Forty or so minutes later I smelled them as they emerged. An explosion of cilantro, lime, and garlic wafting through the grease-slicked kitchen was the dinner bell that brought the cooks close, plastic quart containers and forks in hand, for a meal we ate standing up or crouching at our stations. The cook who made them didn't speak English and I was too self-conscious to stumble over my Spanish, so I never found out what made his bean and rice bake so aromatic and special.

This quick-to-put-together pilaf of black beans, rice, cilantro stems, toasted cumin, garlic, and lime Citrus Shrine is my full-flavored attempt at the same dinner bell of aromas. It's a welcome one-pot companion to tacos—a meal we have a lot in our house in the name of ease. But when you pair tacos with a pot of beans, a skillet of rice, and all the accoutrements that make the taco-eating experience complete, you end up with a lot of dishes to wash. Try this pilaf instead and get everything in one pot.

3 tablespoons extra-virgin olive oil, divided

1 cup long-grain white rice

2 teaspoons whole cumin seeds

3 garlic cloves, sliced thin

2 quarters Citrus Shrine preserved lime rind (page 140), white pith removed, cut into strips

1 teaspoon kosher salt

1 (15-ounce) can black beans, drained and rinsed

⅓ cup chopped cilantro stems

3 cups chicken broth or water

1 Preheat your oven to 350°F. In a 12-inch ovenproof skillet, heat 2 tablespoons of the olive oil over medium heat. Add the rice, cumin, garlic, and Citrus Shrine strips. Sauté for about a minute, taking care that the rice gets toasted a bit and the cumin grows aromatic. Stir in the salt, black beans, cilantro stems, and broth. Bring that up to a simmer and transfer the skillet to the middle rack of your oven. Bake for 30 minutes. The rice will have absorbed the broth and the pilaf will largely be done.

2 To gild the lily, put the skillet back on your stove over medium heat. Drizzle the remaining 1 tablespoon oil around the edges of the skillet and let the pilaf sit there undisturbed for 2 minutes. The rice on the bottom will crisp up and give the pilaf a variety of texture. Serve warm.

Margaritas with Salt Inside

makes 1 pitcher, enough for 4 cocktails (with simple syrup to spare)

There's nothing I like better than a perfectly tart margarita on a hot day. But let's be honest, mouth-puckering, salivation-worthy margaritas are not the norm in our nation's temples to "ACP" covered in queso dip. Too often they're a weird green color, watered down yet tooth-achingly sweet. And as much as I long for the balance offered up by salt's edge, it's often iodized table salt clumped clumsily on the rim of a goblet, and it rarely does what I want it to.

I'm not going so far as to say I've improved on a classic cocktail. If made properly, a true margarita is untouchable. What I have done here is broaden lime's influence on the drink. By simmering a simple syrup of sugar and lime Citrus Shrine, I've added the sunny notes of citrus rind and the thirst-inducing ones from its salty, funky pulp.

I've suggested tequila as the liquor here, but if the whole pitcher were for just me, I'd choose mezcal. If you're on the fence about this smoky, distinct sister to tequila, these margaritas make a more measured introduction to the spirit than a shot.

4   quarters <u>Citrus Shrine</u> preserved lime rind (page 140), white pith removed, plus more rind for serving

1   cup granulated sugar
⅔   cup fresh lime juice
⅓   cup fresh orange juice
1½ cups silver tequila or mezcal

1 Slice the Citrus Shrine rind into thin strips and roughly chop the pulp. Put all that in a small saucepan with the sugar and 2 cups water. Bring it to a boil, then reduce the heat to low and simmer for about 10 minutes. Leave the pulp and rind in the syrup once it's done. I like candied rind and salty pulp discoveries in my margarita. If you don't, you can certainly strain those out.

2 Once the syrup has completely cooled, put ½ cup of it in a quart jar with the citrus juices, the tequila or mezcal, and 1 cup ice. Screw on the lid and shake it like a mustachioed mixologist wearing a vest. Pour the margaritas over new ice and float a few strips of lime rind on top.

COLLARDS BREAK CHARACTER

For as long as I can remember I've fought against type. My dad owned one of the largest farms in our rural community, so I did everything I could to act the opposite of a landowner's daughter. I gravitated toward friends who lived in trailer parks, and in lieu of the playhouse with three real rooms in my backyard, I made my 4 x 2-foot closet the make-believe shack I lived in with my daughter, Poodle Mae, who I rescued from the side of the road. When my hall proctor in boarding school coined me the girl from the tobacco farm, I became the school's most enthusiastic consumer of Greek mythology, the Indigo Girls, and the Gap. And when my peers referred to me as the Southern belle during an internship at *CBS Sunday Morning,* I dove into dive bars, wore midriff tops, and challenged my direct superiors just so they knew I did not embody the stereotype.

I've made moves big and small to fight against having myself and those around me put in a particular type of box—one without nuance, one that's not allowed to change, one that only tells a small part of the story. Most recently I drew a line in the sand, stomped my foot, and said my TV show *A Chef's Life* had to end.

When we started making the show, I was a thirty-two-year-old ex-New Yorker running a restaurant with her husband in her hometown. I ran the kitchen, worked the line, did all the ordering, planned all the menus. I was emphatically the chef. I worked with a farmer named Warren who worked with a woman

named Lillie. Over the course of five seasons, Warren, Lillie, and I became part of the fabric of each other's lives as well as the characters people associated with the show. *A Chef's Life* was a warm and wonderful look at Eastern North Carolina's food, culture, and people, and I'm so very grateful to have been at the show's center. But with each passing season I grew more uncomfortable with the image it projected—not because it was bad, but because it didn't evolve. This is not a criticism of the show's director or producers or even me. Rather, our viewership liked what they saw and as a production team we felt pressure to continue to give them a version of that.

Lillie is an African American woman in her sixties. She worked most of her life in a nursing home. Her mother was a cook for a prominent white family in the area. Lillie has children, grandchildren, and great-grandchildren. As best I can tell, she takes care of all of them in both big and small ways. She came to work with Warren growing vegetables because a friend of hers, who was his farmhand at the time, had cancer and was too sick to come to work. Lillie filled in for her so the friend wouldn't lose her job. The friend passed away and Lillie continued working with Warren growing vegetables, making deliveries, and running his stand at the farmers' market. She is no-nonsense, practical, hard-working, funny, and warm. She taught me to make biscuits on the first season of the show. I failed miserably and she talked a little junk to me. From that point on, Lillie became known as the witty cook who reminded thousands of middle-aged white people of the black woman who kept their kitchens humming and their houses clean when they were kids. But that's not Lillie.

Warren is a white man in his sixties. He grew up on the farm he now tends. Like a lot of people, he made his living most of his life growing tobacco. When tobacco farming and eventually tobacco subsidies went away, Warren was forced to look at

"The irony is that the show that changed all of our lives didn't allow us to evolve."

his farm differently. Tobacco was such a powerful cash crop. Families could make a real living on a 40-acre tobacco farm, but nothing else you put in the ground to grow is capable of that. Warren started growing vegetables for me and eventually other restaurants in the area. He and his wife turned their farmhouse into an Airbnb to bring in extra income, because vegetables, even organic ones, are not tobacco. He's full of charisma and a pure pleasure to be around. On the surface he's happy-go-lucky, but there is a philosopher who feels a deep responsibility to his children and his land living just beneath his charming smile. On the first season of *A Chef's Life,* Warren takes me through his corn patch. He's barefoot. He's also barefoot when he makes a delivery to the

restaurant later in the episode. From that point forward, Warren became the barefoot farmer trope. But Warren is so much more.

After the first season of the show my life changed a whole lot. I became an author, a public speaker, a fundraiser, a brand ambassador. My new career pulled me in a million directions, none of them toward the kitchen at Chef and the Farmer. But viewers loved to see the down-home struggling chef with a Southern accent who worked the line, cooked dinner for her family, and doted on her parents. They wanted me just as they had discovered me. They wanted Lillie to don an apron and talk junk while she taught me to cook. They wanted Warren to walk barefoot through his fields with a piece of hay in his mouth. So that's what we did...when the cameras rolled. But in the off time, the real time, Warren invested in growing hemp in hopes that a new cash crop would make life as a farmer more sustainable. I apologized to my cooks and my team for being absent but making it look as if I were not. And Lillie privately pondered when fame would mean more than taking photos and signing autographs.

The irony is that the show that changed all of our lives didn't allow us to evolve, and eventually that became too much for me. I felt like we were the collards of the greens world, pigeonholed into a life slow-stewed with cured pork—suitable for nothing else, misunderstood, underestimated. I wanted people to see we were more, less, and different than the way we'd been typecast. So I did the thing. I stopped the show and went about making a new one.

Somewhere South is not about me or Warren or Lillie. Instead its lens looks outward at a variety of cultures that make up the American South. It represents my interests as a student and storyteller. It doesn't hinge on any one personality, or a set of caricatures. It's about people. How we are different, and ultimately how we are the same. It's about how place and circumstance shape us, and how we shape place. It's about how our foods, our traditions, and our minds continuously evolve.

Collards Break Character

serves 4

I stumble around the question of how I find inspiration for new dishes because generally the process is more research than revelation. But when my friend Von Diaz made her collards braised in coconut milk on an episode of my show *Somewhere South*, I was blown away by the idea of collards braised in anything other than porky pot liquor. Von's collards landed in my bowl dark green, earthy, and a little bit bitter against a white backdrop of mellow, comforting coconut milk. They were familiar but different and I was totally inspired.

Von sautéed her collards in oil before she got to the business of stewing them. Her reasoning was that it gave the individual leaves distinction in the same way that toasting rice before you make risotto makes each grain stand out. I thought this step was bogus at first, but when I sat down with my bowl of slippery collard soldiers aswim in a sea of coconut milk, each leaf emerged on its own and my mind was changed.

My version is a flavor-packed side dish with green curry paste, ginger, and onion for aromatic, round depth and the rind and pulp of lime Citrus Shrine for its funky elegant brine. At the last minute I throw in lots of herbs and lime juice because for me their high notes are what make the heat, sweet, and mellow qualities of curry stand out. If you want to bulk it up to be more main event than side, serve it over rice.

Thanks, Von, for turning my head and having me look at collards through a different lens.

1 medium yellow onion, sliced thin (1 cup)

1 tablespoon minced fresh ginger

1 teaspoon kosher salt, divided

2 tablespoons extra-virgin olive oil or coconut oil

4 garlic cloves, sliced thin

¼ cup green curry paste

4 quarters Citrus Shrine preserved lime (page 140), white pith removed, pulp and rind roughly chopped

8 cups tightly packed collard leaves, stripped of their stems and roughly chopped

2 (13.5-ounce) cans unsweetened coconut milk

¼ cup fresh lime juice

Lots of fresh mint and cilantro to finish

1 In a 6- to 8-quart Dutch oven, sweat the onion and ginger with ¼ teaspoon of the salt in the oil over medium-low heat. Once the onion is translucent, stir in the garlic, curry paste, and Citrus Shrine pulp and rind and continue to cook for about a minute. Add the collards and the remaining ¾ teaspoon salt and go about coating the greens with the curry mixture. They should wilt down a bit and glisten dark green.

2 Pour in 2 cups water, using that action to scrape up any browned bits that cling to the bottom of your pot. Stew, covered, for about 5 minutes. Remove the lid, stir in the coconut milk, and cook uncovered for another 5 minutes. Just before serving, add the lime juice. Once the collards are in your bowl, throw the herbs on top and submerge yourself in their brand of tropical comfort.

Orange Tzimmes Time

serves 4

My husband, Ben, is Jewish. Not the kind of Jewish that means we go to temple or memorize the Torah, but the kind who exerts his Jewish identity through food. For me, this is an exciting and delicious way to religion. Jewish food traditions are deeply rooted in story, and as a result every ingredient, every technique has meaning. I love that and I love Jewish food...except for gefilte fish.

Tzimmes is a traditional stew made from dried fruit and roots like carrots and sweet potatoes. It's often served for Rosh Hashanah, when sweet stuff suggests a sweet new year. Ben builds his on short ribs that balance the sweet quality of the stew and make it something we crave anytime it's cold outside.

In the last little while I've gotten in on the tzimmes action and punctuate the fruity notes with lots of orange Citrus Shrine and the spicy virtue of horseradish. Tzimmes calls for some work, but it's worth it. And like a lot of stews, it's even better the next day.

3	pounds bone-in short ribs of beef
2½	teaspoons kosher salt, divided
1	tablespoon extra-virgin olive oil
3	small leeks, light green and white parts only, sliced into ½-inch-thick rounds (2 cups)
2	tablespoons minced fresh ginger
5	garlic cloves, smashed and peeled
4	quarters Citrus Shrine preserved orange (page 140), white pith removed, rind cut into strips, and pulp roughly chopped
3	small carrots, peeled and cut into 1-inch-thick rounds (2 cups)

3	stalks celery, cut into ½-inch-thick slices (1 cup)
⅓	cup pitted dried dates, roughly chopped
¼	cup dried cherries
½	teaspoon ground black pepper
2	tablespoons prepared horseradish
	Few sprigs fresh thyme and/or rosemary
2½	cups chicken broth
¼	cup sherry vinegar
1	large sweet potato, peeled and cut into 1-inch cubes (2 cups)
2	small crisp apples, cut into 1-inch cubes (2 cups)

1 Preheat your oven to 350°F. Begin by seasoning the short ribs on all sides with 2 teaspoons of the salt. In a 12-inch braiser or a 6-quart Dutch oven, heat the olive oil over medium-high heat. Add the short ribs and cook until browned all over, about 10 minutes.

2 Once the short ribs are nicely caramelized on all sides, use tongs to take them out and set aside. Pour off all but about a tablespoon of fat from the pan and add the leeks, ginger, garlic cloves, and remaining ½ teaspoon salt. Cook over medium heat for about 3 minutes, until the leeks start to soften and brown a bit. Stir in the Citrus Shrine rind and pulp, carrots, celery, dates, cherries, and black pepper. Cook another 3 minutes to liven up the orange and toast the black pepper. Add the meat back in, along with the horseradish, herbs, broth, and vinegar. The broth should not submerge the meat but instead should climb to just below its crest.

3 Bring everything up to a simmer on the stove. Cover and transfer to the middle rack of your oven and braise for 1 hour 20 minutes. Pull the stew out of the oven and add the sweet potato and apples. Cover again, slide back into the oven, and braise for an additional 40 minutes, until the potatoes are tender.

4 Serve warm straight out of the oven, or chill the stew overnight and reheat the next day. We eat this as is for a one-pot meal, but you could serve it over rice or mashed potatoes.

Squash in Its Raw Wonder

serves 4

No one waits with bated breath for the first summer squash of the season. While people cat-fight over tomatoes, defend the merits of okra, and put their names on waiting lists for sweet corn, summer squash sits shingled at our farmers' markets from late May to September like excited orphans whispering for love.

Why the indifference, I wonder? I think long and skinny, round and squat zucchini, eight ball, cheddar, pattypan, and crookneck squash are pretty exciting in their hues of green, yellow, and orange. My theory is that vegetable medleys at chain restaurants all over our fast-casual nation have darkened people's opinion of the quick-to-sauté, inexpensive filler of a "healthy side."

Summer squash, which are cousins of cucumbers, have much more to offer than the local Applebee's lets on. Because they are more like cucumbers than winter squash, zucchini and the like are elegant and crisp served salad-esque.

I would call this a *crudo* because "crudo" means raw, and that preparation lets the lemon Citrus Shrine, olives, cheese, and oregano do the hard-lifting punchy flavor work, while the squash gets to be the crunchy, refreshing vehicle. It's a look at squash we don't often get. Give it a go and see how elegant this vegetable can be.

2 medium zucchini or squash

2 scallions, sliced thin (¼ cup)

3 quarters Citrus Shrine preserved lemon rind (page 140), white pith removed, sliced into thin strips

⅓ cup fresh lemon juice

1 teaspoon kosher salt

1 teaspoon red pepper flakes

½ cup tasty extra-virgin olive oil

2 tablespoons picked fresh oregano

½ cup Niçoise olives, pitted and halved

½ cup grated Parmigiano Reggiano (use a Microplane)

1 Begin by thinly shaving the squash with a mandoline or vegetable peeler. Combine the squash with the scallions, Citrus Shrine strips, lemon juice, salt, and pepper flakes in a medium bowl. Toss to combine and let it hang out for about 15 minutes.

2 Stir in half the olive oil and half the oregano. Spread the zucchini mixture and all its accumulated juice onto the plates you want to serve your crudo on and top with the olives, the remaining oil, the Parm, and the rest of the oregano.

Party in a Can Bean Dip

Makes 2 cups

No, I'm not talking about beer. A can of beans fuels this party.

It struck me a long time ago that beans make an incredible base for dips, spreads, soups, and even sauces. Chickpeas and hummus alerted me first, then canned cannellini beans told me about their thin, docile skins that go unnoticed when blended up. With this nugget of news tucked under my wing, I stopped shaming myself for buying beans in a can instead of stewing beans in a pot, because those beans were just gonna end up in a blender with more assertive, flavorful ingredients that need the bean's basic-ness to round out their pronounced personalities.

This changed a lot of things for me. For one, I always have a few cans of beans in my cupboard. Pureed, they're like a personal assistant who's all-around better for you than the last assistant ever was. She highlights your best qualities and smooths the edges around your worst. She doesn't yet know how much she's worth, so her services are a bargain. And best of all, she's comfortable hanging in the background. If it weren't for how much better she made your life, you wouldn't even know she was there.

As the base for a dip, canned cannellini beans provide a protein- and fiber-rich platform to support bold flavors. Citrus Shrine of every hue adds a savory quality that fresh zest does not, so I've paired preserved lemon with my rekindled love for intense sun-dried tomatoes and bracing olives.

This is, of course, a great sauce-dip in your kitchen. But what I want you to take away is that you can flavor your can party any way you like.

Quirky Furki, soy sauce, sesame oil, rice vinegar, olive oil

Red Weapons, Lime Citrus Shrine, olive oil

LGD, avocado, lime, **Lemon Citrus Shrine,** honey, olive oil

For instance, you could add tahini, hot sauce, honey, roasted red peppers, and anchovies, and for the fatty element, olive oil, sour cream, nut oils, Greek yogurt, or fresh cheese. And if you make my kitchen MVPs, you'll unleash the potential for endless next-level parties. Here are some other combos you might want to consider:

- 1 (15-ounce) can cannellini beans, drained and rinsed
- ½ cup Castelvetrano olives, pitted
- ⅓ cup sun-dried tomatoes packed in oil, drained, plus 2 tablespoons of their oil
- 1 quarter Citrus Shrine preserved lemon rind (page 140), white pith removed
- 1 tablespoon fresh lemon juice
- 1 garlic clove, peeled
- 1 teaspoon kosher salt
- ⅔ cup extra-virgin olive oil

1. Combine all the ingredients in your most powerful "tearing shit up" device and let it rip for a good 2 minutes. I know that feels like a long time in a blender, but I think it's only because blenders loudly remind you they are working. Set a timer and step away if need be.

2. Once all is smooth, the dip is ready to lap up with flatbread, chips, or vegetables, although I think it is better the next day. Just make sure you bring it to room temperature before eating so it's the best it can be.

HEADS up If you thin the dip out with a little water or olive oil, you've got a creamy sauce for fish, chicken, lamb, and roasted vegetables of all kinds. I cannot emphasize how major this is. A healthful dip, a spread, a sauce—all from a can of cannellini beans. I can't.

Can-Do Kraut, R-Rated Onions, sour cream, Parmigiano Reggiano, hot sauce, olive oil

Sweet Potential, V's Nuts, tahini, lemon, hot sauce, olive oil

Recipe above

Herbdacious, greek yogurt, anchovies, capers, Lemon Citrus Shrine, lemon juice, olive oil

Rock Me Don't Shake Me Lemon Pie

makes one 8-inch pie

They say there's a chocolate person and a lemon person in every relationship. I'm the lemon person and this is my pie. The starting place is lemon chess pie with a butter crust. I love the simple custard that balances sweet, sour, and creamy. But I'm haunted by a slice of Shaker lemon pie I had years ago, and that memory made me tinker with the classic.

Shaker lemon pie is packed with so many thin slices of lemon it makes even the most devout lemon people pause. Clearly, I enjoyed my slice. But Ben, a chocolate person, was horrified and confused. It was too much for him, and I understood why. I wanted less of the bitter stuff, but not for the chewy rind to go away entirely. I needed to be rocked by lemon rather than shaken.

So here you go, lemon people. A creamy lemon custard with no pith to shake you, no seeds to surprise. Just elegant, chewy rind to rock your lemon world.

PIE CRUST

- 1 cup all-purpose flour
- 1 teaspoon granulated sugar
- ¾ teaspoon kosher salt
- ½ cup (1 stick) unsalted butter, cold, cut into cubes
- Up to ¼ cup ice water

LEMON FILLING

- 1⅔ cups granulated sugar
- 1 tablespoon cornmeal
- 1 tablespoon all-purpose flour
- ½ teaspoon kosher salt
- 5 tablespoons unsalted butter, melted
- 5 large eggs
- ⅔ cup heavy cream
- ¼ cup plus 3 tablespoons fresh lemon juice
- 3 tablespoons fresh orange juice
- ½ teaspoon vanilla extract
- 2 quarters Citrus Shrine preserved orange rind (page 140), white pith removed, cut into very thin strips
- 4 quarters Citrus Shrine preserved lemon rind (page 140), white pith removed, cut into very thin strips

1 **Make the Crust:** Preheat your oven to 325°F. In a medium bowl, whisk together the flour, sugar, and salt. Add the butter and incorporate with a pastry blender or a large tined fork until the mixture looks like very coarse cornmeal. Add only enough of the ice water to encourage the dough to come together. Using your hands, form the dough into a ball, then press into a disc. Cover with plastic wrap and let it rest in the fridge for at least 1 hour. Overnight works too.

2 Once the dough is rested, roll it out into a thin 10-inch round using as little flour as possible. Fit the dough into an 8-inch pie pan and cut off the excess. Crimp the sides with a fork and lay a piece of parchment or foil over top of it. Put it in the freezer for a minimum of 15 minutes to prevent shrinkage in the oven.

3 When you're ready to blind-bake the crust, put a layer of dry pasta or beans on top of the parchment and bake on the middle rack of your oven for 12 minutes, until it firms up a bit. You're not looking for golden-brown color here.

4 **Make the Filling:** While the crust blind-bakes, whisk the sugar, cornmeal, flour, and salt in a large bowl. Using a wooden spoon, stir in the melted butter followed by one egg at a time, stirring well after each.

5 Trade your wooden spoon for a whisk and work it until the mixture is thick and lightly colored. Whisk in the cream, lemon juice, orange juice, vanilla extract, and all the Citrus Shrine.

6 **Assemble and Bake the Pie:** Put the blind-baked shell on a rimmed baking sheet and pour the filling into it. It will be quite full and, depending on your pie pan, you may have a bit of filling left over. Pour it into an ovenproof ramekin and bake for a secret snack.

7 Slide the pie onto the middle rack of your oven and bake for 1 hour 10 minutes, or until a skewer inserted into the middle of your pie comes out clean. The top will be deep golden brown and your kitchen will smell like a freshly baked sunny day.

CHAPTER SIX

COMMUNITY Organizer

Sweet • Punchy • Pointed • Kind

Community Organizer's story started about five years ago.

I had espoused a deep love for pickling and preserving on my show, *A Chef's Life*, and people from everywhere were sending me gifts like jams, jellies, bread and butter pickles, and chow chows. I also got more eccentric offerings like canned deer meat, watermelon kimchi, pickled bologna, and sweet cucumber preserves stained scarlet with Red Hot candies.

In the mix I also received an 8-ounce jar of something called "pea helper." It came in a package with no return address, but a handwritten note that said, "Stir this into a pot of peas. Our family loves pea helper," told me what to do. The note made no allusion to who this pea helper–loving family was or what went into the much-loved help, but—more curious than suspicious—I took the note's advice and stirred a little over half of her into a pot of peas just before they were done.

Please note that although I'm known to exalt less sexy ingredients like said field peas, they're not something I get all over myself to eat. But these peas were different. They had sweetness that pulled up the legume's earthy baseline. Their broth carried hints of onion and garlic that made them taste complex and less boring. And they had acid, not just the vinegar-finished kind, but the more mellow vegetal variety that's the result of tomatoes and peppers stewed as one.

I didn't know exactly what she was, but I knew Ms. Pea Helper had really *helped*. She had organized the pot to taste like its best self. She didn't steal the spotlight from the folks who were there first, or simply mask blandness with a new overpowering flavor. From my perspective she didn't have a lot to work with in this single ingredient pot of peas, but using her slow-simmered talents, she managed to support, encourage, and accentuate all the tiny legumes' attributes. She made them interesting enough to eat as a meal.

And then it dawned on me. Her name and purpose were probably inspired by that American classic, Hamburger Helper. If you're not privy to Hamburger Helper's kitchen convenience niche, it's a preservative-fortified flavor packet that adds dimension to, and in the end makes a meal out of, ground beef. Voilà! I now knew Ms. Pea Helper's name shortchanged her. What could she do with a greater group of ingredients? What kind of magic could she make in a more diverse community? The answer would be zero if I couldn't figure out how to re-create and rename her.

I turned to the Internet, community recipe collections, and old-school country cooks, but what I learned is that when you try to figure out how to make pea helper, you get little more than woeful looks. Undeterred, I thanked baby Jesus I hadn't dumped the entire jar of mystery in my pot of peas and I called on its contents and my palate to do the research.

With the knowledge of how she performed in that pot of peas and just from the hue of her, Ms. Pea Helper reminded me of sofrito, the flavor base made by stewing onions, tomatoes, and garlic in oil. Sofrito is the foundation for a lot of Spanish, Portuguese, and Italian cooking, and I knew Ms. Pea Helper was a not-so-distant cousin. But there were differences, too. I could see and taste the summer-garden greenness unique to bell peppers. The fact that I could visually pick out ingredients at all set Ms. Helper apart from her old world relative, who is typically

cooked down to a homogenous rust-colored paste. And I'd be in denial if I didn't recognize Ms. Helper's ketchup-like qualities. Having unsuccessfully tried to replace Heinz with homemade, I know brown sugar and vinegar are responsible for ketchup's addictive tang.

Still, the aromatics and spices that defined Ms. Pea Helper's personality remained a mystery. She had the kind of oomph and ahh that grows out of things you see in a pickling spice packet, but she didn't polarize with clove, anise, or heat. She could shapeshift, so I decided I'd take a small leap and give her a few colors from which she could be a chameleon. Onions and garlic, because a lot of foundations start there. Peppers and tomatoes, because I could see their shape in the original, and bay leaves because they never hurt anybody—these things would ensure her charisma but keep her moderate and measured.

Now she needed a new name. "Pea" anything wouldn't work for a world of reasons, and "helper" felt more like life support and less like a cure. I needed to choose a name that demonstrated her abilities to bring individual ingredients together, to direct their purpose, to make them greater than the sum of their parts. I needed to make sure her name made it clear she wasn't the main event—that it indicated you wouldn't enjoy eating her from a spoon. For a moment I decided on Mrs. President. Then I considered how her power emerged resolutely from the background rather than loudly taking center stage, and I took a side step to Community Organizer. It best quantifies her role, highlights her strengths, and positions her place as the foundation that lets something else shine. If it once suited Barack Obama, it would certainly suit her. ➧

Community Organizer

HERE'S WHAT'S IMPORTANT

- I call for fresh tomatoes here because I prefer their flavor in the end product, but you can and should use canned tomatoes if that's all you've got.

- Don't fixate on the type of vinegar or sugar I've suggested. Red wine vinegar and dark brown sugar are my first picks for this, but I've made Community Organizer with all the shades of sugar and a bevy of different vinegars. Stay away from rice wine vinegar, though. It's too sweet and not quite tart enough.

- Onion is important, not the type of onion.

- Community Organizer will keep in your fridge for 1 month, in your freezer for 3 months, and in jars that have been canned in a hot water bath till the cows come home.

20 medium plum or canning tomatoes (about 4 pounds)	2 teaspoons kosher salt
½ cup extra-virgin olive oil	2 teaspoons red pepper flakes
2 large or 3 medium yellow onions, diced	1 cup packed dark brown sugar
10 garlic cloves, sliced	1 cup red wine vinegar
6 to 8 medium bell peppers of any color, seeds, stems, and ribs removed, diced	3 bay leaves

1. Bring a large pot of water to a boil and set up an ice bath nearby. Using a small knife, make an X on the bottom of each tomato. Drop the tomatoes into the rapidly boiling water and let them sit for about 30 seconds, or until you see their skins start to split. Pluck the tomatoes out and drop them into the ice bath. Once they've cooled enough to handle, peel them and cut into small dice, reserving all the collected juice.

2. In a 6-quart Dutch oven, heat the olive oil over medium heat. Add the onions, garlic, bell peppers, salt, and pepper flakes. Cook for about 30 minutes over medium-low heat, stirring from time to time to make sure there's nothing burning on the bottom. They will deepen in color but shouldn't brown.

3. Add the tomatoes plus all their liquid and the brown sugar, vinegar, and bay leaves. Bring this up to a boil, lower it to an excited simmer, and cook until the contents of the pot have reduced by half. This can take anywhere from 45 minutes to a little over an hour.

4. Pluck out the bay leaves and note Community Organizer's bright, sweet, and focused attributes. She's ready to do her thing now, but if you'd like, you can put this in jars and can them in a hot water bath for 10 minutes. Community Organizer makes a great shelf-stable gift. Otherwise you can keep your Community Organizer in the fridge in a sealed container for up to a month or in the freezer for up to 3 months.

MAKES 4 PINTS

1 braising liquid for hearty greens like kale, chard, and collards

2 blended as a topping for meatloaf

3 flavor foundation for tomato-based vegetable soups or chili

4 starting point for meaty braises

5 topping for scrambled eggs or breakfast tacos

6 sauce for pasta with either cheese or meat or both

7 ground meat flavoring for tacos

8 melted with cream cheese and sausage to make a dip

9 medium for reheating leftover meat or vegetables

10 addition to grilled cheese

LEGUME LESSON

Given Community Organizer's origins as an aid to field peas, it's important to honor the legume family and all the good its members bring to our kitchens. After all, legumes also known as beans, peas, and lentils are an integral ingredient all over the world. Dirt cheap, comforting, packed with protein, full of fiber, and wildly versatile, I believe legumes are the food of the future.

If you don't believe me, consider the blue zones. Blue zones are pockets of population around the world where people tend to live longer. One of the common threads between these groups, which are scattered from Loma Linda, California, to Icaria, Greece, to Okinawa, Japan, is that they eat some type of legume at least once a day. And while we wring our hands at all the damage we as humans do to the planet, legumes give back to the land and add nutrients to the soil in which they grow. When seasoned a certain way, legumes fool us (at least some of us) and stand in for meat. When blended and used for their creamy qualities in a dip or as a thickener in a soup, legumes show off as rich and luxurious.

I try not to choose favorites, but there's really no down side to a legume. Still, as ubiquitous as beans, lentils, and peas are, they're misunderstood. I'd like to do what I can for the planet and its people so I'll turn to bullet points to clear up our shared confusion:

- **You do not have to soak dried legumes of any kind before you cook them.** In fact I'd argue you're doing the legumes a disservice with a soak. One argument is that soaking dried beans or peas shortens the cooking time, but I've done the tests and if soaked beans cook significantly faster than bone-dry ones I need a new timer.

- **Different legumes call for different ratios of liquid.** Check the bag or the Internet to determine how much you need, and know you can always add more wet stuff as they simmer.

- **Don't add salt at the start.** Salt in its pure form toughens the skin and makes for unevenly cooked beans and peas. Instead, once your legumes are cooked through, add a generous amount of salt to the pot and let the beans sit and soak it up for about 10 minutes. There is a little bend in this rule as a lot of country cooks use broth laced with salt-cured pork to cook their beans. This seems to be okay as long as any excess salt is rinsed away before you throw the pork in the pot.

- **Add aromatics** like smashed garlic, onions, carrots, celery, bay leaves, or herbs of any kind to the liquid you use to simmer legumes. You can be willy-nilly with this part of legume cookery, adding whatever vegetable scraps you have on hand—with one major caveat. Acid added at the start can toughen the bean or pea's skin, so if you're gonna season your legumes with vinegar, citrus, or tomato-laced condiments like Community Organizer, add it when they are almost done.

- **Cook legumes slowly.** Gentle, persistent heat unlocks their creamy qualities and helps them hold their shape. Plus, more time at the simmer means more time to soak up flavor from the broth. One way to achieve consistent temperature and therefore superior beans is to bring them up to a boil on the stove, then cover and transfer to the gentle heat of a 350°F oven.

- I'm not here to hate on canned beans. I always have a can or two in my cupboard for when the need for beans sneaks up on me. As illustrated by Party in a Can Bean Dip (page 164), I lean on canned beans often to make dips. But always, always, *always* rinse canned beans before you use them. The thick liquid they float in is like snot packed with sodium.

  After all that, I doubt you need a recipe, but out of respect for Ms. Pea Helper, I'll give you one.

"It's important to honor the legume family and all the good its members bring to our kitchens."

Organized Peas (or Beans)

makes 6 cups

The artist formerly known as pea helper makes her mark here. Everything is optional except for the peas or beans, the salt, and the Community Organizer, so don't overthink it. What I want is for you to feel free as a bird to throw in scraps of onion, half a carrot, or herbs of any kind. The point is that basic peas plus Community Organizer equals special stuff.

1 (1-pound) bag dried field peas or beans of any kind (peas, beans, or lentils)

Broth or water

Aromatics of your choice, like onion, carrots, celery, or garlic (optional)

Herbs you have hanging around, like rosemary, oregano, thyme, or sage (optional)

1½ teaspoons kosher salt

1 to 2 cups Community Organizer (page 176), depending on how much help you want

1 tablespoon unsalted butter

❶ Rinse the peas, beans, or lentils with cool water and pick out anything that looks as if it doesn't belong. Put them in a large Dutch oven and cover with about 2 inches of water or broth. Cut the aromatics and herbs of your choice, if you're using, into large hunks that you can pick out when the beans are done and throw them in. (Diced vegetables make this feel like soup rather than beans.) And if you don't throw in any aromatics at all, that's fine too, as Ms. Community Organizer will flavor them up just fine.

❷ Bring the contents of your pot to a boil, then lower it to a creeping simmer. Cook, covered, checking occasionally to make sure the beans are submerged in liquid but just barely.

❸ The time you need to cook the beans or peas will vary (check the package instructions), but once they're cooked through, all tender and creamy, pick out the chunks of aromatics and herbs and stir in the salt. At this point you have a basic pot of beans ready for any number of recipes.

❹ Add the Community Organizer and let things simmer another 5 minutes. Stir in the butter and serve.

Bake Beans Again

serves 4

Baked beans are one of the United States' culturally distinct side dishes. They're a crowd pleaser that stand for summer and backyard barbecues. But nine times out of ten the baked beans we eat alongside slaw, potato salad, corn on the cob, hot dogs, and hamburgers are dumped out of a can and heated in the microwave. They never see the dry, persistent heat of an oven and wouldn't recognize a bath of rendering pork if faced with one. I've got a problem with that, and I think we as Americans can do better.

If you go to the minuscule trouble of baking beans uncovered in an actual oven, you'll notice the step creates a variation of textures that makes them more showstopper than afterthought. The beans on top dehydrate and caramelize with the help of the sugars in the sauce. They form a crust for the creamy, porky, sweet beans underneath. They're equally as addictive at room temperature as they are piping hot out of the oven, maybe even more so. That makes them an ideal choice for cookouts that call you to the yard not the kitchen. Perhaps that's why baked beans became a thing in the first place.

Let's take back, and take pride in, our baked beans. Instead of a quick placeholder on a paper plate, make our culture's classic backyard BBQ side dish something both kids and adults get excited about. Dare I say we need to make baked beans great again?

¼ cup extra-virgin olive oil

⅓ cup diced country ham or prosciutto; or 4 ounces bacon cut into little chunks

½ teaspoon ground black pepper

4 cups cooked pinto, cannellini, or lima beans (from about 2 cups dried, page 181, or canned)

½ cup liquid reserved from cooking the beans

1½ cups Community Organizer (page 176)

1. Preheat your oven to 350°F. In a 12-inch ovenproof skillet, heat the olive oil over medium heat and add the ham or bacon. If you've chosen ham, let it cook for about 30 seconds, or until it just begins to wake up and sizzle. You don't want it to crisp up or dry out; instead your goal is to flavor the oil. If you've chosen bacon, render it for about a minute, or until it's about halfway done and still a little flabby.

2. Add the black pepper to the porky player in your pan and toast it for a few seconds. This step brings the black pepper to life and wakes its flavor. Stir in the beans, the reserved cooking liquid, and the Community Organizer.

3. Slide the skillet onto the middle rack of your oven to bake. The mixture will be loose with liquid and you'll doubt my claim above that the beans on top will dehydrate and form a crust, but talk to me when the skillet emerges. It'll take about an hour. You will marvel at what beans baked in the oven can be.

Broccoli Soup for Cheese Lovers

makes 2 quarts

My daughter Flo is a cheese hound. It's not a new interest. As long as she's eaten solid food, cheese has been the thing Flo sniffs out and scarfs up like there's an impending planet-wide shortage. As her mom, I've tailored the meals I make to suit her taste for the stuff. I don't cook mac and cheese every day or give her hunks of cheese as a snack. Instead I use cheese to my advantage. If a vegetable, even a green one, is cheese-adjacent she's more inclined to eat it. And even though that vegetable is often cloaked in curds and whey, Flo is still eating a vegetable and I am a good mom.

While it enlists three cheeses so its name speaks to Flo, this soup is healthy and fairly light. No flour binds it and no cream works toward its luxury. Instead Ms. Community Organizer comes in and acts like the boss she is, binding the mineral depth of broccoli with the wide funk of smoked provolone and the salty point of Parm. I do the rest with a crown of crushed Cheez-Its, because guess what, I'm a Cheez-It hound.

6 to 7 cups roughly chopped broccoli (about 2 small heads)

4 cups chicken or vegetable broth

3 cups milk

2 cups Community Organizer (page 176)

2 teaspoons kosher salt

1½ cups shredded smoked provolone, smoked Gruyère, or another smoked melting cheese

½ cup grated Parmigiano Reggiano (use a Microplane)

Crushed Cheez-Its as garnish

1 The fact that you have to use a blender to make the soup smooth is offset by how simple it is to put the soup together, so let your equipment aversions go for a minute and bear with me.

2 Combine the broccoli, broth, milk, Community Organizer, and salt in a 6-quart Dutch oven. Cover and bring to a boil over medium-high heat. Cook for 10 minutes. Stir in the smoked cheese and Parm and cook 5 minutes more.

3 In batches, transfer the soup to a blender and process until the soup is totally smooth. I don't care what kind of equipment you have, hot stuff in a blender is a hot mess waiting to happen, so start with a little soup and see what and how your blender handles it. I always hold the top with a towel to protect my hand, but do what you want. I've warned you.

4 Once you've blended all the soup, reheat it in a pot before you ladle it into bowls and top with crushed Cheez-Its.

NACHO NORMAL BOOK TOUR

My first book tour was the stuff of legend. I had honed my eccentricities for thirty-seven years and I felt anything I did should reflect my stubborn passions. I wasn't about to fly around to food festivals and set up tables in tasting tents only to sign books for disillusioned, slightly drunk people with plastic wine glasses dangling around their necks. Under no circumstance was I amenable to hosting book dinners at other people's restaurants where the tickets cost $120 and I had to search for the food processor and the dish pit in every new kitchen. Even worse would be attending dinners where other people cooked my food and I looked on, horrified, at their interpretations of it. And I sure didn't want to ship air-dried sausage, proper cornmeal, or muscadine grapes to places that didn't have those things—which would have been just about everywhere.

I had written a big book I was proud of, and I wanted to share it and my food on my own terms, from my own kitchen, in a buzzworthy yet approachable way. Sounds impossible, I know, but not if you consider a food truck.

O Sara Lee, as she lamentably came to be known, was born a bread truck. 500,000 miles later we selected her for our kitchen on wheels because she was the biggest, cheapest truck we could find. We appointed her with a six-burner range, a fryer, combi oven, three refrigerators, and a 36-inch standing freezer. If that list of equipment doesn't sound like overkill, consider that I didn't even have a combi oven in my restaurant kitchen—

but my food truck was gonna roll with one. Also think about how long it takes to freeze a freezer and imagine trying to do it running on a generator. Most troublesome, though, was an issue that came to light only once we were on the road. O Sara Lee was built to carry bread, the lightest foodstuff there is. And we had weighed her down with more than a thousand pounds of equipment.

Book tours, even lame ones, are not free. I was lucky that Little, Brown, my publisher, agreed to give me a reasonable stipend to travel around the country on airplanes in the name of selling and signing books. They had not, nor should they have, planned to buy a food truck and pay for its elaborate ride around the country. Some people are motivated by money. I'm motivated by the word no, so at the "no" from Little, Brown I set out to pay for O Sara Lee and her tour by different means. I got sponsors. Duke's mayonnaise, Whole Foods, UNOX (the combi oven company), and even the tourism arm of North Carolina signed on to support my truck tour and its band of challenge zealots. We planned events at independent bookstores, grocery stores, and colleges, and set up a website to sell tickets. The ticket paid for a book, a "meal," and a moment with me. The moment with me cost about $5 and those dollars were gonna turn "no" into "let's go."

The plan seemed simple to me. Casey Atwater, our chef de book tour and truck driver, would oversee the cooking. We'd have a rotating menu of chicken and rice under an herb salad with chicken cracklings, Tom Thumb sausage with field peas and rutabaga relish, and Eastern North Carolina fish stew with hardboiled eggs and white bread. We'd serve apps like baked grits with pimento cheese and salsa or fried collards while people waited in line. For dessert we'd scoop buttermilk sorbet topped with macerated fruit or serve pecan chewy pie squares with whipped cream as people left.

Months before we set sail, Casey contacted health inspectors in all twenty-five towns we would visit, because our mobile kitchen would require an inspection everywhere we landed. To further check that box he reached out to friends of mine who ran restaurants in each town to ask if they would act as our commissary kitchen, or the place we went to wash dishes and refill our potable water. He started working on the relish, fruit preserves, pecan pie, and shrimp stock for the stew—basically anything that could be canned or frozen before we got on the road.

Once on tour, we planned to rely on a cook named Michelle Gans who had worked with me for years. She'd do all the food prep back home, and hand it off to a roster of cooks from my restaurants, who would drive out to meet us on the road. Two at the time, they'd spend a week with us then be tagged out by two fresh faces from home. This meandering heavy gaggle of a book tour would last nine weeks.

Maybe it wasn't so simple after all.

On October 2, 2016, the least lame, most ambitious cookbook tour in history got on the road. O Sara's sides had been wrapped with sponsors' logos and images of the book cover. Its backside donned a blow-up of my mayonnaise-dripped face eating a BLT. My husband, Ben, and Casey drove O Sara Lee to Nashville. Madison and Holley, the tour directors, along with two cooks from the restaurant, followed. Behind them was the crew for *A Chef's Life,* who came to film what could be fascinating to watch.

From the start the truck had problems. O Sara Lee lumbered, lurched, and smoked, and all but refused to traverse the North Carolina mountains. On flat land she agreed to a max of 50 mph and when faced with an incline said hell no to anything above 30. The freezer wouldn't freeze and the generator went kaput. It was clear we had a long and arduous nine weeks ahead. We kept up with our elaborate menu for the first little bit, but even when O Sara was running smoothly, she made everything harder. It took longer to get where you were going, to get settled when you got there, and to clean up. But the truck and her trouble aside, it was being forced to wash collards in the bathtub of an Airbnb that was the straw that broke the camel's back, and we made the decision to simplify. This was not an easy place to arrive. I had made such a huge deal out of the book tour. It had sponsors for Christ's sake. It couldn't fail, but we couldn't go on as we had. The elaborate menu was out of question, but people had already bought tickets to an event with the expectation the food would be representative of what I wrote about in the book, so we could simplify but no one could know we had. Thankfully we had an idea that would snatch victory from the jaws of defeat.

What kind of dish is no one ever mad at? What takes a little of this and a little of that and makes it seem ridiculously decadent? Nachos. Casey would become our Jesus and our scattering of Tom Thumb chunks, stewed tomato relish, smashed butterbeans, and tart buttermilk would be his bread loaves.

Problem is, I was technically the chef and I had never really made nachos. I had enjoyed them at casual restuarants for years, yes, but made them? No. So my first ones looked like the first time I made pizza or the first time I folded dumplings. There was too much stuff and not enough infrastructure to support it. Our learning curve was steep and short. My challenge zealots and I ended the longest nine weeks of our lives with a keen understanding of nacho science. Since then, nachos have become one of my favorite things to eat around the coffee table for movie night. As we learned, they leave really only one pan to clean and they generally make people happy. I never thought I'd be indebted to nachos, but somehow I believe I am.

Nacho Normal

serves 4

1½ cups cooked beans (from about ¾ cup dried, page 181, or canned)

4 ounces (about 2 cups packed) fresh spinach

2 cloves garlic, smashed and peeled

1½ teaspoons kosher salt, divided

3 tablespoons extra-virgin olive oil, divided

4 cups cauliflower, riced or cut into small pieces

1½ cups Community Organizer (page 176)

2 tablespoons unsalted butter

1 bag tortilla chips, or enough chips to fully cover a large rimmed baking sheet

2 cups shredded pepper Jack or Colby cheese

½ cup sour cream

3 scallions, sliced

½ cup chopped fresh cilantro

❶ Preheat your oven to 400°F. Put the beans, spinach, garlic, ½ teaspoon of the salt, and ½ cup water in a blender and process until smooth. Heat 2 tablespoons of the olive oil in a skillet over medium and add the bean mixture. It will be pretty loose, so this process is about cooking it down to achieve proper refried bean viscosity (aka sludge). It's usually about 5 to 10 minutes.

❷ While the beans reduce, heat a 12-inch skillet over medium heat with the remaining 1 tablespoon olive oil. Once the oil shimmers, add the cauliflower pieces plus the remaining 1 teaspoon salt and let the cauliflower brown without shaking the pan for about 3 minutes. Stir in the Community Organizer and let everything cook together for about a minute. You want the organized cauliflower to heat through, but please stop it short of mushy. The point is to have distinct cauliflower pieces mingled in sauce. Stir in the butter, turn off the heat, and go about assembling your nachos.

❸ Spread a thick layer of chips over the largest baking sheet with sides you have. If all you have are small baking sheets, use two. The chips can overlap. You don't want to see any of the baking sheet peeking up from underneath the chips. They need to form a unified base for all the toppings. Spoon and dot the cauliflower mixture evenly over your base, then follow with the beans and finally the cheese.

❹ Slide the baking sheet onto the top rack of your oven and bake for about 12 minutes to melt the cheese and make the nachos nachos. Bring the melted glory out of the oven and dollop sour cream over top. Finish with a shower of scallions and cilantro and serve these suckers straight from the baking sheet.

Fast Road to Fancy Pork Scaloppine

serves 4

The headline here reads: *Three main ingredients marry one of my heroes to make a remarkable meal in minutes. Or, It looks like she spent hours in the kitchen but we have evidence to show she stalked frenemies on Instagram in the early evening. Or, Don't fret if you live in rural America. Walmart has everything you need to make a noteworthy dinner.*

Inspired by pork scaloppine and chicken marsala, this recipe tells all the stories above. It's the type of dish that made me want to write this book in the first place, because it shows you that with a little forethought you can fashion a fast, distinct meal with actual personality anywhere—and it doesn't take skill or fancy equipment to do it.

- 1 pound pork loin or 4 small boneless pork chops
- ⅓ cup all-purpose flour
- 2 teaspoons kosher salt, divided
- 2 tablespoons extra-virgin olive oil
- ⅓ cup Castelvetrano olives, pitted
- ½ teaspoon ground black pepper
- 1½ cups **Community Organizer** (page 176)
- 6 to 7 fresh sage leaves, roughly chopped or left whole
- 2 tablespoons fresh lemon juice
- 2 tablespoons unsalted butter

1 If using a whole hunk of pork loin, slice it into four equal-size "chops." Put each chop between two pieces of plastic wrap and gently pound them thinner using the fat end of a wine bottle or the smooth side of a meat mallet. When you're done pounding, your cutlets should be ⅓ inch thick.

2 Season the flour with ½ teaspoon salt and sprinkle the remaining 1½ teaspoons on both sides of the pork. Dredge the seasoned pork cutlets in the flour, making sure they are lightly dusted rather than clumped with flour.

3 In a 12-inch skillet, heat the olive oil over medium-high heat until shimmering. Use tongs to lay the floured cutlets in the pan and brown them on the first side for roughly 3 minutes. Flip them over to brown on the opposite side. As the chops lay on their second side sizzling, add the olives, black pepper, and Community Organizer. Let that come up and boil for about a minute before stirring in the sage, lemon juice, and butter. Serve immediately, or at least soon.

Egg in a Cup in a Microwave

serves 4

I first ate eggs cooked in a coffee mug at my high school boyfriend's house. A little loose and studded with bacon, they were his dad's breakfast trick and the one food memory I took away from many meals with Andrew's family. I do have a memory of a joke Dr. Wagoner told about margaritas and how they were like breasts—one's not enough and three are too many. He told us that at dinner, but I don't think that makes it a *food* memory.

Anyway, because it was high school I thought I'd marry Andrew and I'd learn to make Dr. Wagoner's famous mug eggs some time before Andrew and I had kids. But I did not become a Wagoner and my almost-father-in-law never showed me his trick.

Lucky for you I figured it out on my own, and even may have improved on Dr. Wagoner's original. Basically, eggs, crumbled bacon, cheese, and Community Organizer all go in a mug. They whiz around in the microwave for a total of a minute and out comes a handheld, satisfying, perfect-for-the-car breakfast. CO casts a ketchup effect here, ringing both sweet and tart bells. She is what keeps your mug in the mug, coming back for more—well, she and bacon.

My kids love this because I guess it's more fun to eat something out of a cup than from a plate. I'm a fan first because it's surprisingly tasty, second because it's a cinch to make, and third because when we eat it in the car (which is always) there's no crumbs to clean up and no mess to mention.

Thanks for the trick, Dr. Wagoner.

1 teaspoon unsalted butter

2 large eggs

2 tablespoons milk

2 tablespoons grated cheese of your choice

½ teaspoon kosher salt

2 grinds black pepper

3 tablespoons Community Organizer (page 176)

1 slice cooked bacon

1 Rub the inside of the mug with the butter. Crack the eggs into the mug and add the milk, cheese, salt, and pepper. Stir things around a little with a fork, but don't go wild like you would if an omelet was your goal. If you leave some distinct ribbons of white and yolk rather than whisk them to a homogenous pale yellow, the finished product eats more like broken soft boiled eggs and I like that.

2 Once the eggs and cheese sitch is ready, swirl in Ms. CO and crumble the bacon over top. Put the mug in the microwave and let her go 30 seconds. Bring the mug out, stir its contents a time or two, and put it back in for another 30. Depending on the power of your microwave, your breakfast may be done at this point. The eggs should be set, if a little runny. If that's not the case, give them another stir and an additional 30 second spin. Stir once more before smiling down into your breakfast.

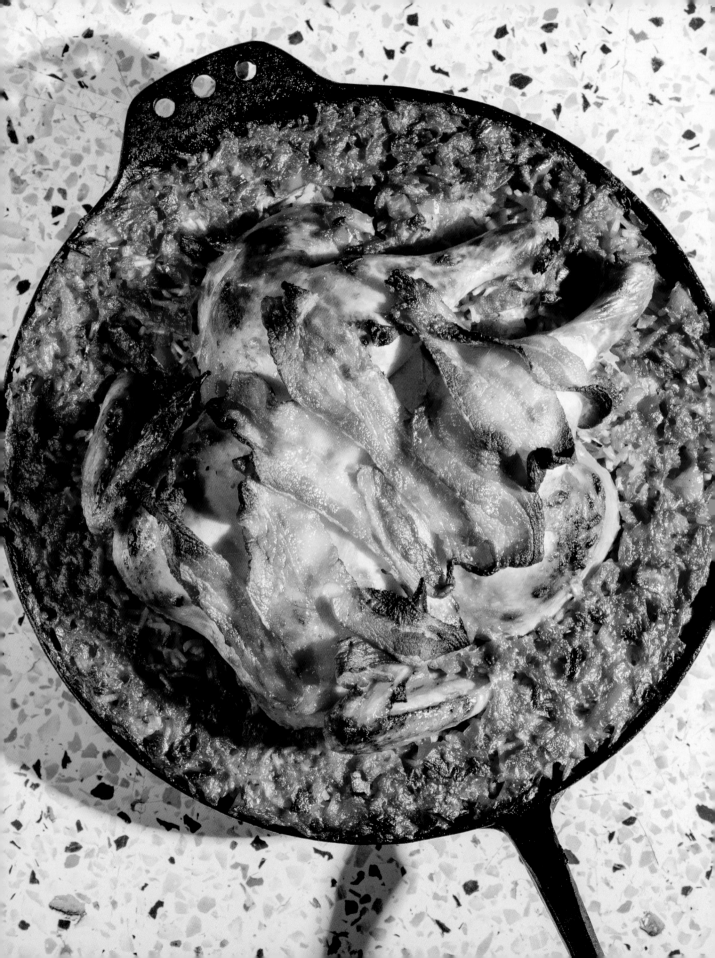

All About That Rice... with Chicken

serves 4

I have a penchant for roasting chicken on top of things. I love it because the technique does so much and calls on only one pan to do it. My roast chicken deep dive is also strategic, because I believe the ability to cook chicken in a variety of ways is one of the most valuable skills a home cook can develop. That's why I beat you over the head with it in this book.

So now that you know where I'm coming from, add brown rice to the bread (page 29), cauliflower (page 60), and grits (page 110) that are already on the list of things that get immeasurably better under the rendered drippings from a chicken as it cooks. Honestly, I thought I had exhausted the technique and chosen the ingredients that benefit from it the most, but trapped at a beach cottage with only a chicken, some brown rice, and a pint of Community Organizer, I discovered my favorite matchup yet.

Timing and the type of rice are really important here. You need legit brown rice that takes about 45 minutes to cook. If you are uncertain about the type of rice you have, look to the instructions on the bag. You also need a spatchcocked chicken because a chicken butchered this way will cook faster and provide the largest rendering blanket for your rice. Spatchcocking sounds scary, but all it requires is that you cut on both side of the chicken's spine to remove it from the bird. Then splay the bird out so it's flat. Voilà! Add "spatchcock doctor" to your resume.

1½ cups brown rice

1½ cups Community Organizer (page 176), divided

3 teaspoons kosher salt, divided

1 (3- to 4-pound) whole chicken, spatchcocked

1 teaspoon ground black pepper

4 slices thick-cut bacon

1. Preheat your oven to 475°F. In a 12-inch ovenproof skillet, bring the rice, 1 cup of the Community Organizer, 1 teaspoon of the salt, and 3⅓ cups water to a boil.

2. While the rice comes to a boil, season the chicken all over with the remaining 2 teaspoons salt and the pepper. Rub its skin with the remaining ½ cup Community Organizer and lay the slices of bacon over the chicken's breast.

3. Once the rice starts to boil, let it cook on the stove for 5 minutes. Then lay the chicken on top of the rice and transfer the skillet to the middle rack of your oven. The chicken will sink a little and that's okay. It will reemerge as the rice takes hold of the water and end up perched on top.

4. Bake for 30 minutes, then check the bacon and take it off if it's crisp. Have it as a snack or crumble it overtop the finished dish. (Once it has fully rendered it will have given all it can to the chicken and the rice. Plus the breasts need to be naked a bit to brown.) After another 10 minutes or so in the oven, when the internal temperature of the chicken, taken between the joint of the thigh and breast, reads 165°F, bring the skillet out and put it back on the eye of your stove. (That's the burner, for those who don't know.) Remove the chicken to a cutting board.

5. Over medium heat, cook the rice for 3 minutes more to crisp it around the edge of the pan. Carve the chicken and serve with the rice.

Barbecue Potatoes

serves 4

Barbecue and all the things you serve with it are hot topics in North Carolina, where arguments are positioned according to which end of the state you call home. I'm from the east, a place where the barbecue rules are strict. We believe in vinegar-based sauce, sweet slaw, and chewy cornbread. That's pretty much the variety you'll see at barbecue shacks across my region, but a few spots serve an oddity that can best be described as BBQ potatoes.

I'm not a fan, as the potatoes I've tried seem as if they were dumped from a can and simply heated in sauce, but the food fixer in me imagined a better barbecue potato—something more like *patatas bravas* from Spain. These potatoes—boiled, roasted till crisp, and then roasted some more with a fiery tomato sauce—are one of Spain's most famous tapas.

Here I've combined barbecue potatoes' flavors with patatas bravas' technique in a hugely satisfying potato dish you can eat as a side or share as a starter. I like to eat them with toothpicks because that makes me feel Spanish, but a fork works too.

1½ pounds small round potatoes (the ones usually sold in a netted bag)

3 tablespoons extra-virgin olive oil

2 teaspoons kosher salt

½ cup Community Organizer (page 176), pureed in a blender

1 teaspoon ground black pepper

Crumbled feta, optional

① Preheat your oven to 400°F and bring a large pot of heavily salted water to a boil. Drop the potatoes in the boiling water and cook for about 15 minutes. You want them just cooked through but not falling apart. Scoop the potatoes out and let them cool to the point that you can handle them.

② Using your hand and a flat surface, smash the potatoes one at a time so they split open and some of their flesh is exposed. You want the potatoes to hold together, so be gentle but direct with your smash.

③ Once you've had your way with all the potatoes, toss them with the olive oil and salt. Spread them onto a baking sheet and slide that onto the middle rack of your oven. Roast for 25 to 30 minutes. They should be crisp and browned in spots.

④ Pull the baking sheet out of the oven and carefully toss the potatoes with the pureed Community Organizer and the black pepper. Slide them back into the oven and roast an additional 20 minutes, until they look almost glazed. Serve warm with crumbled feta overtop if you're feeling extra.

Lasagna Primavera

makes one 12 x 8-inch lasagna

When I was about seven years old, lasagna became "the thing" my mom made for special occasions. This wouldn't be noteworthy except that until this point, the Howards ate exclusively inside the lines of a rural Southern farming family because everything else was, in my dad's words, "foreign." But one night, to my dad's chagrin and my delight, my mom's cookware went to bed casserole dishes and woke up lasagna pans.

When I think back on it, Mom's lasagna period was pretty brief, but its Italian-ish halo made me feel more sophisticated and less like a bumpkin. Layering the noodles, sauce, and cheese at my mom's side made me feel accomplished, like a little helper rather than a pest. And serving it at birthday parties or at covered dish lunches meant I could have more cheese and fewer vegetables. When our family's collective lasagna period ended abruptly with the discovery of good-enough frozen Stouffer's, I never layered lasagna by my mom's side again.

My lasagna period looks a little different than hers. It's less traditional because I fancy myself a nonconformist. It's packed full of vegetables and sauced with Community Organizer. But it's bound with cheese because that, along with the noodles, seems to define the dish. My lasagna is delicious and comforting and still a labor of love. Best of all, there's no good-enough frozen version out there to replace it.

3 tablespoons extra-virgin olive oil

8 cups diced mixed veggies, such as zucchini, corn, mushrooms, and/or eggplant

2½ teaspoons kosher salt

½ teaspoon red pepper flakes

5 ounces fresh spinach (about 2 cups packed)

4 cups Community Organizer (page 176)

1 cup ricotta

1½ cups grated Parmigiano Reggiano (use a Microplane)

1 large egg

1 (10-ounce) box no-boil lasagna noodles

16 ounces fresh mozzarella, diced

1 Preheat your oven to 350°F. In a 12-inch skillet, heat half the olive oil over medium heat till it shimmers. Cook the veggies in two batches so they have space to caramelize in the pan. Add half the diced veggies, 1 teaspoon salt, and ¼ teaspoon red pepper flakes and sauté until caramelized, about 10 minutes. Transfer the browned veggies to a plate and do it again with the remaining olive oil, veggies, pepper flakes, and 1 teaspoon salt.

2 Combine all the sautéed veggies in the pan. Add the spinach and wilt over medium heat. Stir in the Community Organizer plus 1 cup water and bring it up to a simmer. Cook the mixture for 5 minutes, until the liquid reduces and becomes saucy.

3 In a medium bowl, combine the ricotta, Parm, egg, and remaining ½ teaspoon of salt. Stir to combine.

4 To assemble your lasagna, spoon a thin layer of sauce in the bottom of a deep 12 x 8-inch casserole dish or lasagna pan (or whatever it's called in your house). Follow up with a layer of uncooked noodles, then a thin layer of sauce. Top the sauce with a layer of mozzarella and then a layer of the ricotta mixture. Continue layering in that order, reserving enough mozzarella to finish with a good smattering on top.

5 Put your lasagna on a rimmed baking sheet to catch any bubbled-over spillage. Bake it uncovered on the middle rack of your oven for 1 hour, until it's bubbling and browned on top and at the edges. Let it rest 10 minutes before jumping in there to serve.

CHAPTER SEVEN

Herb-dacious

Full • Round • Herbal • Nuanced • Fatty • Smooth

Every time I go to the grocery store and see those tiny plastic containers of herbs hanging next to the lettuce I get agitated.

Then when I look to the side and see squeezable tubes of pureed basil and mint, my blood pressure spikes. Why would you only need six leaves of basil, and why would you pay $3.00 for them? And what is in that tube exactly? Would mint feel good about the way she emerges from it? I don't think so.

The truth is that we all need to be cooking with more herbs. They do something no other category of plant can. With virtually zero calories, herbs deliver floral, sweet, spicy, and aromatic flavors to food. They turn birthday balloons into hot air balloons with the flick of a wrist. Trust me, if you introduce more herbs into your repertoire your food will taste better and you will end up eating healthier, more well-rounded meals.

The problem is that you're not going to introduce more herbs to your food if your options come in those plastic sleeves or get squeezed from a tube. You gotta go bigger. Buy the herbs in bundles. Most grocery stores offer parsley, cilantro, mint, and basil this way. Or better yet, buy the herbs in dirt and plant them at home. All you need is a windowsill and you can have an herba-copia all year long.

Once you get on the herb train you'll find you have herbs to spare. A quarter bundle of mint waits to turn brown in the corner of your produce drawer. A handful of dill sits patiently for the next crab cake you fry. Your basil plant longs to bush out and make more basil, but you won't stack your next caprese for at least a week. Don't waste these green petals of taste. Blend them up. Bind them with fat, funk, and sunshine, and make an herb delivery system that's just about the handiest thing you'll find in your fridge. That's what I call being Herbdacious.

Herbdacious is gonna remind you a lot of pesto or pistou, depending on your relationship with either Italy or France. But while both of these classic sauces make use of mostly basil, Herbdacious is more inclusive. Olive oil-poached garlic blended with a combination of soft herbs like mint, cilantro, tarragon, dill, basil, and chervil make Herbdacious an herb delivery system that's round, robust, and mellow all at the same time. It's both garlic confit and herb puree. It's marinade, ingredient, sauce, and slather. Herbdacious goes in, on, and around dishes in a way that leaves a mark on your mind because it makes things taste better. Maybe more than any other flavor hero in this book, Herbdacious speaks up and calls out to be included in dishes because it doesn't add texture, big doses of acid, heat, or umami. It adds *dimension*. It's background music and melody. It's personality and rhythm. Herbdacious delivers. ➤

Herb-dacious

HERE'S WHAT'S IMPORTANT

- Garlic is a tough subject. I never, ever use the pre-minced stuff in a jar, and I don't like food that comes from a tube (unless it's tomato paste), so you know where I land on squirtable garlic. I have some strong feelings about the pre-peeled whole cloves of garlic that are readily available in most grocery stores. On the one hand, pre-peeled cloves are incredibly convenient and can save you a fair amount of time. But often they have a strong smell and are sort of wet and translucent when you buy them. That means they're on the verge of rotten, and cooked or raw, rotten is bad. Even at their freshest, pre-peeled cloves taste different—not bad, but different.

- For this recipe, and for every recipe generally, I recommend you buy whole heads of garlic, peel the cloves yourself, and proceed. But all that being said, you should know that I know so much about pre-peeled garlic because I have a bag of it in my fridge at this very moment.

- I call for "leaves" of basil and parsley here, but don't be afraid to use the tender sections of their stems. Generally I cut the bottom off the sprigs and consider the rest appropriate when things get blended as Herbdacious does. The stems of soft herbs like these have flavor too and shouldn't be wasted.

- Herbdacious will keep in a sealed container in your fridge for 2 weeks and for up to 3 months in your freezer. Ice cube trays are a super clutch way to store convenient portion-ready servings.

2   heads garlic (about 20 cloves), peeled
⅔   cup extra-virgin olive oil
1   cup packed fresh basil leaves
¼   cup packed fresh parsley leaves
¼   cup tightly packed fresh dill, mint, chervil, or cilantro
¼   cup roughly chopped scallions, green parts only
½   cup grated Parmigiano Reggiano (use a Microplane)
3   tablespoons fresh lemon juice
   Grated zest of 2 lemons
1½   teaspoons kosher salt

1 In a small saucepan, bring the garlic cloves and olive oil up to a simmer over very low heat. If it begins to sizzle and boil, pull it off the heat and let cool slightly before you return it to the hot eye of the stove. The idea is to slowly poach the garlic in the oil rather than fry it. This could take as long as 20 minutes if you keep the heat low. The garlic will be soft and just slightly browned.

2 This garlic confit plus its oil are kitchen heroes on their own and can be used anywhere you want mellow garlic notes. You could stop this recipe right here and save those little garlic bombs in the fridge for a month, submerged in oil. Pureed, the cloves are especially useful as a means to thicken and add flavor to sauces.

3 But you don't get to Herbdacious by calling it quits early. Once the garlic confit is completely cool, put it and all the remaining ingredients in the most powerful blender you have and let it rip until the mixture is smooth and green. Store Herbdacious in a sealed container in your fridge for up to 2 weeks, or in your freezer for up to 3 months.

MAKES 2 CUPS

1 mix with mayo for a BLT or a BLP (that's a bacon, lettuce and peach sandwich)

2 slather on corn on the cob, steak, chicken, pork or fish

3 garnish soups, especially tomato, potato, and brothy vegetable ones

4 drizzle on bowls of beans or grilled or sautéed vegetables of any kind

5 spoon over baked potatoes with shaved Parm and olive oil

6 use to add dimension to guacamole or avocado toast

7 dot on tomato or watermelon salads with creamy cheeses

8 slather on bread with cheese for garlic bread

9 use as green base for pizza

10 use to dress pasta or grain salads, deviled eggs, or egg salad

11 whisk into vinaigrettes

12 toss with stale bread and toast for croutons or bread crumbs

Fancy as a Clam

serves 4

In my humble opinion, clams are the most dynamic and elegant of the bivalves. Don't get me wrong, I slurp oysters, sear scallops, and steam mussels with the best of them, but clams bring so much brine, so much sea, to everything they touch, they are a prince among their peers.

Served raw and cold, they cleanse the palate and make you forget all the other fruits de mer. Breaded and fried, they're meaty with chew. And when steamed, clams do something miraculous. They make a broth that's salty and assertive, a brine that begs to tango with butter and lemon, a foundation that's come to define the linguini and chowders of our world.

A bowl of steamed clams with a hunk of bread speaks to me every season of the year, but when summer hits, I zero in on the perfect balance of salty clams steamed with sweet corn. It's one of my favorite combinations on the planet, and as best as I can tell the only way to improve it is with a generous swirl of Herbdacious and a cold glass of crisp white wine.

 ATTENTION While you can use frozen or canned corn for this recipe, it's really best if you're able to cut corn from the cob in an effort to scrape and collect the corn milk from its kernels. Do what you can, but note my suggestion.

3 tablespoons unsalted butter, divided

2 leeks, white and light green parts only, sliced into ½-inch-thick rounds

1 teaspoon kosher salt

½ teaspoon red pepper flakes

2 cups sweet corn (from about 3 ears), plus any milk you can scrape from the cob

1 cup white wine

3 pounds littleneck clams (4 to 5 dozen), rinsed well under cold water

⅓ cup Herbdacious (page 206)

3 tablespoons fresh lemon juice

Rustic toast to sop, dip, and scoop

1 In a 12-inch skillet fitted with a lid or a 6-quart Dutch oven, melt 2 tablespoons of the butter over medium heat. Add the leeks, salt, and pepper flakes and sweat for about 5 minutes. Stir in the corn and cook for another 3 to 5 minutes. Add the white wine and bring everything to a simmer.

2 Throw in the clams and cover. Cook for 5 minutes. Then peek under the lid to see how things are opening up. Once about three-fourths of your clams have opened, remove the lid and stir in the remaining 1 tablespoon butter, the Herbdacious, and lemon juice.

3 Serve the clams and the sauce with lots of toasted bread to make the most of everything.

Meatloaf's Big Makeover

serves 4

I've been thinking a lot about meatloaf lately. I didn't grow up eating much of it, but was always aware of its odd reputation. It is an American classic, after all, but for a dish that sustained bellies and stretched protein during the lean years of the Great Depression, meatloaf's name somehow suggests a lack of creativity. Even though it sits in a cultural category with hot dogs, hamburgers, and apple pie, meatloaf's image is lackluster, forever tarnished by its ties to school cafeterias. And although I personally love ketchup, it seems unfair that the most exciting thing about meatloaf gets squirt from a bottle.

All these mixed meatloaf messages got me thinking that meatloaf needs a makeover. I'm certain a lot of you will disagree, but know I'm not trying to replace or improve on the original. Still, Ms. Meatloaf deserves another outfit in her wardrobe, so here goes.

Meatloaf mounted with Herbdacious, studded with olives, and smothered in a sun-dried tomato sauce seems like an appropriately fresh face for a dish that conjures such nostalgia. It pays homage to her drive to satisfy and comfort, but like putting avocado on a hamburger or kimchi on a hot dog, this makeover gives meatloaf a new look, and a reason to celebrate her contributions to the cuisine we call American.

1 tablespoon extra-virgin olive oil

2 large yellow onions, diced small (2½ to 3 cups)

2½ teaspoons kosher salt, divided

1 teaspoon ground black pepper

½ cup (7.5-ounce jar) sun-dried tomatoes, with their oil

1½ cups (12-ounce jar) roasted red peppers, drained

2 tablespoons honey

2 tablespoons red wine vinegar

2 large eggs

½ cup sour cream

⅔ cup Herbdacious (page 206)

1 cup pitted and roughly chopped kalamata olives

2 tablespoons Worcestershire sauce

2½ pounds ground beef

½ cup bread crumbs or crushed saltine crackers

1 Preheat your oven to 325°F. In a 10- to 12-inch sauté pan or skillet, heat the olive oil over medium heat. Add the onions, 1 teaspoon of the salt, and the black pepper. Sweat for about 10 minutes, until the onions are translucent and soft.

2 While the onions sweat, combine the sun-dried tomatoes, roasted red peppers, honey, vinegar, and ½ teaspoon salt in the bowl of a food processor and blend until smooth.

3 In a large bowl, whisk the eggs, sour cream, Herbdacious, olives, and Worcestershire. Add the onions, beef, bread crumbs, and remaining 1 teaspoon salt. Gently mix to combine. If you mash and knead this into submission you will not be happy with the texture of your meatloaf, so treat it with kid hands.

4 Line a baking sheet with parchment paper or foil and dump the meat mixture overtop, then shape into a rectangular block about 3 x 3 x 12 inches. Spread the tomato mixture on top of that, taking care to cover the sides. It will seem like a lot of sauce, but that's intentional. I like sauce. Slide the baking sheet onto the middle rack of your oven and bake for 1 hour, till it's cooked all the way through. Bring the meatloaf out and let it cool for a few minutes before slicing.

That's Impressive Leg of Lamb

serves 6

Large pieces of meat cooked whole grab just about everybody's attention. Whether for a chicken making a browned, crisped-skin entrance from the oven or a beef rib roast that stands tall on a platter, onlookers generally pause, peer, and pay respect to the cook who transformed that large piece of protein into a magnetic object.

For me, the shock factor and the seductive draw of a hunk of meat is never greater than the one cast by a leg of lamb. With a bone that juts out of its round, caramelized thigh and an intoxicating game-laced perfume, leg of lamb announces *I am special, pause and take note of me.*

This one shows off Herbdacious's talents as a marinade. Lamb is lean and legs are muscles that work hard, so this cut of meat benefits from a long soak in something that will tenderize, add flavor, and protect as it cooks. Mounted with tangy yogurt that lends acid, Herbdacious does all these things and flirts with the mild, barnyardy funk we know and love from lamb. Roast it in the oven or, better yet, char it with care on the grill. Whatever you do, make sure there's an audience when this impressive piece of meat makes its entrance.

½ cup Greek yogurt

½ cup Herbdacious (page 206)

1 (roughly 7-pound) leg of lamb

1½ teaspoons kosher salt

1 teaspoon ground black pepper

1 The day before you want to cook your lamb leg, whisk together the yogurt and Herbdacious in a small bowl. Then rub the lamb with the salt and pepper followed by the Herbdacious-yogurt mix. Slide the whole gloppy mix into a large zip-top plastic bag or a covered baking dish and marinate in the fridge for a minimum of 4 hours, or up to 12 hours.

2 An hour before you want to cook the lamb, bring it out of the fridge to come to room temperature. Then preheat your oven to 350°F. Put the leg of lamb, fat cap up, onto a baking sheet that is ideally fitted with a rack.

3 Slide the baking sheet onto the middle rack of your oven and roast for about 1 hour 15 minutes. Test the internal temperature with a meat thermometer at the leg's thickest part. Once it reads 130°F for a rosy-pink medium, bring the lamb out of the oven and let it rest for 15 minutes. This will be the most difficult part of the whole lamb event because everyone will stand and gawk at how beautiful it looks and how intoxicating it smells, so have your guests set the table as the impressive piece of meat rests.

Tomato Gravy to Me

serves 4

Southern food purists and Italian American grandmas may raise their eyebrows at my inclination to call this gravy. It's not a flour-thickened sauce made from meat drippings that's spooned from a cast-iron pan and puddled over rice. And it's not a Sunday tomato-and-meat tradition that simmers all day and represents a culture's story in a new land. But it is a thick, rich, flavorful sauce that makes just about anything more enjoyable to eat under its cover. To me that spells gravy. The list of things it complements is pretty long and ridiculous, but for starters consider spooning it on something plain like simple grilled fish or chicken, or make a brunch plan and dollop it on cheese grits, then top that bowl-of-happy with a fried egg. And don't forget pasta.

- 1 yellow onion, halved and sliced thin with the grain
- 2 tablespoons extra-virgin olive oil
- 1 teaspoon kosher salt
- ¼ teaspoon red pepper flakes
- 4 cups grape or cherry tomatoes (2 dry pints)
- 1 cup vegetable or chicken broth or water
- ⅓ cup Herbdacious (page 206)
- 1 tablespoon unsalted butter
- 2 tablespoons fresh lemon juice

1 In a 10- to 12-inch skillet or heavy-bottomed sauté pan over medium heat, sweat the onion in the olive oil with the salt and red pepper flakes. Once they are soft and slightly caramelized, mound them at the edge and add the tomatoes to the skillet bottom. Let the tomatoes sit, suffer, and blister for a few minutes. They will brown in spots and blister in others. Once some of the tomatoes have started to split from their skins, add the broth you've got (or water), stir it all together, and simmer until the mixture has reduced and thickened. Just before serving it on top or underneath something, swirl in the Herbdacious, butter, and lemon juice.

Chicken Salad Worth Discussion

serves 6

Chicken salad is an under-discussed yet important member of American cuisine. Smooth and chunky chicken salads ride in coolers to the beach, football games, and picnics all over our nation. You find chicken salad in every deli, and I'm pretty sure our affinity for cooked chicken slicked with mayo fueled the mayonnaise fire for a number of years.

But for a dish so integral to our culture, we don't talk about chicken salad a whole lot, and I understand why. Even if you dot yours with walnuts and apples or you favor pickle relish and celery, chicken salad in its truest sense just isn't that interesting. You like it or you don't. You make it or you buy it. It's just kind of...*there*, in all its whiteness.

This, however, is chicken salad worthy of discussion. To be perfectly transparent, I had planned to make a more traditional chicken salad with Herbdacious folded into a mayo-based dressing, but that day I ran out of mayo and decided I was hungry enough to trash the project in lieu of something quick to eat.

The result was a revelation and celebration of chicken salad that's luminous, compelling, and, dare I say it, delightful. While traditional chicken salad bound by mayo is muted and spreadable, this is green, fork-ready, and loud. When the crunchy bits in other chicken salads seem like afterthoughts, here the salted cucumber and pickled red onion feel like valued teammates.

Give chicken salad the kind of credit all American classics deserve. Make a version worth talking about.

1 small red onion, halved and sliced super-thin with the grain (about ⅔ cup)

2 teaspoons kosher salt, divided

2 teaspoons granulated sugar, divided

⅓ cup red wine vinegar

1 English cucumber, halved lengthwise and sliced super thin

4 boneless, skinless chicken breasts (about 2 pounds)—likely the only time I will ever recommend the use of these

2 tablespoons extra-virgin olive oil

3 tablespoons fresh lemon juice

½ teaspoon ground black pepper

⅓ cup Herbdacious (page 206)

❶ Begin by pickling the onions. This requires at least an hour, but you get a gold star if you do it the night before because they'll really have an opportunity to grow mellow and bright with some extra time. Either way, toss the sliced onions with ½ teaspoon of the salt, 1 teaspoon of the sugar, and all the vinegar.

❷ While you're at it, in a separate bowl toss the sliced cucumber with ½ teaspoon salt and the remaining 1 teaspoon sugar. Let this hang near your onions for whatever time works in your world—either on the counter while you prepare the rest of the salad or in the fridge overnight.

❸ Preheat your oven to 350°F and toss the chicken breasts with the remaining 1 teaspoon salt and the olive oil. Put them on a baking sheet, slide that onto the middle rack of your oven, and roast till a meat thermometer shows they've reached 160°F, about 25 minutes.

❹ Bring the chicken breasts out of the oven and let them cool to room temperature.

❺ Once they've cooled, cut them into ½-inch chunks and toss with the lemon juice and black pepper in a bowl. Drain the red onion and cucumber and throw that in the bowl too. Finally, toss it all with the Herbdacious, taste it, and tell someone how freaking surprised you are by this chicken salad.

CHEF'S MIX

There are those who are born with the desire to be parents and those who are on the fence about it. I was most definitely a fence-dweller all the way through my twenties. Career-driven and a wee bit selfish, I didn't see where or how a baby might fit into my brand of being. Plus, I never really relished the company of other people's kids. I had a fair amount of experience with eight nieces and nephews to coo at and cuddle, and I babysat in high school and was even a nanny in college. But I chose those jobs because they were easy, unsupervised means to make money while keeping my schedule flexible. It's telling that I can't remember the names of any of the kids I babysat, but that twenty years later I do remember the parents, their jobs, and their relationships like I was in their living rooms yesterday.

When I turned thirty my temperature changed. It was that clock they talk about, the biological one ticking to tell me that if anything inside me wanted to be a mom, and not an old one, I'd better get busy. Never one to do anything halfway, I got pregnant with boy-girl twins at thirty-two.

In all the ways, I was so very lucky. Ben and I had made healthy carbon copies of ourselves—a girl who looked just like me and a boy who was the spitting image of him. Having been on bed rest with the time and attention to read far too many parenting books, I worried I wouldn't connect with my babies or I wouldn't be able to breastfeed. I worried my touch wouldn't comfort them or that my maternal instincts would prove dull. But I was wrong about all that. From the beginning Theo and Flo felt like they were of me rather than mine. We connected, and I mothered just fine. We were a one-shot family of four, complete with a dog and a full set of grandparents.

Early on, work started to compete for my attention. I felt like I had three babies. Two whose needs could often be passed on to a grandparent or nanny, and one whose tantrums could only be calmed by me. And so it went, this push and pull between being a mom and a career woman. The endless shuffling of guilt—guilt when I was at work because I missed my babies' and their daily milestones at home, guilt when I was at home because I knew my team was suffering at work. Guilt because I knew I could make the decision not to have a TV show, not to write a book, not to open another restaurant in favor of being home more with my kids. Guilt because that's not what I chose to do. I kept telling myself, "They're just babies now. They don't know I only tucked them in twice this week." I convinced myself that when they got old enough to hold memories I'd be home more. I'd bring them to work with me, on trips with me. I could be an unconventional mom and still be an engaged one. These are the things I told myself to wipe the guilt away. What I didn't acknowledge was that while my babies weren't making memories, my mind was a steel trap of lost moments and regret.

It's not to say I was an absent, disengaged parent. I most definitely was not. I did all the things—fed them, rocked them, read and sang to them. I was particularly good at snuggling and loving on them. But at the end of the day it wasn't enough. I worried I had imposter syndrome around motherhood. All the mothers I had known seemed content just to be mothers. They looked into their children's eyes and saw their own future. I didn't see that. I was sure my maternal GPS had a glitch.

I saw other moms on the floor in dramatic, giggle-filled acts of make-believe. I watched them willingly play dress-up and decorate doll houses while I simmered farro, sweet potatoes, and turkey to blend for baby food. Theoretically I wanted to play. I just wanted to fill ice cube trays with perfectly balanced toddler meals more. That seemed like an extension of my work, a way my career could make my kids' lives better in the moment. I could ensure they'd be good eaters or at least have a healthy start, and I patted myself on the back every time Flo identified beets roasting with her nose or requested barbecue tofu for dinner. I was a very good mom in some ways, but I was preoccupied by the idea that I had a very limited window of time to capture my career and make it what I wanted. And I knew the work of it was happening while my kids were making memories.

In third grade Theo had to draw a picture of his family and write a few sentences about what he loved to do most with each member. Just the premise of the assignment had me worried like I'd be the one graded on the assignment, not him.

I loved him. I talked to and listened to him. I scratched his back and sang "You Are My Sunshine" to him before bed. I went to his games and drove him to school. I watched movies and listened to hip-hop with him, but I couldn't think of anything we *did* together. We didn't play kickball or put together Legos. We didn't go fishing or to Disneyland or bike-riding. I went on book tours and business trips instead. With this assignment my mother-fraud would be uncovered for his teachers, his classmates, and me to see.

When he finished the assignment, I took a deep breath and read how Theo loved to play basketball with his dad, how he loved to play Uno with his sister, and how he loved to cook with me. It was a perfectly good answer and for everybody looking on, it made perfect sense. But it wasn't true in the way he meant it. Despite my profession and all the expectations that come with being both a chef and a mom, I had never made much of

"And so it went, this push and pull between being a mom and a career woman."

a point to cook with my kids. They never seemed interested. I was never interested. I hadn't taken the time to slow down and show them my world. I'd thought about it, sure, but I resolved we'd do it when they were older, when I had more time, more patience, when they raised their hands and asked for it. And right there on that page I saw that Theo was asking. He's always been very keen to recognize people's expectations of him, and he knew people expected him to love to cook with his chef of a mom. I had to make it right.

The first time was a grand gesture. One that would make his statement true and show off his love for cooking with Mom. One that I knew we could accomplish together, without a big mess or a big fail: Chex Mix for his teachers at Christmas. But not just any old Chex Mix with its recipe taken from the back of the box. We made Chex Mix fit for a chef and her son. Chef Mix for both of us.

Chef Mix

makes 6 cups

There are three reasons Chex mix is my favorite snack food. First, and I know this goes against a lot of hand-in-the-snack-bowl rules, I like that you can pick out the elements you enjoy and leave behind the ones you don't. Second (but related), I feel as if I'm saving calories when I eat this snack dotted with cereal because I never eat all of it. I don't get down with pretzels or the nuts, so it's basically diet food. And third, my roommate's mother used to bring us bags of homemade Chex mix whenever she visited and I've never forgotten how much better it can be when you make it yourself.

So here I am with my own version of the perfect road food, conversation starter, and customizable snack that's got something everybody likes: Chex mix, Herbdacious edition.

2 tablespoons unsalted butter, melted

6 tablespoons Herbdacious (page 206)

1 teaspoon kosher salt

2 cups Chex of any kind

1 cup Cheez-Its

1 cup nuts of your desire

1 cup roughly broken saltine crackers

1 cup roughly broken bagel chips

1 Preheat your oven to 325°F. In a small bowl, whisk the melted butter with the Herbdacious and salt. In a large bowl, toss the Herbdacious-butter mixture with everything else. Don't do this gently. Do it like you want every morsel of carb and protein covered in Herbdacious butter and you don't care if a few pieces break in your pursuit.

2 Spread that mixture out onto your largest baking sheet and slide that onto the middle rack of your oven. Bake for 8 minutes. Bring it out and toss the soon-to-be snack mix around so it toasts evenly, then slide the baking sheet back in the oven for an additional 6 minutes, until crisp and toasty.

3 Bring it out. Let it cool. Then snack, but know, for reasons I can't explain, that the herby cohesiveness that makes this Chex mix distinct only emerges the next day. What you don't eat will keep to great pleasure sealed in a container for up to 2 weeks.

Caesar Me Convinced

makes 2 cups

Caesar salad is one of those things I love to hate. Not because the emulsification of lemon, anchovies, Parm, and oil suggests our country's mediocre way of interpreting Italian food, I just loathe Caesar's legacy because so many Caesar salads are so dang bad. We've somehow managed to take an idea with delicious intentions and strapped a band of don't care around it. A Caesar is often a throw-away—a salad doused in cheese to hide the lettuce it refuses to exalt. It's a way to get a crouton on the menu. It's a lazy choice for those of us who don't want to make a real meal decision. But Caesar salad doesn't have to be that way.

Go after it with your Caesar. Chill the lettuce. Squeeze fresh lemon. Get crazy with some zest if you can. Grate the Parm right over top, and give the emulsified, anchovy dressing of your dreams a serious chance at special. Herbdacious her.

ATTENTION If I recommend a piece of equipment to do something you could otherwise do by hand, it's because that gadget makes the work much much easier. So, while it is totally possible to employ only a cutting board, knife, bowl, and whisk to emulsify this dressing, I highly recommend you lean on a food processor or blender to do the work. Emulsification by hand is a pain in the rear. End of story.

5 anchovy fillets packed in oil

1 tablespoon red wine vinegar

1 tablespoon fresh lemon juice

1 tablespoon Dijon mustard

1 garlic clove, peeled

1 large egg yolk

1 teaspoon kosher salt, divided

¼ cup Herbdacious (page 206)

¼ cup vegetable oil

½ cup finely grated (on a Microplane) Parmigiano Reggiano, divided

2 to 3 heads romaine lettuce, split lengthwise, chilled

Grated zest of a lemon, for garnish

Croutons, for garnish

❶ In the bowl of a food processor or blender, combine the anchovy fillets, vinegar, lemon juice, Dijon, garlic clove, egg yolk, and ¼ teaspoon of the salt. Turn on the motor of whatever gadget you've got and let her rip till the mixture is smooth. With the motor still running, start to drizzle in the Herbdacious a few drops at the time. Once the Herbdacious is fully incorporated, slowly drizzle in the vegetable oil. At this point the dressing should be creamy and thick. That's what "emulsified" looks like.

❷ Transfer your Caesar dressing to a bowl and stir in ¼ cup of the Parm. Cover and refrigerate for at least 30 minutes before serving.

❸ When you're ready, bring your split romaine heads out of the fridge and toss them with the remaining ¾ teaspoon salt and half the dressing. Arrange them on a plate and drizzle the rest of the dressing on top, then cover with the remaining ¼ cup Parm and the lemon zest and croutons if you like.

❹ This dressing is one of my favorite creamy things in this book, but know it's best the day it's made. So in the event you have some left over after your salad, consider it as a dip for vegetables, a sauce for skewers of meat, or a slather for a piece of toast.

This Is 40 Fettuccine

serves 4

When I turned forty I did something extravagant and quite possibly beyond my means. I rented a villa, a baller one, on the Sorrentine coast of Italy for three weeks. The first week I invited my sisters and their families to join. The second I hosted a group of college friends, and the last week we welcomed people I work with and happen to love.

What you learn when you stay put in one residential part of Italy for that long is that they eat what they eat and not much else. There's no sushi to cleanse your palate, no burgers to remind you of home, and no bistecca Fiorentina because that's from Tuscany and you're in Campania.

I thought I knew the food of that region. In addition to the setting, it was caprese salad, fritto misto, and linguini with clams that made me choose the spot nestled between Amalfi and Sorrento to celebrate. But when you stay somewhere long enough and you eat deep into that region's cuisine you learn about the dishes that haven't yet made a splash on this side of the Atlantic.

One such dish, and the one that will always take me back to my fortieth birthday, is spaghetti alla Nerano. As its name suggests, it comes from a tiny town called Nerano nestled in a cove on the Amalfi coast. The setting stuns. The people are chic and the pasta is simple. Spaghetti tossed with fried zucchini, cheese, and basil shouldn't be that memorable, but in Nerano, it is.

½ cup extra-virgin olive oil

5 small zucchini or 3 large, sliced into ¼-inch-thick rounds

1 teaspoon kosher salt, plus more for salting the pasta water

½ cup Herbdacious (page 206)

11 ounces dried fettuccine

1 cup finely grated Parmigiano Reggiano or provolone del Monaco (use a Microplane)

1 Bring a large pot of salted water up to a boil.

2 In a 12-inch skillet, heat half the oil over medium heat. Add half the zucchini and half the salt and pan-fry until many of the zucchini rounds are golden brown. Transfer the cooked zucchini to a bowl and follow up with the remaining olive oil, zucchini, and salt in the same way.

3 Once you've fried all the zucchini, put half of them in a blender with the Herbdacious and buzz that mixture until smooth. Reserve the remaining zucchini rounds to throw into the pasta at the end.

4 Meanwhile, cook your fettuccine. The idea is to drain it just before it's done as it will continue to cook a bit in the sauce. This seems to be a tricky feat for us Americans, so just do your best and aim for something other than noodle mush. But before you drain the fettucine, dip a mug in and reserve about a cup of the starchy cooking water.

5 Combine the drained noodles, the zucchini puree, ⅔ cup of the cheese, and about half the reserved pasta water in the skillet. Cook over medium-high heat, tossing, for about 3 minutes and marvel at how the zucchini puree starts to cling to the pasta to make a sauce. At the last minute, throw in the fried zucchini slices and the remaining ⅓ cup cheese. If you need to thin things out or add silk to your sauce, toss in a little more pasta water.

Juicy & Bright Citrus Salad

serves 4

Whenever I get bent out of shape about all the root vegetables and general brown-ness winter weather brings to our plates, I think about citrus and I can cook another day. Not the preserved citrus I pray to (beginning on page 140), but the oranges, tangelos, grapefruit, and clementines that are literally and figuratively the bright spots of our coldest months.

There is absolutely no better way to freshen up a heavy spread or highlight a simple piece of skillet-seared fish than with a juicy wet salad of citrus slices and supremes layered with ribbons of fennel. It functions like a brief respite from winter's reality—like a trip to Tulum in February. Then Herbdacious enters and her big expressive tone makes the sun shine brighter and daylight last longer.

Don't skip this one and don't put her in a corner either. Serve her center stage with roast chicken as a foil, or layer her with fresh mozzarella or stracciatella cheese for a winter riff on a summer caprese. I want you to make this so many times you could teach a class on how to supreme fruit.

1 small red onion, peeled	3 tangerines or clementines
½ cup red wine vinegar	1 head fennel
2 teaspoons kosher salt, divided	½ teaspoon red pepper flakes
2 ruby red grapefruit or pomelos	¼ cup fresh lemon juice
3 oranges of any variety	½ cup Herbdacious (page 206)
	⅓ cup tasty extra-virgin olive oil

① Using a mandoline or a knife, slice the red onion into thin-as-you-can rings. Put them in a small bowl and stir in the vinegar and ½ teaspoon of the salt. Let this hang out while you prepare the rest of the ingredients. It will actually improve with more time, so feel free to pickle the onions a day, even a week in advance.

② To prepare the citrus, put on a podcast and settle into a trance state. I actually find the act of turning whole citrus into wedges and rounds meditative, so I'm really not kidding with that instruction. Begin by cutting the top, bottom, and sides away from the citrus flesh. You should remove the rind as well as all the white pith.

③ Once you've removed all the skin from the fruit, grab a big bowl and decide which fruit you want to supreme and what you'd like to slice. I like a variety of shapes and sizes so I do a little of both across the board. No matter what you decide, do all of this work over the bowl so it collects the juice as well as all the cut fruit. To *supreme* (cut citrus into clean, membrane-free wedges), slide a paring knife just inside a wedge section, then turn the edge of the knife up and push the naked wedge out of its crease. If you find a certain type of citrus has a lot of seeds as you whittle away, slice it into rounds from the top and bottom till you hit the seed cavity, then cut four sides of flesh from around it. That way you still end up with neat pieces.

④ Once you've had your way with the fruit, turn to the fennel. For this I really like to use a mandoline, but I understand others' fear of the instrument. Just make sure you remove the root and any tough outer layers. Then go about slicing the tender, moist section of the stalks. If fennel fronds are your thing, reserve them for garnish. Then slice the root as thin as you can manage.

⑤ Lift the onions out of the vinegar and put them and the fennel in the bowl with the fruit and its juice. Season it all with the remaining 1½ teaspoons salt and the pepper flakes. Let that hang out for about 10 minutes. Then stir in the lemon juice, the Herbdacious, and the olive oil. Serve in a vessel with a rim to contain the juicy sauce, because the juicy sauce is life.

Mashed Potatoes' Second Coming

makes about 12 potato cakes

One of the most common food questions asked on the Internet is what to do with leftover mashed potatoes. My first inclination is to answer "heat them up," but evidently people want more. These potato cakes wrapped in bacon with their shatteringly crisp sides and fluffy floral guts are just that. Had mashed potatoes for supper? Form and fry these patties the next morning and make them a base for a Benedict or as a starch with scrambled eggs. Want mashed potatoes for lunch? Put these in a puddle of chicken soup in lieu of noodles or crackers. Or just serve them with a dollop of sour cream and a dot of Herbdacious, and nobody will suspect a leftover lurks inside.

3 cups cold mashed potatoes	1 teaspoon baking powder
1 tablespoon sour cream	1½ teaspoons kosher salt
⅓ cup Herbdacious (page 206)	1 teaspoon ground black pepper
⅔ cup all-purpose flour, plus more for dusting	2 8-ounce packs sliced bacon
	6 tablespoons unsalted butter

❶ In a large bowl, mix the mashed potatoes with the sour cream and Herbdacious. In a smaller bowl, stir together the flour, baking powder, salt, and black pepper. Dump the dry mixture into the wet and mix with a spoon to combine. It will be a sticky dough. Let it sit in the bowl for about 5 minutes to let the flour get comfortable with the potatoes. Then flour your work surface and dump the mixture out.

❷ Flour the top of the dough a bit and press it into a ¾-inch-thick disc. Use a biscuit cutter or even your knife to cut the dough into rounds or triangles—whatever suits you—and place the cakes on a baking sheet. Gather together and then press out the remaining dough and cut out additional cakes. Use flour all along the way to keep the dough from sticking. Refrigerate the cakes, covered, for 15 minutes, or up to overnight before pan-frying them.

❸ Lay two slices of bacon on your work surface so they form a cross. Put one potato cake in the center of the bacon cros and fold the edges up to meet at the center. Now you have a potato bacon package of sorts. Continue with the remaining potato cakes and bacon. Once you've wrapped all of them, refrigerate seam-side down for 15 minutes, or up to overnight, before pan-frying.

❹ Heat a 12-inch, heavy-bottomed skillet over medium heat. Add 2 tablespoons of the butter. Once it's melted and starting to bubble, add half the potato cakes bacon seam down. Take care that they don't touch. You'll need enough room to get in there with your spatula to flip them when the time comes. Cook the potato cakes gently on the first side without disturbing them for about 5 minutes. Flip, add another tablespoon butter, and cook on the other side an additional 5 minutes. The tops and bottoms of the cakes should be brown and crisp but overall they will feel fragile and a bit delicate. Transfer them to a plate, then follow up in the same way by cooking the remaining cakes in butter. Serve warm.

ATTENTION The art of putting these together is a simple one, but if your mashed potatoes are runny, you'll need to add a little more flour to force things together, so don't take the measurements here as gospel. Use your noggin.

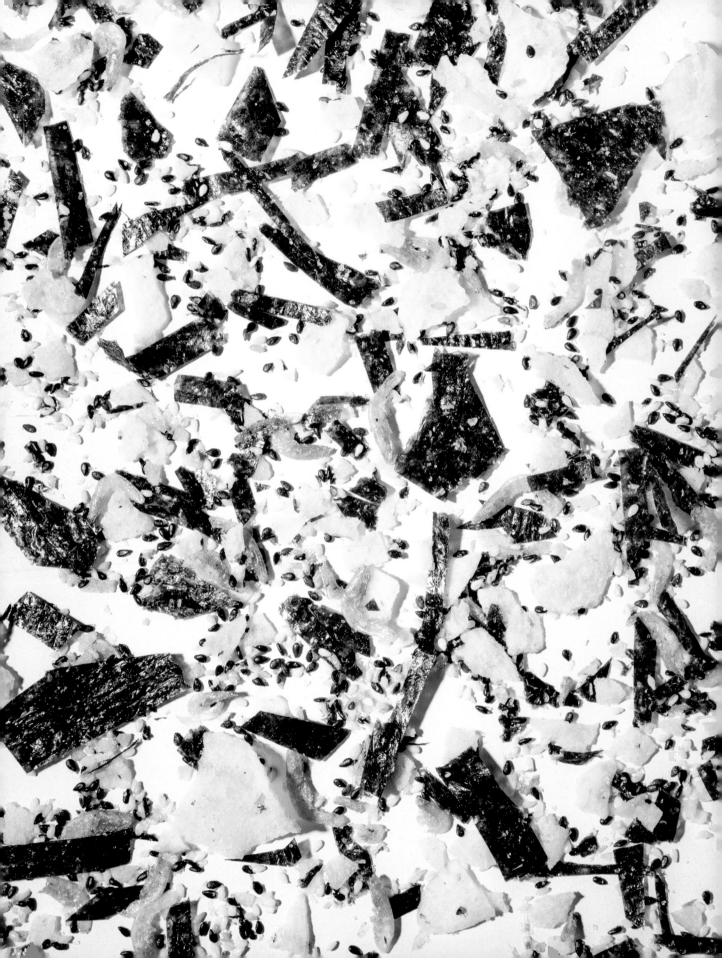

CHAPTER EIGHT

Quirky Furki

Umami • Sea-driven • Textured • Funky

This flavor hero might be a bit outside the lines of what you expect from me.

My Quirky Furki is a tweaked version of the Japanese seasoning *furikake,* and I'm a white woman so superglued to the food of the American South that anything other than collard greens and cornbread raises red flags about authenticity. That's precisely why Quirky Furki matters. This book reflects the food I eat, the food I cook for my family, and the type of food that excites me. And guess what? I study, cook, and eat all kinds of cuisine because they teach me a lot about flavor, technique, balance, and the shared pleasure everybody everywhere gets from a good meal. What's more, as a parent of kids growing up in a rural area, where diversity is easy to miss, when I celebrate people, traditions, and foods from different cultures, it lets my kids know we are in fact not the center of the universe.

I've never been to Japan, but for a long time I've studied that country's refined food traditions from the rims of ramen bowls, from the catbird seats of sushi bars, and from the pages of books. There's hardly a cuisine on the planet I admire more. And as best I can tell, people in Japan sprinkle furikake on rice, fish, and vegetables with the same fervor we squirt ketchup on french fries in the U.S. Generally a means to amplify subtle flavors and add intriguing texture, furikake comes in a multitude of variations that seem to mirror the tastes of the person who sprinkles it. Mine is no different.

My Quirky Furki calls on the usual suspects in the furikake canon. Sesame seeds, seaweed, dried fish, salt, and sugar are the basics found in nearly every version. I use those and tweak their presence a bit by toasting the sesame seeds with sesame oil to heighten their nuttiness. I favor tiny dried shrimp in lieu of bonito flakes because I enjoy the girth and texture they provide. And I point up those umami rich flavors with turbinado sugar and flaky salt because their larger particle size makes sense in the mix. But the ingredient that puts the quirk in my furk and gives my version of the seasoning both an acidic hit and a base from which to begin is salt-and-vinegar potato chips.

Yes, I hinge the success of this flavor hero on Cape Cod brand salt-and-vinegar potato chips. There's no behind-the-scenes brand sponsorship. I haven't lost my mind and forgotten how to cook. I just happen to think these potato chips have an unmatched approach to texture, salt, and acid, and make a smart addition to a lot of things that yearn for their unique crunch.

Because its foundation is sesame and seaweed, Quirky Furki amplifies seafood, but please don't pigeonhole it. Rather, imagine it as punched-up salt you'd use anywhere salt makes sense—on top of soft stuff like avocado or eggs; whipped with butter and melted on toast, baked potatoes, or cooked proteins; or folded into things like burger meat or casseroles as a means to layer flavor. My experience is that Quirky Furki makes a dramatic entrance when I use it to finish dishes, but when layered and cooked into things, it's much more nuanced and elegant.

Like all my pantry players, Quirky Furki is a pleasure to have around. She keeps for an eternity, makes a welcomed gift, offers easy excitement to weeknight meals, and, if paid attention to, will make you a more confident, nimble cook. ⬧

Quirky Furki

HERE'S WHAT'S IMPORTANT

- I like to use white sesame seeds because it's easier to see how they're coming along when you're toasting them (and most specifically whether or not they have burned), but if black sesame is all you have, that's fine too.

- Turbinado sugar is important here not because of a flavor distinction among sugars, but because of its particle size. It's more granular and less moist than other sugars, so it doesn't sink to the bottom of the mix or soften things up.

- If you're using shrimp rather than bonito, save the oil you fry the shrimp in and use it to sauté vegetables or scramble eggs or pan-fry fish. It's full of flavor and will add depth to simple recipes. I do recommend you store it in the fridge. Like all flavored oils, it has the potential to go rancid if exposed to lots of sunlight or warm temps.

- Quirky Furki will keep in an airtight container at room temperature for 1 month.

1 cup vegetable oil (not needed if you use bonito flakes)

2 cups dried tiny shrimp, or 2 cups bonito flakes

10 sheets (one .88-ounce package) dried seaweed or nori

2 teaspoons toasted sesame oil

1 cup white sesame seeds

5 ounces (about two-thirds of an 8-ounce bag) salt-and-vinegar potato chips (I like Cape Cod brand)

3 tablespoons flaky salt

3 tablespoons turbinado sugar

❶ Fry the Tiny Shrimp: If you are using bonito flakes instead of dried shrimp, skip down to toasting the nori. Heat the vegetable oil in a Dutch oven over medium heat while you set up a plate lined with a few layers of paper towels nearby. Drop one shrimp in to see if the oil is ready. If it sizzles immediately, go ahead and drop half the shrimp in the oil. Fry for about 30 seconds, or until the shrimp darken slightly in color. (You're looking for a toasted crustacean color, not a dark, burnt earth color.) Using a slotted metal spoon, scoop the shrimp out of the oil and put them on the paper towels to drain.

❷ You may not enjoy the way the shrimp smell at this point, and you may not appreciate the shrimp's flavor on its own. Don't let this deter you and don't make the executive decision to just leave the shrimp out of the mix. I don't salivate at their smell or individual taste either, but I love the sum of all these parts enough to dedicate a chapter to it, so trust me and move forward.

MAKES 4 CUPS

3 Fry the remaining shrimp. Drain them on paper towels and remove the oil from the heat. When it's cool, treat the oil like you would garlic oil, and store it in a jar in the refrigerator.

4 **Toast the Nori:** If you have gas burners, using tongs, hold one sheet of nori horizontally about 2 inches above the open flame of your stove to toast. Each side will require about 3 seconds, during which the nori sheet will shrink slightly, lighten in color, and may even catch fire. All of these transformations are okay, but blow out the flame if you cause one, and set the sheet aside. Continue toasting the remaining sheets. Once they cool they should be rather brittle and misshapen.

5 If you don't have a gas burner, you can toast the nori in a 500°F oven directly on the rack in a single layer for about 4 minutes. The point is that the nori will grow more brittle and aromatic post-toast.

6 **Toast the Sesame Seeds:** If you can multitask over an open flame, put the sesame oil and seeds in a 12-inch skillet to toast over medium heat while you work the nori. If you are using a smaller skillet, you will need to toast the sesame seeds in batches. The point is for the seeds to pretty much be in a single layer, so with a little tossing and stirring all the seeds meet heat and toast evenly. Once your pan is hot, this will only take about 30 seconds.

7 Some people like to do this in the oven. If this is the route you want to go, preheat your oven to 375°F, spread the seeds out evenly on a baking sheet, and set your timer for 10 minutes. (I choose the stovetop because I hate heating my oven for such a small task and I like to keep my eye on the seeds as they toast.)

8 However you want to go about it, toast the sesame seeds and do it well. Once they're done take them out of the skillet or off the tray. Otherwise the residual heat will continue to brown the seeds you've worked so hard to perfectly toast.

9 **Pull the Quirky Furki Together:** Now it's time for the food processor. Basically you are going to process the shrimp, nori, and potato chips separately. Don't worry about cleaning the food processor in between ingredients. They will all end up together, and their union starts here.

10 Begin with the shrimp. They will take about 10 seconds with your processor on full tilt and what was 2 cups of fluffy fried crustaceans will emerge as 1 cup of shrimp crumbs. Dump that into a large bowl and move on to the nori.

11 Cram all the nori sheets in the food processor. Fasten the lid and let her rip. Toasted nori is more stubborn than dried fried shrimp so this will take a bit longer and will require some pulsing to get all the sheets chopped somewhat evenly. What you're looking for is about 1½ cups finely chopped pieces, none of which should be bigger than a petite hand's pinkie nail. Dump the chopped nori into the same bowl with the shrimp crumbs.

12 Now for the potato chips. Put the salt-and-vinegar chips in your food processor and blend for about 5 seconds, or until what you have is potato chip crumbs. Not potato chip dust...potato chip crumbs.

13 Now you have a decision to make. You can add the potato chips to the bowl with the shrimp and the nori, then stir in the sesame seeds, salt, and sugar and call it done. Or you can put all the ingredients, including the sesame seeds, salt, and sugar, in the food processor and blend together until the mixture is a uniform crumb.

14 Both versions have their appeal. The stirred, less-uniform one allows you to visually appreciate the elements that make up the fun ingredient you've made. It also provides more crunch to the Quirk. Because of this I generally prefer this version as a topping. The further processed Furki is more uniform and married in a way that delivers a cohesive flavor profile. It's easier to measure and works better as an ingredient rather than a topping (except on popcorn!). If you want to be ready for whatever opportunity presents itself, blend half and leave half as is.

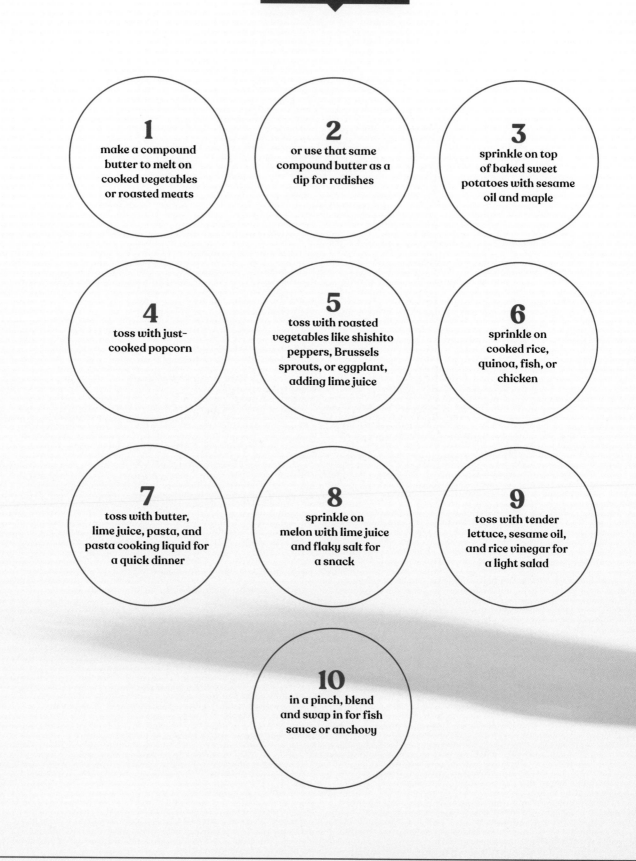

1
make a compound butter to melt on cooked vegetables or roasted meats

2
or use that same compound butter as a dip for radishes

3
sprinkle on top of baked sweet potatoes with sesame oil and maple

4
toss with just-cooked popcorn

5
toss with roasted vegetables like shishito peppers, Brussels sprouts, or eggplant, adding lime juice

6
sprinkle on cooked rice, quinoa, fish, or chicken

7
toss with butter, lime juice, pasta, and pasta cooking liquid for a quick dinner

8
sprinkle on melon with lime juice and flaky salt for a snack

9
toss with tender lettuce, sesame oil, and rice vinegar for a light salad

10
in a pinch, blend and swap in for fish sauce or anchovy

Gingered Cabbage in a Quirky Cream

serves 4 to 6

I always have a head of green cabbage in my fridge. It's cheap, of consistent quality in the grocery store, full of stuff that's good for you, and versatile once you get it home. All that being said, I find a lot of people don't know what to do with the humble vegetable. They understand it stewed and soft, or crunchy and cold. Beyond that, cabbage is a mystery.

If you're one of those people who looks at a head of cabbage and can't see anything but slaw, listen up. For years, my cabbage seared over high heat with ginger, garlic, and pepper flakes has made my dinner guests scratch their heads with the question, "What's happening here in this cabbage situation?" They can't understand how something that's pretty bland on its own can take on such a wild and creamy, caramelized, popcorn character. They assume it must be chef wizardry they'll never master. I assure them it's stupid easy. They roll their eyes and then, for the first time in their lives, they request an encore from cabbage.

All that hoopla is even before Quirky Furki enters stage far left with plain-as-day water, plus cool cream and silky sweet butter. In concert with the already noteworthy cabbage, they put on a show that tastes like it took forever to nail. It hits all the notes, sings all the songs, does all the dances, and unlocks the limitless potential of formerly misunderstood Mr. Cabbage.

❶ Cut the cabbage into quarters, remove the core, then cut the quarters into rough 1-inch strips. Put 3 tablespoons of the butter and the ginger in a 12-inch skillet over medium-high heat. Lay the cabbage overtop and press it down so it's firmly planted on the skillet's bottom. Don't worry about breaking the cabbage into individual leaves. This will happen naturally as it cooks. Scatter the pepper flakes, 1 teaspoon of the salt, and the garlic overtop. Under no circumstances should the garlic be on the bottom with the ginger. Over high heat, ginger caramelizes and develops a deep, pleasant character, but in the same environment, garlic burns and becomes bitter.

❷ Let the cabbage sit and sizzle for 3 minutes. I know this is hard, but whatever it takes, access the discipline inside of you and don't shake or stir a thing. After 3 minutes, lift up a little cabbage along the edge of your skillet. Is it brown in spots? If the answer is yes, then toss the mound of cabbage around, add the remaining 1 teaspoon salt, and let it sit and sizzle once again for 3 minutes. After 3 minutes, toss the cabbage once more and cook for a final 3 minutes. After 12 minutes total in your skillet at a sizzle, the cabbage should be brown in spots, translucent green in others, and have both a soft and toothsome texture.

❸ At this point it's ready to eat, but for the purpose of this book and for the good of humanity we are going to go a step further. With the heat still on, add 2 cups water and work to scrape up those browned bits I mentioned earlier. Bring it up to simmer and whisk in the remaining 2 tablespoons butter and the cream. Cook for 1 minute just to let the cream acquaint itself with the cabbage. Scoop the brothy cabbage into bowls and scatter with as much or as little Quirky Furki as you like. It should mingle with the creamy broth, transforming it in a wizard kind of way.

1 small or ½ large head green cabbage	2 teaspoons kosher salt, divided
5 tablespoons unsalted butter, divided	6 garlic cloves, sliced
3 tablespoons minced fresh ginger	½ cup heavy cream
½ teaspoon red pepper flakes	Up to 1 cup Quirky Furki (page 236)

HEADS up The amount of cabbage and the size of your skillet are very important here. Use a 12-inch, heavy-bottomed skillet and make sure a carpet of cabbage covers the bottom and mounds in the center. Usually when I want you to caramelize something, I urge that your ingredients don't touch and have room to breathe. That's not the case here. It will take longer for the cabbage to cook to the texture we want, so we are going to encourage caramelization in a slightly different way.

Scrambled Eggs with Tomatoes & More

serves 4

A few years ago I read a touching story by Francis Lam about the ubiquitous comfort food of his family's kitchen, scrambled eggs with tomatoes. Francis is the son of Chinese immigrants and in an effort to connect with the warm feeling certain food memories wrap around us, his adult self set out to re-create the dish. Problem was, recipes for the simple preparation were almost impossible to find in cookbooks, and an inquiry to his mother for direction would be, in Francis's words, "like asking her to explain how to tie shoelaces."

I love to cook but what I love even more is finding common threads between cuisines— threads that connect us and demonstrate how we're all more alike than different. In Francis's story I saw myself and my mom's chicken and rice. A dish that showed up on my family's table multiple times a week when I was a kid, a bowl of comfort that coddles my soul, and a recipe so simple nobody took the time to write it down: Chicken and rice is my scrambled eggs with tomatoes. And of course, I've reinvented it for my own version.

Please forgive me, Ms. Lam, but I've now tweaked your recipe a bit, swapping in sherry vinegar for Shaoxing wine, because sherry vinegar is easier for me to find. And I added Quirky Furki to lend texture and nutty umami to your already perfect combination. Adulterating time-honored dishes people already love is a habit I have. Just ask my mom.

- 6 large eggs
- 1 tablespoon sherry vinegar
- 1 teaspoon kosher salt
- ½ teaspoon ground black pepper
- 3 tablespoons extra-virgin olive oil
- 4 scallions, thinly sliced, divided
- 3 to 4 plum tomatoes, peeled and crushed (or 1 cup canned tomatoes with their juice)
- 2 tablespoons ketchup
- 1 teaspoon cornstarch whisked with 2 tablespoons water
- 3 to 4 cups cooked rice
- ⅔ cup Quirky Furki (page 236)

1 In a medium bowl, whisk the eggs, sherry vinegar, salt, and black pepper to form a homogenous mixture.

2 In a 12-inch skillet, heat the olive oil over medium-low heat and add the scallions, reserving a small handful for garnish. Sauté for about 30 seconds. Add the eggs and lower the heat a bit more. Let the eggs sit and set just a bit before stirring so you have some big pretty curds in your scramble. Then go about cooking your eggs the way you normally would, but scoop them out of the skillet just before they are completely done.

3 Add the tomatoes, ketchup, and cornstarch mixture to the skillet. Raise the heat to medium and bring the tomatoes up to a simmer. The juices should thicken and establish a sauce that smells like tomato-forward ketchup after about 2 minutes. Carefully stir in the eggs and cook 30 seconds or so more. Serve the soft, comforting scramble over rice and under a scattering of scallions and Quirky Furki.

Tuesday Lunch from Monday Supper

serves 1

We live across the road from my parents, and while most of the food transfers go from our house to theirs, on Monday nights my mom cooks an entire side of salmon to share with the Knight-Howards across the street. Her method is simple. She uses a skin-on side of fish and puts it skin side down on a baking sheet, squeezes a bunch of lemon juice overtop, sprinkles it with salt, and slowly bakes it at 300°F till it's flaky.

We all eat what we can, but because an entire side of fish is a lot, we always end up stashing a bit in the fridge. Now, I'm well aware that last night's cooked, cold salmon doesn't raise a lot of heartbeats, but I've developed quite an affinity for it—as well as a method for elevating this particular leftover. Here are my guidelines for enjoying Mom's salmon, followed by a recipe for perhaps my most favorite combination.

- Never, ever reheat leftover salmon.

- Break it into bite-size chunks rather than attempting to enjoy it whole.

- Add extra acid like lemon or lime juice—and lots of it.

- Pair the soft fish with crunchy fresh stuff like shaved radishes, blanched asparagus, or sugar snap peas instead of lettuce or cold grains. Tossing leftover fish with cold quinoa or leaves of butterhead seems like hiding it. Setting cold salmon against snow peas or sliced cucumbers celebrates it.

- Sauce what's becoming a pretty special salad with something creamy and assertive like Caesar dressing or punched up mayonnaise.

- Anoint the reimagined wonder with textured, in-your-face flavorful stuff like Quirky Furki, garlic bread crumbs, or flaky salt.

4 ounces chilled cooked salmon, broken into bite-size chunks

¼ cup thinly shaved radishes

½ cup sugar snap or snow peas or other similar crunchy green vegetable, blanched and shocked

Half a juicy lemon or lime

2 teaspoons extra-virgin olive oil

½ teaspoon kosher salt

2 tablespoons Miso Mayo (page 258), Tartar Sauce (page 148), or LGD Goes Ranch (page 18)

3 to 4 torn mint leaves

¼ teaspoon flaky salt

2 tablespoons Quirky Furki (page 236)

1 In a medium bowl, gently toss the salmon, radishes, and whatever bright green crunchy vegetables you choose with the citrus juice, olive oil, and salt. On the center of the plate on which you plan to eat the salmon, smear the creamy, flavor-forward sauce. Mound the crunchy vegetables and soft salmon situation on top of the sauce smear and scatter the torn mint overtop. Sprinkle with the flaky salt and the Quirky Furki and enjoy your lunch.

Fried Dollar Bills

makes as many as you like

I was once put off by the idea of a "signature dish." Good food was *new* food, to me, and I worked hard not to be known for this or that. Then fried collards happened and I ate my words. They hit our menu and never left. Here's why:

- They're unexpected, crunchy, earthy, salty, and satisfying.

- They are stupid easy and super quick to make.

- They're as good cool as they are hot.

- Collards are always high quality and available in my area.

- They were a big hunk of our profit margin—hence the name.

    I want to include a word about my friend and book agent, David Black. I had plans to tell a story about his dog Rascal (aka his second child) and a secret ham hock I had stored in my suitcase the first time I stayed at his home in Brooklyn—you know, like any smart traveling professional person does. While David and I were out one day, Rascal became so violently and mysteriously ill that David's wife, Melissa, feared the worst and took her to the hospital. Turns out she hadn't eaten anything poisonous, just something incredibly salty. You can guess who was responsible. But since Rascal survived, so did I.

    Ham hocks no longer agree with David, either; he eats mostly vegan these days. Since he taught me how to turn my stories and recipes into business as a writer, I'm sending these dollar bills his way.

Collards

Peanut or vegetable oil, for deep frying

Finely ground <u>Quirky Furki</u> (page 236)

Kosher salt

❶ Remove the stems from your collards. Then cut the collard leaves into 1-inch strips. Add the oil to your Dutch oven, paying attention to the very important safety note below. Heat the oil over medium heat until a thermometer reads 350°F.

❷ Before dropping the collards in the oil, line a large bowl with paper towels and fetch a nice long pair of tongs. This is going to go superfast, so you need to have all your gear within arm's reach.

❸ To test the experience and your tolerance for it, drop one or two collard strips into the oil and immediately place the lid on top. The collards will pop and crackle for a few seconds. Once they've quieted, take the lid off and pluck the collards out with tongs. Put them in the bowl to drain and season them with the Quirky Furki and a little salt right away.

❹ Keep your eye on the temperature of the oil and follow up by frying small handfuls of collards in the same fashion. The bigger the handful, the more violent the crackle and pop. Don't get cocky. Keep your batches small. Season each batch as it comes out of the oil. The Fried Dollar Bills will be good and crisp at room temperature for hours.

 HEADS up We use a commercial fryer for this, but you can use a large Dutch oven fitted with a lid or a small at-home deep fryer if you have it. The ideal home Fried Dollar Bill situation is an outdoor turkey fryer, but I recognize that is a highly specialized piece of equipment.

The important thing is to make sure there are at least 4 inches between the top of your frying oil and the rim of your pot. Although the process is simple, the collards pop and act the fool when they fry, so if you have too much oil it can bubble over the rim and that's a bad situation. If you don't have your wits about you this can be dangerous. By which I mean...don't drink and Fry Dollar Bills!

INSPIRATION STRIKES

Our paths to inspiration are all different. I hear a lot of people say things like, "I'm inspired by the harvest." Or "...the colors at the farmers' market," or "...the hard work of my community." But those answers don't ring true to me. I'm inspired to *smile* at all that stuff, but I don't buy a tub of cherry tomatoes because they're pretty. And as ashamed as I am to admit it, the diligence and drive of others have never inspired me to do much more than marvel at their determination.

For me, inspiration starts with purpose. What is it that I want to do? Then I look at the parameters that limit how I might do it. That part stops people who think we can only be inspired by something great: a strong team, a delicious meal, a pupu platter of ingredients to choose from. Abundance inspires. Freedom inspires.

It's just the opposite for me. I am my most creative when my purpose meets constraints. Perhaps that makes me a problem solver, not an artist, but even Rembrandt had limits to work his magic. My cocktail for inspiration may not be for everyone, but since I find myself constantly inspired, I think it's a recipe I should share. Here's a snapshot.

It's a Sunday morning and I'm slowly pushing my cart at the Piggly Wiggly. I want to develop some recipes with Quirky Furki. (That's my purpose.) The Piggly Wiggly closest to home caters to country folks. There's variety, but it's in pork products, cornmeal, collard greens, and cans. In short, it's not the grocery store of your dreams when you're looking to highlight a condiment inspired by Japan. (These are my parameters.) I've gathered beef for skewers, ground pork for meatballs, and spinach for broth when I spot a stack of Hawaiian rolls out of the corner of my eye. Suddenly the connection between Hawaii, Japan, and Spam screams at me and a lightning bolt of an idea shoots down from the fluorescent lights of the Pig. I see my Quirky Furki as the star of a revamped tailgate classic—ham, cheese, and poppy seed party rolls. (That's inspiration.)

Pushing my cart now at full NASCAR speed, I round the canned meat aisle just as I question the nutritional wisdom of Spam. I quickly access my guilty love for bologna, turn my cart on its back wheel and barrel toward the deli meats. Laser-focused, I push past grandmas and store clerks and recall with delight that whole pineapples are one of six or so fruits this Piggly Wiggly sells fresh. Doubling back to grab butter, I'm stopped when the need for cheese pops in my head and I tally the choices the Pig's limits provide. Provolone it is, but I also grab what Velveeta calls mozzarella just to be safe. (This is how I act when I get inspired.)

With all my party-roll players piled on top of the packages of beef, pork, and spinach I went to the store to buy, I hightail it to the checkout line overcome with desire to birth this brilliant idea. But just as the turtle in front of me counts his change to pay for his honey bun, I'm struck with the worry I don't have mayonnaise at home. It's something I worry about often and the concern is valid, but I am not about to give up my place in that snail of a line. Instead, I see someone across the store who looks sort of familiar, and yell to ask if she'll grab me a jar of Duke's mayo. She sees I'm rabid and flustered, so she helps me out. I pay, scurry to the car, and race toward these baked and buttery Party Rolls.

And that's how I find my inspiration.

Inspiration Strikes Party Rolls

makes 12 rolls

¼ whole pineapple

⅓ cup unseasoned rice wine vinegar

½ cup (1 stick) unsalted butter

¼ cup Quirky Furki (page 236)

2 teaspoons Dijon mustard

1 package of 12 Hawaiian rolls

¼ cup mayonnaise

8 thin slices provolone

6 thin slices bologna

❶ Remove the core from your pineapple and discard. Cut the pineapple into slices that are roughly as thick as the slices of provolone. You will need just enough pineapple slices to make one layer inside your sliders. Marinate the pineapple in the rice vinegar for about 30 minutes.

❷ Preheat your oven to 350°F. Melt the butter and stir in the Quirky Furki and Dijon.

❸ Drain the pineapple and shake off any excess vinegar. Slice the entire slab of rolls through the center to separate the top of the slab from the bottom. Put the bottom section on a large baking sheet. Spread the mayo evenly over that half. Shingle four slices of cheese over that. Top with a layer of pineapple, followed by the bologna. Finish with the last four slices of cheese, then cap with the bread lid. Pour the Quirky Furki butter evenly over the top.

❹ Bake on the middle rack of your oven for 20 minutes. The cheese should be melted and the tops of the sliders should be browned and a bit crisp. Cut into individual rolls and serve.

Meat on a Stick Is a Sure Thing

serves 4

I do a fair amount of entertaining, and for a long time the food at my parties flexed my chef muscles and made me look clever rather than wise. I served big blobs of mozzarella poached in marinara sauce, then fetched club soda for stained shirts all night long. I furiously cracked crab claws and shucked raw oysters, struggling to keep up while my guests nibbled on crackers. I fried and reheated dumplings in batches so everybody's dumpling came to them warm. And I watched with disappointment as guests discussed but did not eat the dried mullet roe grated over radishes that represented my POV as an ambitious chef. At the end of these parties I wilted into my couch disillusioned and disheartened at how hard it was to have a good time at an event I planned in the name of fun. If you know me, or even if you don't, you can probably tell by now that if I'm at a party I *need* to be the life of it. So, always the problem solver, never the quitter, I decided I would shift my approach. No longer would I push the limits of my guests or myself. My parties and the food I fashioned for them would be sure things. Things just about everybody likes: handheld foods that don't make a mess in my house or on your clothes, snacks that are tasty at room temperature, hors d'oeuvres you can identify from across a crowded room.

As a result of this realization, I cube, marinate, and thread a lot of meat onto skewers. Everybody knows what meat on a stick is and what to do with it. We love dragging it through a sauce and we seem to enjoy the carnal act of gnawing at something handheld.

Don't be fooled by my no-nonsense approach to entertaining. I may err on the side of ease but I'm not a sellout. It's imperative that people leave my party with remarkable memories of my food.

This meat on a stick, marinated in miso, vinegar, and brown sugar and then dredged in Quirky Furki, is slightly off center, unexpected, attractive, and, without a doubt, a sure thing.

1	pound flatiron, skirt, or flank steak; or 1 pound boneless skinless chicken thighs
2	tablespoons red wine vinegar
2	tablespoons extra-virgin olive oil
2	tablespoons red miso paste
2	teaspoons light brown sugar
1	teaspoon hot sauce
½	teaspoon kosher salt
1	lemon, halved
⅓	cup Quirky Furki (page 236)
	Flaky salt, for garnish

1 Cut the meat into 1-inch-wide strips. In a small bowl, whisk together the vinegar, olive oil, miso, brown sugar, hot sauce, and salt. Pour this mixture over the meat, massage the two, and let this sit for an hour.

2 Preheat a grill or grill pan over medium-high heat. Thread the meat onto skewers and sear on all sides until cooked through and caramelized. Squeeze the lemon overtop and dredge one side of each skewer in the Quirky Furki. Sprinkle with flaky salt and serve warm.

Pork Meatballs Bobbing in Broth

serves 4

It's not fair to call this a soup because it's really all about the meatballs. Think of the broth as a light, wet, lime-spiked jacuzzi for orbs of moist, seasoned ground pork. You should have a meatball in every bite and feel right about it. And in these meaty balls of umami you'll see Quirky Furki's abilities as a baseline seasoning. She's not sprinkled on top. She's not even visible. She doesn't scream, "I'm here! Taste how exciting I am!"

Instead, folded into the meatballs to define their personality, Quirky Furki seasons the meatballs and flavors the broth as they cook. This recipe shows that as talented as she is out front, Quirky Furki is equally powerful in the background. Slurp these for a light lunch or serve as a fun starter at an elegant dinner.

1	pound ground pork or turkey
¼	cup grated (on a Microplane) fresh ginger, divided
6	cloves garlic, grated (on a Microplane), divided
2	tablespoons grated (on a Microplane) yellow or red onion
⅓	cup Quirky Furki (page 236)
1	tablespoon soy sauce
2	teaspoons light brown sugar
1	teaspoon kosher salt, divided
1	large egg white, lightly beaten
2	tablespoons extra-virgin olive oil
1	small yellow onion, halved and sliced thin (about ⅔ cup)
¼	teaspoon red pepper flakes
6	cups chicken broth
1	tablespoon fresh lime juice
	Fresh basil, mint, and/or cilantro, for garnish (optional)

1 In a medium bowl, mix the ground pork or turkey with half the grated ginger, half the garlic, all the grated onion, the Quirky Furki, soy sauce, brown sugar, ½ teaspoon of the salt, and the beaten egg white. Make sure you have a well-mixed meat paste, then go about rolling that into 1-inch balls. You'll end up with about 20 of them when all is said and done. Slide them in the fridge to firm up while you prepare the broth.

2 In a Dutch oven or large saucepan, heat the olive oil over medium heat. Add the sliced onion, pepper flakes, remaining ginger and garlic, and remaining ½ teaspoon salt. Sweat for about 5 minutes, or until the onion is translucent and limp. Add the broth and bring to a simmer. Cover and cook for 10 minutes.

3 Gently drop in the meatballs. Cover again and simmer for 15 minutes, until they are cooked through. Just before serving, add the lime juice and any herbs or tender greens you choose.

Please Forgive Me Steamed Rice

makes a scant 4 cups

I struggle with rules, even time-honored, culturally connected ones like furikake's general purpose as seasoning for rice *after* it's cooked. I wanted to know what would happen if I steamed the seasoning's seascaped nutty notes into the rice *while* it cooked. I knew this departure might break the rules of furikake as an endgame seasoning and even challenge the notion of rice as something purposefully plain, but the idea nagged at me and I resolved to try it in private to quiet my question.

I wasn't gonna tell anybody because it was really just an experiment, but now I'm here asking for forgiveness for fiddling with a classic because this rice was a revelation. It's not in-your-face and fun like plain rice with a party on top. Instead it tastes like furikake went to charm school and came back refined. Elegant, subtle, and scented, serve this anywhere you want rice that's a bit more than a blank canvas.

1   cup jasmine rice
½   teaspoon kosher salt

2   tablespoons finely ground Quirky Furki (page 236)

1 Rinse and swish the rice around in water and drain. Do this about three times total, or until the water runs clear. Combine the rice, salt, and 1⅓ cups water in a 2- to 3-quart saucepan fitted with a lid. Bring the rice to a boil over high heat. Lower the heat to a gentle simmer and cook for about 9 minutes. Remove the lid.

2 Stir in the Quirky Furki, cover once more, and cook for another minute. Take the saucepan off the heat but keep it covered and let it sit for about 10 minutes. Remove the lid, fluff the rice with a fork, and serve.

HEADS up

For this recipe you'll need the version of Quirky Furki that took a turn in the food processor and is more powder than crumb.

Roasted Butternut Squash with Miso Mayo

serves 4

If you only Quirky Furky once, please do it here. You don't even have to do it with butternut squash. I just chose her because she too often gets treated like cauliflower, mushrooms, okra, broccoli, or Brussels sprouts who have the ability to crisp up in the oven before becoming soft from its indirect heat. But butternut squash requires a hot jump start on the stove to encourage caramelization's texture. So if using a vegetable other than butternut, assess the vegetable you choose and treat her the way she wants to be treated.

And for the love of food that tastes good, roast vegetables properly. If you choose cauliflower, don't pile cauliflower on top of cauliflower or you'll end up with steamed, soft, lackluster cauliflower. If you bring enough Brussels sprouts to the party to require two baking sheets, rotate those sheets halfway through their time in the oven so they cook evenly. Season generously and while the vegetables are still warm.

Above all else, make sure there's sauce at the party. Miso mayonnaise spiked with lemon and vinegar is the lube that makes this more soiree than side dish. But anything creamy that doesn't clash with Quirky Furki's sea-driven notes will work.

BUTTERNUT SQUASH

- 1 butternut squash, peeled, halved, seeded, and cut into 1-inch-thick half-moons
- 2 tablespoons extra-virgin olive oil
- 2 teaspoons light brown sugar
- 1 teaspoon kosher salt, divided
- ½ teaspoon ground black pepper

MISO MAYO

- ⅔ cup mayonnaise
- ¼ cup red, yellow, or white miso paste
- 3 tablespoons fresh lemon juice
- 2 tablespoons rice wine vinegar
- 2 tablespoons soy sauce
- 2 tablespoons honey
- ¼ cup Quirky Furki (page 236)

1 **Roast the Squash:** Preheat your oven to 375°F. In a large bowl, toss the butternut squash with the oil, brown sugar, ½ teaspoon of the salt, and the black pepper. Heat the largest ovenproof skillet you have over medium heat for a couple minutes. (Starting the squash in a hot pan will encourage caramelization before the squash becomes squishy soft.) Add the squash in a single layer; the pieces can touch but they should not overlap. Once they are settled and sizzling, transfer the skillet to the middle rack of your oven and let them roast there undisturbed for 15 minutes.

2 After 15 minutes in the oven, flip the butternut pieces over in the skillet and roast an additional 15 minutes. Take the skillet out of the oven; the squash should be caramelized and brown in spots and cooked through. Season them with the remaining ½ teaspoon salt and transfer to a platter or a rack to cool.

3 **Make the Mayo:** Whisk the mayonnaise with miso, lemon juice, rice vinegar, soy sauce, and honey.

4 To serve, adorn the squash with the Quirky Furki and miso mayo.

CHAPTER NINE

V's Nuts

Crunchy • Spicy • Sweet • Earthy

If your kitchen is the room in the house you gravitate toward,

the one that pulls you with magnetic force through its door, then you likely already know nuts to be more than just a snack. If you cook with confidence, you probably throw toasted nuts into salads, grind them into pesto or romesco sauces, and dot muffins and cakes with their fatty crunch. You may even have a nut of choice, the nut of your kitchen. Whether they're B's nuts, C's nuts or D's nuts, you respect walnut's texture, almond's fat, and pistachio's taste.

And even if you don't cook for the love of it, you probably revere nuts for their protein, their fiber, their antioxidants. Dare I say avocados are the only competition nuts have in the ring of ingredients that are at once virtuous and sinful? And no other food straddles the lines of savory and sweet, baked and raw, whole and pulverized with as much grace, as much finesse, as the mighty nut. I feel the same way about nuts that I feel about herbs. Cook with them more, eat more of them, and you'll find yourself enjoying a healthier, more exciting diet all around.

V's Nuts are a heat and sweet means to that end. They exude charisma that warrants inclusion in places nuts have never gone before. Pecans coated with frothy egg whites infused with spice, then roasted till crisp, V's Nuts will become your snack addiction and ingredient friend.

Anywhere you insert them, they add more than naked nuts can. Roughly chopped, whole, or ground into a nutty cayenne dust, V's Nuts scream, "Look at me! I can add crunch to that. I can add fat to that. I can add spice and even sweet to that. I can make all that taste better. And don't worry, I won't overshadow with my wit or undermine with my enthusiasm, I'm not funky or tart. I don't bring umami and I don't taste of a specific place. I'm a team player. Ingredients like me. You will like me." That's what V's Nuts would say if nuts could talk. ➧

V's Nuts

HERE'S WHAT'S IMPORTANT

- The V's Nuts recipe calls for pecans because pecans have long been the nut of my kitchen. But if you march to the beat of another nut, know that almonds, walnuts, hazelnuts, and macadamias work well too.

- Lots of times I tell you it's okay to play with the combination of spices or fudge on their measurements. Not here. Not for the purpose of the recipes that follow. V's Nuts should be a precise degree of spicy and sweet, so don't take liberties unless you're just looking to them for a snack.

- Worcestershire sauce contains anchovies. To make these nuts vegetarian, swap out the Worcestershire for the soy sauce of your preference

- Be aware that different nuts bring varying amounts of fat and freshness and will therefore roast differently. So don't measure their doneness by the number of minutes they spend in the oven. Rather, to tell whether or not they are properly roasted, tap them with a wooden spoon. If they sound flat and hollow, they are ready to come out and cool. If your tapping makes a muffled, full sound, roast them a bit longer.

- V's Nuts will keep in a sealed container in your pantry for a month. I don't recommend storing them in the fridge because the moist nature of that environment can alter their quality.

2   **large egg whites**
½   **cup granulated sugar**
2   **teaspoons cayenne**
2   **tablespoons paprika**
1½ **teaspoons kosher salt**

2   **teaspoons Worcestershire sauce**
4   **cups pecan halves or pieces (or other nuts as above)**

① Preheat your oven to 350°F. In a bowl large enough to hold all the ingredients, whisk the egg whites with all your might until they form soft peaks. You can of course use an electric mixer for this, but the volume of egg whites here is small, and I usually save that gadget for larger batches.

② In a smaller bowl, stir the sugar, cayenne, paprika, and salt to combine. Whisk the spice mix plus the Worcestershire into the egg whites. Then stir in the pecans, making sure the egg white mixture coats every nook and cranny of every nut. Line a large baking sheet with parchment, foil, or, in the best of scenarios, a Silpat silicone mat, and spread the nuts in a single layer overtop.

③ Slide the baking sheet onto the middle rack of your oven and bake for 10 minutes. Bring the baking sheet out and stir the nuts over and around. Spread them back into a single layer and put them back in the oven for an additional 10 to 13 minutes. When the egg white mixture has dried and is no longer sticky and your nuts make a flat sound when tapped with a wooden spoon, V's Nuts are ready to come out of the oven.

④ Allow the nuts to cool on the baking sheet for about an hour, then put them in a sealed container for storage. They will keep there at room temperature for 1 month.

MAKES 4 CUPS

NO BRAINERS

1 snack on 'em

2 fold into granola

3 toss in a salad

4 stir into chicken salad

5 roughly chop and put in a grilled cheese

6 blend into soups

7 sprinkle on sautéed vegetables

8 crown avocado toast

9 sprinkle on baked sweet potatoes

10 chop and fold into cookie dough

11 top ice cream

Waldorf Salad Redo

Serves 4 to 6

I'm drawn to salads built around a combination of fruit, nuts, and cheese. The fatty, pointed softness of gorgonzola, Parmigiano Reggiano, or chèvre set against the sweet textural interplay between crisp fresh fruit and earthy nuts—those things make salads satisfying.

I happen to be someone who seeks satisfaction in my salads, so I tend to flip the standard salad ratio on its head in favor of much more stuff and much less lettuce. In my salad-verse it's almost as if the lettuce exists to stretch the fruit, nuts, and cheese rather than support them.

That's why I love a Waldorf salad, where grapes, apples, and walnuts come together in a mayo-slicked juicy event that doesn't feel particularly healthy but doesn't feel particularly not. I've zhuzhed this classic up a bit with V's Nuts, of course, but I've also added a smattering of romaine to give the fruit and pecans room to breathe, and added punctuation with the sharp angle that is blue cheese.

½ cup thinly sliced red onion

2 tablespoons red wine vinegar

1 teaspoon kosher salt, divided

⅓ cup mayonnaise

⅓ cup sour cream or full-fat plain Greek yogurt

¼ cup buttermilk

3 tablespoons fresh lemon juice

2 tablespoons Dijon mustard

1 tablespoon honey

2 medium apples, cut off the core and into rough 1-inch cubes

1 cup seedless green grapes, halved

3 stalks celery, sliced thin (1 cup)

1 cup V's Nuts (page 266), roughly chopped

1 head romaine lettuce, white and light green parts only, cut into 1-inch pieces

1 cup quality blue cheese, such as gorgonzola or Maytag, crumbled

Torn fresh mint and basil, optional

❶ In a bowl large enough to hold the finished salad, combine the red onion, red wine vinegar, and ¼ teaspoon of the salt. Let this hang out and get acquainted while you prepare and chop the rest of the ingredients.

❷ In a smaller bowl, whisk the mayo, sour cream or yogurt, buttermilk, lemon juice, Dijon, honey, and ¼ teaspoon of the salt. Set aside.

❸ Once the red onions have kind of wilted under the will of the vinegar and salt, stir in the apples, grapes, celery, V's Nuts, romaine, remaining ½ teaspoon salt, and blue cheese, plus the herbs if you've got them.

❹ At this point you can mix the dressing with everything. The result will be delicious but it won't be pretty, so I like to serve the Waldorf naked with its dressing drizzled over top.

A note about ROMAINE

I pretty much always have a head of romaine lettuce in the organized clutter of my fridge. I appreciate its crunch, its refreshing subtle taste, and its structural ability to hold up to dressings of all kinds. Often I separate the green leafy tops from the mostly white crunchy core because the two parts have different strengths. I toss the more fragile green tops with leafy salads, wilt them with garlic like spinach, or fold them into broths at the last minute to add something vegetal and fresh (like the Pork Meatballs Bobbing in Broth on page 254). And I reserve the core, often called the heart, for recipes like this one, where I want the romaine to provide crunch, levity, and girth. Romaine is an always available, affordable, versatile workhorse. Don't underestimate its potential.

THIS ONE'S FOR MIKE

I'll start by saying my experience with editors is limited. I've now written one very large book plus the one you're reading right now, but the first things I wrote that someone else edited were for magazines. Those editors did what I thought all editors were designed to do: They pointed out when something didn't make sense. They questioned my tone, corrected my grammar, and in some cases massively pissed me off by removing large sections of text or flip-flopping my stories around without any warning of their antics. There wasn't a lot of conversation along the way about what something could *become*—just terse reactions to what it already *was*. But my book editor, one Mr. Mike Szczerban, moves through my work in a different way. He pushes and pulls, questions and listens. It's a delicate dance, even clumsy at times, that feels like friendship, mentorship, and partnership.

He wasn't there at the start, though. I was lucky enough to kind-of select my first book editor, a polite man named Michael Sand at Little, Brown, but before our honeymoon was even over, the editor I cherry-picked had left for an opportunity elsewhere. I was told it happens all the time, but as insecure with my writing as I was, it felt oddly personal—like my first few pages had driven him away. I was anxious about being assigned a rando from who knows where. Lucky for me the assignment was a fortuitous one.

I met Mike under the most awkward of circumstances. We were filming *A Chef's Life,* and the director who lives to see me squirm thought it would be brilliant for me to meet my new editor in person for the first time on camera. What I remember is that Mike was abnormally sweaty, wiping his forehead every 30 seconds with what must have been a soaked handkerchief. He was soft-spoken and thoughtful, and I could see he was nervous. I felt so bad for putting him in this highly exposed position that I barely balked when he called my prose "discursive."

I liked Mike right away, but that didn't mean I trusted him. He had already assigned my style a loosely negative word whose definition I had to look up to understand fully, so I decided I'd keep things close. What if this guy didn't like my approach? What if he didn't appreciate my voice? What if he squashed my dreams of being an author, demanding I enlist a co-writer instead of doing it myself? No. No. No. I would control this situation, write the book, and send it to him tied up in a bow right at the deadline. That way there would be no time for him to try and swap my words out for someone else's. And that's what I did.

I kept Mike at bay while I wrote, sending him only the recipes and headnotes I knew no food lover could question. Then on the day it was due I sent the massive 250,000-word manuscript to him. He called me a few minutes later, breathless, and said I did good. All he had read so far were the pages about the equipment and products I prefer, but he said it was good. "Good" was not really what I was going for, but I was encouraged enough to wait out the month it took Mike to surface again without additional medication, so I'm glad he gave me that. When Mike did pop up in my inbox again, he said it was time to talk.

I was nauseous at the prospect. I would have preferred for him to just send me edits, my soul on the page marked through in red, so I didn't have to actually listen to his critiques. But no, Mike wanted to talk and so we did. What ensued was not at all what I had feared. In his soft, teddy-bear tone of voice he apologized for taking so long (the first of many such beginnings) and congratulated me on what he called a "joy to read through." Maybe talking wasn't so bad. The coming weeks were a joy for me, too, as we went through the book line by line and Mike asked questions and pushed me to question how we could make the book better. How we could elevate my voice in ways I hadn't considered. How we could make the narrative heart of the book, a story about my grandma in a nursing home and the fig tree outside it, resonate more.

I recall only two arguments over the course of the gentle walk-through. One about a chicken-tomato-macaroni dish. I won that one. The other about whether or not the word "nab" was a widely understood term for savory snack crackers with filling. He got a point there. Through the design, photography, publication, and book tour, Mike guided me—and my understanding of what an editor does expanded exponentially. All in all, we built so much trust and respect for one another that Mike and his wife, Kristen, joined me and twenty of my other favorite people in Italy for my fortieth birthday. That's saying something.

Then there was Pleasantly Plump. I don't know whether or not to put Pleasantly Plump in italics because *Pleasantly Plump* was never published, but I intended it to be my second book. A narrative cookbook about body image, Pleasantly Plump was also the name my grandma used to call me when she really wanted to call me fat. Mike did not like the idea. Nor did he like the name. He argued I wasn't the person to write that book. On that I disagreed 1,000 percent. Who was he to tell me I didn't look the part to write about my own issues? Then he argued a cookbook about body image sounded like a pool party about drowning. To that I had to admit Mike had a valid point.

I continued to throw ideas his way. I even wrote a fleshed-out proposal with recipes, headnotes, and essays...twice. Mike never said no, but he never said yes. He wanted me to push more—to come up with an idea that was original, distinct, one that didn't suffer from a sophomore slump or try to replicate what the first book did. I wanted the same, but I was incredibly frustrated. He said, "When we get to an idea that really works, we'll know." I took issue with his use of "we" since *I* was bringing him ideas and *he* was returning them with questions.

Along the way, he offered up that he'd love to see me make more of the kinds of recipes that scratch a common itch for people cooking at home, ones that would leave people saying, "You have to make Vivian's meatloaf, Vivian's mac and cheese, Vivian's banana bread." Dishes everybody Googles and wants a fresh take on—simple, comforting things that made people feel like winners in the kitchen. Dishes I should embrace. I was beginning to think Mike was not editing me. He was pushing me. Where, I didn't know exactly, but I felt unpleasantly pushed.

So when I came to Mike with the idea for *This Will Make It Taste Good,* I did it over the phone. I was exhausted by my futile exercises in proposal-writing and pretty convinced he was gonna pooh-pooh anything other than *Deep Run Roots Part Deux with More Mainstream Recipes.* But he didn't. He listened to me excitedly explain the premise of the book, punctuated by the proposed title. Then he made me wait under a long, loaded, Mike Szczerban pause, and said, "I like it. The title may be too long, but I like it."

I guess all the pushing was because Mike recognized the word "no" was a powerful motivator for me. He knew I didn't just want to write another book. I wanted to write a better, more original one than the first. And he was certain I could when I was sure I couldn't. Mike believed in me more than I did myself. In the end I got the title. Mike got his banana bread. I hope he's the one who edit-pushes me as long as I write books.

V's Roasted-Banana Nut Bread

makes one standard 10-inch Bundt loaf

4 to 5 ripe bananas

2 cups all-purpose flour

1 tablespoon baking powder

¼ teaspoon baking soda

1 teaspoon kosher salt

½ teaspoon ground cinnamon

½ teaspoon ground nutmeg

½ cup (1 stick) unsalted butter at room temperature, plus more for greasing your pan

⅓ cup packed light brown sugar

⅓ cup granulated sugar

2 large eggs

Grated zest and juice of 1 orange

1 cup V's Nuts (page 266), roughly chopped

1 Preheat your oven to 350°F and grease the pan with butter or nonstick cooking spray.

2 Place the ripe bananas (peels still on) on a baking sheet and roast for about 20 minutes. The bananas will become quite soft and dark brown and something akin to banana syrup may even leech out from the skins. Once you see these cues, bring the bananas out, let them cool, and lower the oven's temp to 325°F.

3 In a medium bowl, whisk together the flour, baking powder, baking soda, salt, cinnamon, and nutmeg. Set that aside.

4 In the bowl of a standing mixer, cream the butter and both sugars on high speed until light and fluffy, about 2 minutes. Lower the speed a couple notches and add the eggs one at a time, making sure the first is incorporated before adding the second. Follow up with the orange zest and juice.

5 Once the mixture is homogenous, add the dry ingredients in two batches. Take care not to overmix, because while we call this bread, it's really more like cake and should be treated as such.

6 Once the dry ingredients are incorporated, peel away the banana skins and fold the banana pulp and any syrup that accumulated on the baking sheet into the "cake" batter. (You should be working with roughly 2 cups of banana). Follow up with V's Nuts, making sure both the banana and the nuts are evenly distributed throughout.

7 Turn the batter into your pan and slide onto the middle rack of your oven. Bake for 1 hour, or until a skewer inserted into the middle of the bread comes out clean. Allow the bread to cool for 20 minutes before turning it out of its baking dish.

V'S NUTS

273

Kim's Invention Ice Cream

makes 1 quart

If you think V's Nuts only matter for their texture, make this ice cream. It's an invention of our long time pastry chef, Kim Adams, who took to steeping all kinds of things in cream about ten years ago in an effort to expand our original ice cream repertoire at Chef and the Farmer. While several of her concoctions, like coriander-basil and curry-lime ice cream, worked as novelties, this one rose above, and we make it every fall.

Through some feat of steeping, it tastes like the most elegant expression of pecan laced with a liqueur-like sweetness that is inherent to certain lucky nuts (like the pecan, almond, and walnut). It's smooth, luxurious, and creamy like all ice cream should be—but with a hint of cayenne's heat and a whiff of paprika's smoke: an ice cream that's round and craveable.

The only downside is that once V's Nuts steep, they've donated everything they've got to the worthy cause of dessert, and they're not suitable for much else. So take a cue from Kim and make this ice cream the star of a sundae, adding salted caramel and extra nuts for crunch.

2   cups heavy cream

2   cups whole milk

1   cup roughly chopped V's Nuts (page 266)

½   cup granulated sugar

8   large egg yolks

❶ In a medium saucepan, combine the cream, milk, nuts, and sugar and heat over medium just until the sugar dissolves and little bubbles form around the edge of the pan. Take the saucepan off the heat and let its contents cool to room temperature. Refrigerate the nut and dairy mixture overnight to allow the ice cream's flavor to develop.

❷ The next day, place the yolks in a medium bowl and whisk until they lighten in color. Reheat the cream-and-nut mixture over medium heat to just under a boil, then pass the hot cream through the finest strainer you have into a medium bowl. Discard the now limp, flavorless nuts. Whisking as you go, add about a quarter of the cream mixture to the eggs. Once that's fully incorporated, whisk in about a quarter more, then do this one more time.

❸ Return the tempered yolk mixture plus the remaining cream back to the saucepan and set that over medium-low heat. As it heats, whisk frequently. The yolks will cook and thicken the ice cream mixture and you may see a little bit of curdling around the sides of the pan; this is okay. Once the mixture has thickened and coats the back of a spoon, about 10 minutes, pass it through the finest strainer you have. Refrigerate the ice cream base overnight for the creamiest end product. If you're in a hurry and want to freeze this ice cream right away, cool it down in an ice bath. When you're ready, dump the ice cream base into your frozen dessert machine and follow the manufacturer's instructions to freeze.

❹ You can enjoy the ice cream right away, but it should really spend several hours in the freezer to firm up. This is unbelievable with chocolate cake and a drizzle of salted caramel, or combined with vanilla ice cream in a sundae.

Little Bit Scrappy, Little Bit Rock 'n' Roll... Parfait

serves 4

If I were a flavor hero, this would be my motto. I do things, make things, and generally operate with the high-intensity, maximum-impact approach of a rock star. But I achieve my loud, look-at-me riffs with something more like a ukulele strung with fishing line than a cherry-red electric guitar. This recipe is the spoonable breakfast version of that character trait. It enlists basic and plain, poofs it together with one thing that's special, and there you have it, Mick Jagger in the morning.

This scrappy show starts with plain Greek yogurt sweetened with ripe banana, thinned with fresh orange juice, and brightened with zest. That's my answer to all the sugar-packed, fake-tasting yogurts out there, and is, in itself, a stunt you need up your sleeve.

Then there's the fruit. Why do we always put naked fruit on our yogurt? We dress lettuce before we eat it, and squeeze lime on our avocado. Fruit needs some help, too. Add a little citrus, a tiny bit of honey, maybe even an herb, and the tired apples and waning blueberries you've languidly plopped in your parfaits wake up and matter.

And then there's the crunch: the carb, the element that satisfies. This is where I could get fancy, but fancy is hard to keep up, so I enlist any kind of breakfast cereal, mix it with V's Nuts, and call it granola on the fly. That's right, mine are scrappy means to a rock 'n' roll result.

2 cups plain Greek yogurt (not fat-free, please)

2 of the ripest bananas you've got

Grated zest of 1 orange

⅓ cup fresh orange juice

2 cups cut-up fruit of your choice (from melon and berries to apples and oranges)

Juice of 1 lemon or lime

1 tablespoon honey

¼ teaspoon kosher salt

Fresh mint or basil, torn (optional)

1 cup cornflakes, Chex, Cheerios, or any other basic cereal you have hanging around

½ cup V's Nuts (page 266), plus more if you like

1 In a blender, blitz the yogurt, bananas, and orange zest and juice until totally smooth. In a medium bowl, toss the fruit with the lemon or lime juice, the honey, salt, and herbs. In another bowl, crush the cereal a bit and stir in the V's Nuts.

2 Make this the parfait all the airport parfaits of your past could have been and layer the yogurt, fruit, and cereal-nut mixture in four glasses or bowls. Or just divide the yogurt among four bowls, spoon on the fruit, and scatter the cereal-nut mixture over top.

Very Versatile Smear of Stuff

Spiced Pecan, Sun-Dried Tomato Romesco

makes 2 cups

You may have tucked your love for sauces made with sun-dried tomatoes away with your fanny pack from the '90s, but I did not. They're an intense mouthful of pucker that somehow taste like Tuscany and Olive Garden at the same time, and I really like that.

Blended with V's Nuts, Parm, olive oil, lemon, and an herb of your choice, sun-dried tomatoes mellow and define this romesco-esque sauce that's really almost a dip. Once you break the seal on Very Versatile, you'll long for the way it renders fish more meaty, meat more delicate, and vegetables more satisfying. Slather it on perfect toast and somehow perfection gets better too.

Craveable, versatile, and easy to make, assuming you've got V's Nuts lying around, Very Versatile should be in your fridge—full stop. It'll keep at least 2 weeks in the fridge, covered with a thin layer of olive oil.

⅔ cup sun-dried tomatoes packed in oil, drained, plus ¼ cup of the oil from the jar

½ cup V's Nuts (page 266)

½ cup chopped fresh basil, parsley, chervil, or mint; or 2 teaspoons chopped fresh rosemary, thyme, oregano, or sage

⅓ cup extra-virgin olive oil

3 tablespoons fresh lemon juice

2 garlic cloves, peeled

½ teaspoon kosher salt

½ cup finely grated Parmigiano Reggiano (use a Microplane)

❶ Combine everything but the Parm in the bowl of a food processor and let her rip. Once the sauce is the texture of coarse sand, put it in a bowl and stir in the cheese.

INVITE these guests to the PARTY

2 tablespoons orange or lemon Citrus Shrine (page 140) or 3 tablespoons Herbdacious (page 206) in lieu of the picked herbs

V'S NUTS

Lunch-at-My-Desk Quinoa Salad

serves 2 to 4

Twenty years ago, when I was in the advertising world and actually worked at a desk, I ate cheese toast and eggplant parm for lunch while I wrote emails to the Food Network begging them for a job chopping vegetables on the set of any show they'd let me. Fatigued from my bread and cheese palooza and the general monotony of my job, I'd follow up my meal with a trip on the elevator down to a vacant floor to take a nap in an abandoned cubicle. I was not a good advertising exec.

I imagine if I were a twenty-something doing the 9-to-5 in today's world of grain bowls and protein boxes, my eggplant parm would have morphed into a salad that looks like this one. Perfect for the waist-minded working person who packs their lunch, this bowl of quinoa, chopped kale, V's Nuts, cranberries, and salty cheese sits in a sherry vinaigrette and improves as it marinates. It's a salad that makes me wonder if my afternoons would have been more productive, more advertising-minded, if it were my desk fuel instead of cheese toast. I wonder, but I'm afraid I already know.

3 cups cooked quinoa (or other cooked grain)

3 cups finely chopped kale

1 cup roughly chopped V's Nuts (page 266)

1 cup dried cranberries

1 cup grated Parmigiano Reggiano (use a Microplane)

2 teaspoons kosher salt

¼ cup sherry vinegar

2 tablespoons fresh lemon juice

2 tablespoons maple syrup or honey

⅓ cup extra-virgin olive oil

1 In a bowl large enough to hold all the ingredients, mix the quinoa, kale, nuts, cranberries, Parm, and salt.

2 In a smaller bowl, whisk together the sherry vinegar, lemon juice, maple syrup or honey, and olive oil. Pour that over the salad and toss.

3 You can eat the salad right away, but it benefits from an extended mingle together. If you'd like to make this a more substantial lunch, add leftover chicken or salmon.

Worth-the-Hype Pimento Cheese

makes 4 cups

In my humble but influencer-minded opinion, pimento cheese has gotten way too much attention. I'd argue it's become the spreadable cheese snack that represents the South, but with its failed promise of "pimento" spice set against its muted flavor, pimento cheese is a disappointment among its peers like deviled eggs, sausage balls, and cheese straws.

No doubt you're not surprised I'm swooping in with a solution to render pimento cheese the queen she should be. All the usual suspects—cheddar, Monterey Jack, mayo, cream cheese, and roasted red peppers—get plumped and promoted with a healthy handful of V's Nuts. Suddenly pimento cheese has texture, spice, depth, and a personality worth the hype she's garnered.

Don't hate on me for the shade I've thrown. Just give pimento cheese another look.

8 ounces sharp yellow cheddar, shredded (roughly 2 cups)

8 ounces Monterey Jack, shredded (roughly 2 cups)

3 ounces cream cheese (roughly ⅓ cup)

⅓ to ½ cup finely chopped roasted red peppers

3 tablespoons mayonnaise

3 tablespoons sour cream

3 tablespoons cider vinegar

½ teaspoon kosher salt

⅔ cup finely chopped V's Nuts (page 266)

1 In the bowl of a standing mixer fitted with the paddle attachment, mix the cheddar, Monterey Jack, and cream cheeses for about 30 seconds, or until they form a big creamy clump. Then add the roasted red peppers, mayo, sour cream, vinegar, and salt and paddle a minute longer. You want everything to come together and essentially warm up a bit. Last but not least, add V's Nuts and paddle just to incorporate.

2 This, and all cheese you want to really taste, is best served at room temperature.

Let's talk about **cheese**

Don't ever let me catch you with a bag of pre-shredded cheese unless you plan to melt it into a dish so basic the cheese doesn't even matter. And please, please, please don't turn to the pre-shredded dark side when what you're making hinges on the quality of the cheese. The pre-shredded stuff is the lowest common denominator in the cheese world, plus it's coated in a non-clumping agent that further solidifies its uselessness. So when it matters (which is always), buy cheese in blocks and break out your grater.

Chicken Breasts I'm Not Mad At

serves 4

Every chance I get, I share my woeful opinion of boneless skinless chicken breasts. Yes, they're a lean, readily available form of protein. And yes, food of all kinds is a gift from the earth that deserves our reverence. But when you remove the skin from the chicken breast, you remove the renderable layer of fat that holds most of the chicken's actual flavor, and then when you detach the meat from the bone, you remove the insulation that keeps it moist as it cooks, both acts stripping the breast of its opportunity to be great.

I wouldn't be so up in arms about people's misguided affinity for the boneless, skinless variety of breasts if it hadn't all but eliminated our ability to find the other kind. In my little town of 20,000 people and four grocery stores, only one meat department offers America's favorite chicken part with skin and bone intact—and I'm pretty sure that Piggly Wiggly only sells it because they grew tired of hearing tirades from the angry chicken breast lady.

If you're in the dark about the merits of skin and bone and breasts, then I implore you to find the lone store in your town willing to sell breasts as nature intended. Then follow my instructions below. All by themselves they'll give you a new perspective on what breasts can be, but with the sauce of V's Nuts blended with lightly cooked onions, they are a weeknight dinner-time game changer.

4 tablespoons extra-virgin olive oil, divided

1 medium yellow onion, halved and sliced thin

4 cloves garlic, sliced

4 teaspoons kosher salt, divided

2 tablespoons tomato paste

2 teaspoons chopped fresh rosemary or thyme

1½ cups chicken broth

¾ cup V's Nuts (page 266)

4 bone-in, skin-on chicken breasts

Grated zest of 1 orange

½ cup fresh orange juice

2 oranges, skin and pith cut away, sliced

1 Preheat your oven to 400°F. In a 10-inch skillet, heat 2 tablespoons of the olive oil over medium heat. Add the onion, garlic, and 1 teaspoon of the salt and cook for about 5 minutes. It's okay if the onions brown just a bit, but you are decidedly not looking for an R-Rated Onion (page 38) situation. Stir in the tomato paste and the herb you've chosen and cook an additional 30 seconds. Transfer the onion mixture to the highest powered blender you have and add the broth and V's Nuts. Let it rip until the sauce is perfectly smooth.

2 In a 12-inch ovenproof skillet, heat the remaining 2 tablespoons olive oil over medium-high heat. Season the chicken breasts with the remaining 3 teaspoons salt and carefully place them, skin side down, in the skillet to brown. You may need to lower your heat to prevent the skin from burning. The hope is that the skin will render into a golden sheath. If the heat is too high, it will brown without ever rendering.

3 Once you've got perfect chicken skin, about 5 minutes, transfer the breasts to a plate for a second and add the nut sauce to the skillet. Position the breasts, skin side up, on top of the sauce and slide the skillet into the oven. Roast for about 14 minutes, or until the breasts read 165°F when an instant-read thermometer is inserted. Bring the skillet out of the oven and transfer the breasts to a clean plate to rest.

4 Over low heat, whisk the orange zest and juice into the sauce in the skillet and, if necessary, reduce the sauce over medium heat until it is dippable and voluptuous. Turn off the heat.

5 After the chicken has rested for about 5 minutes, cut it away from the bone and into medallions to make things easier for those of us who need the help. Stir any reserved chicken juices into the sauce, then shingle the chicken medallions with the orange slices and spoon the sauce over it all.

But-a-Nut Soup

serves 3 (2 cups each)

Every fall, butternut squash soup has a moment. And for years I did my cheffy best to seize it. I stewed butternut with mirepoix, added white potatoes, sweet potatoes, leeks, garlic, and every ingredient I could conjure to make butternut squash soup taste more nuanced, less boring, more exciting. What I ended up with over and over was a muddled bowl of orange that tasted like nothing in particular.

After more than a decade cooking professionally, my focus shifted from fancified techniques employed to grab the attention of other chefs to simple paths toward resolute deliciousness. I started cooking for myself and for my guests, and dishes like butternut squash soup that should be simple became just that.

Here I've leaned into the ingredients we all agree taste, smell, and feel like fall. Ginger, pecans, apples, brown butter, nutmeg, and sage all say *Thanksgiving is on the horizon*, and butternut squash is an orange vegetable that will take us there.

The soup itself is bare bones butternut because I've learned that's the only way butternut really shines. The pyrotechnics come in the relish. Its crunchy, warm, and sweet notes are the foil that make butternut exciting.

❶ Preheat your oven to 375°F. Split the butternut squash lengthwise. Remove the seeds and score the flesh with a knife. Place it flesh side up on a baking sheet and drizzle with the olive oil. Slide that onto the middle rack of your oven. Roast for 1 hour, or until the flesh has started to brown and is easily pierced with a knife. Once the squash is cool enough to handle, scoop out the flesh and discard the skin.

❷ In a 4- to 6-quart saucepan or Dutch oven, sweat the onion, ginger, nutmeg, and ½ teaspoon salt in 1 tablespoon of the butter over medium-low heat for about 5 minutes, or until the onions are translucent and limp. Add the cooked squash, another ½ teaspoon salt, and the broth. Cover and bring to a boil over medium-high heat. Lower the heat and cook at an energetic simmer for about 20 minutes.

❸ While the soup simmers, in a small saucepan or 10-inch sauté pan, cook the remaining 3 tablespoons butter with the leeks and remaining ½ teaspoon salt over medium heat until the butter begins to brown. Add the vinegar and maple syrup and let that bubble for about 10 seconds before removing it from the heat.

❹ Once the soup has simmered for 20 minutes, transfer it to your blender and let it rip (carefully) until the soup is totally smooth. As that's happening, reheat the maple, butter, vinegar mixture and stir the apples, sage, and V's Nuts into it. Serve the soup with a mound of the apple-nut relish in the center.

1	large butternut squash
2	tablespoons extra-virgin olive oil
1	small yellow onion, halved and sliced thin
1	tablespoon minced fresh ginger
½	teaspoon ground nutmeg
1½	teaspoons kosher salt, divided
4	tablespoons unsalted butter, divided
4	cups chicken or vegetable broth
½	cup (½-inch-thick) sliced leek rounds, white and light green parts only
¼	cup cider vinegar
3	tablespoons maple syrup
1	large crisp eating apple, cut off the core and sliced thin
2	tablespoons chopped fresh sage
½	cup roughly chopped V's Nuts (page 266)

A note about apples

You'll notice I use a lot of them. There are at least ten recipes in this book that grab apples by the stem and make the most of their unique qualities. My rabid use of the OG forbidden fruit is not a product of oversight, lack of imagination (obviously), or laziness. Rather I want to drive home the apple's undervalued versatility in savory food, which is coupled with year-round availability and generally consistent quality. Apples add unmatched texture, cherry-red and lime-green pops of color, and a natural fresh sweetness I want you to remember on your quest to make food taste good.

Sin-Tooth Snacks

makes about 20 two-bite snacks

I used to think the adage that you become your parents as you get older was a pattern that played out for some people but would never ever for me. I didn't see myself in any of my mother's behavior. How could I? I'm a rebel of sorts, who cooks and cusses for a living. My mom, Scarlett, is a lady, always put together, polite, and sweet. But about five years ago I started to see a little bit of Scarlett creep into the bull-headed temple of Vivian. I caught myself asking my daughter for a handful of fries just so she wouldn't eat more than she needed. I chased her around with a hair brush and complained she favored hair in her eyes over hair in a tie. I threw Halloween candy away the day after Halloween, and I was shocked when I realized one of my signature sayings had suddenly become "Don't spoil your appetite!"

Today it's clear parts of me have morphed into my mother, and the piece that's most distinctly Scarlett is the way I attempt to manage my spawn's eating habits. But while Mom just hid all the Snickers bars and Oreos and crossed her fingers I wouldn't sniff around to find them, I forgo buying that kind of stuff all together. Instead, I make snacks and treats that portray sinful via chocolate chips and honey, but I bind that sin with redemptive nuts and oats. I make those snacks small: more bite-size than fun-size. The trickery works sometimes. Other times it decidedly doesn't. But these little oat, chocolate chip, V's Nuts squares taste like the no-bake cookies I devoured at other people's houses as a kid. For the most part they appeal to my kid's sin-tooth, and when I'm in a sugar pinch and wish I could ferret out a Snickers bar, they satisfy mine.

1 cup rolled oats

½ cup nut butter of your choice

⅓ cup finely chopped V's Nuts (page 266)

⅓ cup semisweet chocolate chips

¼ cup honey or maple syrup

½ teaspoon kosher salt

1 Dump everything into a bowl and work it together with your hands. Transfer the mixture to the fridge and let chill for about 20 minutes. Bring it out, flatten it into a 1-inch-thick disc, and cut your sin-tooth snacks into little squares. Store in an airtight container for up to a week.

CHAPTER TEN

Sweet
POTENTIAL

Sweet • Fruity • Mellow • Soft

You already have some Sweet Potential in your fridge.

Jellies, jams, and fruit preserves are all kissing cousins that can work the magic in these recipes. And if you're like me, at some point you've gazed at your fridge door dotted with half-empty jars of grape jelly, raspberry jam, and orange marmalade and wondered how many biscuits you'd have to bake to empty those jars and clear some coveted space. That's why, even if you don't go to the tiny bit of trouble it is to make Sweet Potential, you will see something that can help you along in your kitchen. But I beg of you, once you've cleaned out your jelly jars and grown addicted to the delightful power they held inside, make the proper preserves I call Sweet Potential.

First I'd like to demystify the sugared fruit condiment canon so you understand why Sweet Potential is to fruit preserves what Beyoncé is to Destiny's Child. Jelly is essentially fruit juice combined with sugar and pectin to make a clear, cellulite-thick spread. Jelly requires cooking, straining, measuring, and cooking again. It can be melted and used in a lot of these recipes, but pectin never goes away, so the viscosity of jelly is always gonna be a factor. And jelly typically has more sugar than its cousins and less actual fruitiness, so there's that. The most arduous to make and manage with less overall possibility, jelly is the Kelly Rowland in the group.

Jam is fruit cooked with sugar until it becomes spreadable. Jam calls for the least time investment to make and, unlike jelly, the fruit itself is a part of the final product. But jam is muddied and often unremarkable. Jam is the member of Destiny's Child whose name I can't recall.

Sweet Potential is the artist formerly known as fruit preserves. She is plump pieces of fruit suspended in pristine syrup. She's two distinct personalities in one—both Sasha and Beyoncé.

To understand Sweet Potential, to watch as peaches, grapes, apples, or strawberries simmer in the syrup of themselves without falling apart, is to witness sorcery. And all it takes to separate Beyoncé from her band is an overnight snuggle with sugar. It's that step, that simple extended maceration of fruit with sugar, that pulls the essence, aroma, and elegance of the fruit, its juice, from its walls. That juice, mingled with sugar, becomes syrup. That syrup, thickened as it simmers, preserves the integrity of the fruit it surrounds.

Before we got our grapes from Chile and strawberries ripened in hot houses, this is how housewives saved the fruit of the season. Tucked into jars under wax and bobbing in crocks, they spooned out sweet bites of summer when the ground was cold and brown.

Sweet Potential was a treat when there were few, but today we can't look left without treats of some kind coming into view. We're more likely to reward ourselves with an Oreo or a Cronut than a biscuit slathered with preserves. So why persist with the business of sugared fruit preservation? Why go to the trouble when there's so much sweet out there to savor?

Here's why: There's something remarkable about Sweet Potential and the way she distills fruit's flavor into the essence of itself. There's possibility to unlock in her syrup and delightful surprises in her plump pieces. She can do more than we think because all we see when we gaze at her is that she's sweet. But balanced with tart vinegar, lemon juice, or buttermilk, her abilities reveal themselves. Given an edge by the heat of mustard, peppercorns, and chiles of all kinds she becomes a vehicle for spice. Deepened with soy, curry, miso, and cumin she speaks up and requires you to listen. And faced with the funk from assertive cheeses, Sweet Potential shows us her most exciting self. Sweet Potential's talents are largely unsung. Let's celebrate them. ➧

Sweet Potential

I've provided a recipe for a large-ish quantity of Sweet Potential because the work of this is not multiplied by the batch size. Four pounds of fruit requires basically the same amount of work as 2 pounds of fruit, and if I'm going to the trouble to do something like this I generally like to make it count. But you can cut this recipe in half or even thirds with great success.

Sweet Potential will keep in a sealed container in your fridge for 3 months. Contrary to conventional wisdom, because of its high sugar content, it will keep on your counter just fine for at least a week. Or you may can it in a hot water bath and keep it in the pantry forever.

This is a super-simple, three-step process, but there are some nuances related to the type of fruit you choose and what you plan to do with it. Here is what I know on the subject...which is a lot.

- Sweet Potential's recipe calls for a weight of fruit. Always **weigh the fruit** *after* you've trimmed, peeled, or cut fruit away from its core.

- **Apples** and **pears** are among my favorite fruits to preserve. Their flavor is one we already expect in savory food, so the Sweet Potential from these tree fruits is an apt match in lots of recipes. Choose a crisp eating apple like Fuji, Gala, or Pink Lady rather than a tart green apple like Granny Smith. (I don't like Red or Yellow Delicious apples...for anything.) Same goes for pears—the crisper, the better. If you treat them correctly, slivers of apple and pear not only hold their shape, they also maintain a snappy texture that startles palates expecting more applesauce than apple chip. Always, always, always peel the apples and pears you plan to preserve or the skins will toughen and ruin your efforts. Cut them away from their cores and slice them into slivers or small cubes before they macerate. Then I toss the cores in anyway because I like the way they look in the final product.

- **Berries of all kinds** can be preserved whole and don't need to be crushed prior to maceration, but make sure you cut off the caps of strawberries and choose plump, firm blackberries and raspberries. Soft fruit past its prime will cloud the syrup.

- **Figs** are an ideal choice for Sweet Potential because they can be preserved whole and therefore provide dramatic presentation. Leave a little of the stem intact. It will help hold the fruit together. And only choose the firm ones, as soft, past-their-prime figs really want to be jam.

- Like apples, **peaches, cherries, nectarines,** and **apricots** are flavors we're used to seeing in savory foods, so they all make great choices for Sweet Potential. Because of their fuzzy skins, peaches, nectarines, and apricots need to be peeled. To do this, cut a superficial X in the bottom of each fruit and drop them in boiling water for roughly 20 seconds. Then transfer them to an ice bath. Once cool, peel the skins away and cut them into wedges. Other stone fruits like cherries have less aggressive skins and need only to be pitted before they macerate.

- **Muscadine** and **concord grapes,** or **any grapes with seeds and thick skins,** are entirely different

MAKES 6 QUARTS

beasts and more work, but their foxy flavor is worth the trouble. Begin by cooking whole grapes in a Dutch oven or saucepan with just a little water. The skins will pop and open up. Continue cooking until you see the pulp soften and separate from the seeds. Pass the grapes through a sieve. On top you'll have the hulls and the seeds. Underneath you will have pulp. Discard the seeds and put the hulls back in the pan with just enough water to cover. Bring that to a boil, uncovered, and cook until most of the water has evaporated. Combine the hulls and pulp and weigh the mixture. Then add an equal weight of sugar and macerate overnight.

- **Watermelon** is a Sweet Potential gold mine. To preserve its flesh, remove the seeds, cut into cubes, weigh, and macerate with the same weight of sugar, just as you would other fruits. The flesh from melons like **cantaloupe** and **honeydew** works in this way as well. To preserve the **watermelon rind,** peel off the outer green layer and cut the rind into small strips or cubes. Then macerate.

- **Citrus,** like **lemons, limes,** and **oranges,** is a bit tricky. The flesh itself, when cut into supremes without the rind, tends to break down into a bright but pleasant mess once it meets heat. That wouldn't matter so much, but cutting citrus into supremes or slices void of any rind is a lot of work just to have it cook into jam. The more common thing to do is to preserve whole slices of citrus with the rind intact. This approach is suitable for some recipes but the bitterness from the rind diminishes its range quite a bit. To get around this, I like to combine oranges, lemons, and limes with other fruits to preserve, but even here, try to choose citrus with a thinner pith.

- Many times cooks will **add spices** like cloves, coriander, or cinnamon to their fruit preserves to make them more interesting. If you choose to do this, incorporate spices from the beginning as they macerate, then include them as they cook. I've chosen not to embellish Sweet Potential with anything other than lemon slices because the strong flavors from spice make preserves less versatile in recipes. Instead incorporate spices, herbs, and additional flavors for specific recipes as you go.

4 pounds fresh fruit

Up to 4 pounds granulated sugar

1 lemon or lime, sliced thin

1. Once you've peeled, sliced, diced, and weighed the fruit (see above), toss it with an equal weight of sugar, plus the lemon or lime slices, in a Dutch oven. Cover and let macerate overnight. I keep this on the counter because I don't have room in the fridge for something that big and the fruit doesn't mind room temperature for a spell.

2. The next day you'll see a syrup has formed around the fruit. There may still be pockets of sugar that have not fully dissolved and that's totally fine. Transfer the Dutch oven to the stove and bring it up to a simmer over medium heat. I always stir it a bit in the beginning to prevent any sugar from burning, but I've never come close to ruining this and I ruin a lot of stuff, so don't fret.

3. Once it's at a strong simmer, cover, lower the heat slightly, and cook for 15 minutes, or up to 1 hour.

4. For fruits like **strawberries, blackberries, figs,** and **watermelon flesh,** 15 minutes may be all the time you need. For these you want the fruit to shrink a bit and the syrup to take on the pale color of the fruit suspended in it. The preserves don't get better the longer you cook them, so don't be a hero and simmer until the syrup thickens. If you do, your preserves will be sticky and unmanageable once they cool. Let the preserves sit at room temperature at least an hour before you refrigerate them. The cooling process is important as it allows fruits like strawberries and watermelon the chance to plump up with syrup and appear less shriveled.

5. For **apples, pears, citrus,** and **watermelon rinds,** you'll need to cook them a bit longer until *some* of the fruit becomes translucent. This can take up to an hour, so you'll need to keep an eye on the syrup to make sure it doesn't begin to darken into caramel. Just as with the other fruits, you want this syrup to be pale and thin, so adjust it with water as needed. If it seems as if the syrup begins to reduce in volume, add a cup or so of water to ward off thick, difficult-to-work with preserves. Once about a third of the preserves have taken on that clear veneer, turn the heat off and let them cool in the syrup. As they cool, most of the remaining fruit should also wane translucent.

6. Transfer the fruit and syrup into jars, and there you have it. Preserved fruit floating in syrup equals Sweet Potential that will keep in your fridge for basically forever. But this is a book and I can't really claim that, so make the most of your Sweet Potential within 3 months.

1 on biscuits, toast, or drizzled on pancakes

2 as a condiment on a cheese plate

3 sandwiched with mustard on a sausage biscuit

4 spooned over cheesecake...or any cake

5 whisked with vinegar and oil to make a fruit-flavored vinaigrette

6 folded into muffins or sweet breads

7 mixed with mustard and put on a sandwich

8 stirred into yogurt as sweetener

9 used as a sweetener for iced tea, cocktails, or mocktails

10 blended with fruit juice to make popsicles

11 as a topping for ice cream

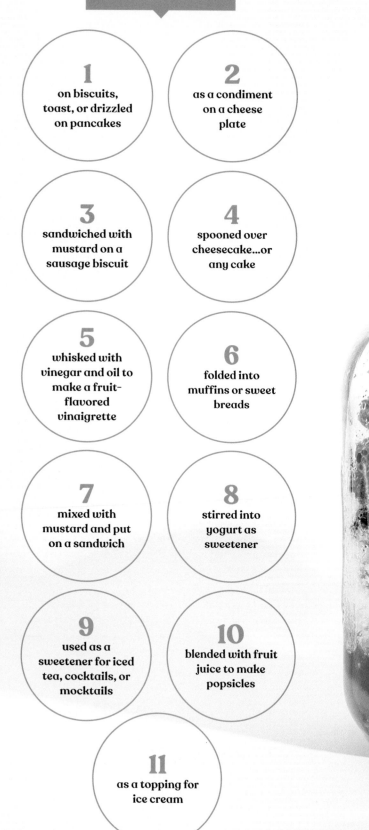

Brussels Sprouts for President

serves 4

Everybody acknowledges that kale, massaged and juiced, had a major moment a few years back and that cauliflower everything is everything these days. But no one remarks on how far Brussels sprouts have come of late.

When I was a kid, Brussels sprouts were the butt of every vegetable joke on TV and the picture of food your parents forced you to eat if you were bad. I never laid eyes on an actual Brussels sprout till I was in my 20s, but I was absolutely certain they were both smelly and slimy. Flash forward to the present day, when Brussels sprouts are so mainstream they've made it past restaurants run by chefs who build altars to lesser loved vegetables and have found their way onto menus at big chains like Outback and Ruby Tuesday.

I'm not sure that means Brussels sprouts have arrived, but we certainly aren't afraid of them anymore. I for one find them to be among the most satisfying green things the kitchen has to offer. They're more substantial than asparagus, peas, and leafy greens, so they're less likely to soften too soon and turn to mush. They have all the potential of cabbage and can be sautéed, roasted, steamed, or fried, or marinated and served raw, but they're in a cute, round little package that makes a plate of Brussels a fun thing to share. And they're meaty in a way most vegetables aren't so they stand up to big flavors and high heat—all the things you'll find here in this dish inspired by the Brussels dish with a cult following from the restaurant Gjelina in Los Angeles.

4 ounces bacon, cut into 1-inch squares

1 pound Brussels sprouts (about 3 cups), trimmed of the root end and halved

1 teaspoon kosher salt

1 tablespoon minced fresh ginger

2 garlic cloves, sliced

3 tablespoons Sweet Potential (page 296)

⅓ cup chicken broth or water

1 tablespoon Dijon mustard

2 tablespoons sherry vinegar or red wine vinegar

1 In a 12-inch skillet, render the bacon over medium heat till crisp. Scoop the bacon out and set it aside. Leave 2 to 3 tablespoons bacon grease in the skillet. Add the Brussels sprouts to the skillet, cut side down, and brown them. It will take 4 to 5 minutes to achieve a char so don't rush it along by stirring like a wild person.

2 Once that side is brown, season the Brussels with the salt and throw in the ginger and garlic. At this point you can scratch your stir itch and move things around a bit with the intent of scraping up the browned bits that have accumulated at the bottom of the pan.

3 After about 30 seconds of that, stir in the Sweet Potential, broth or water, and Dijon. Let this cook down for 4 to 5 minutes, until it appears glaze-ish. Throw in the vinegar and the reserved bacon and serve these bad boys to Brussels lovers everywhere.

Strong Smoothie Game

makes more than you'll drink

Smoothies are part of our morning routine. They're an easy way to frontload nutrition into our kids' day, and as I've mentioned before, we eat a lot of our breakfasts in the car, so a smoothie is the ideal morning roadie.

I wish my kids would accept smoothies that taste like the health and wellness delivery systems they're meant to be, but Theo and Flo are no fools. If they eat or drink something, it's because it tastes good. I inevitably say a Hail Mary as I drizzle something sweet on top of all the healthful stuff in the blender in hopes that the tiny bit of sugar I've added doesn't counteract the good I've attempted.

For a lot of people, the sweet thing they drizzle into the smoothie bowl is honey. If that's your pattern, I beg you to listen. Fruit preserves are interesting because they taste like the essence of the fresh fruit they once were. Somehow strawberries suspended in syrup taste more like strawberry than a strawberry, so when you swap out the honey for fruit preserves you intensify the fruit flavor factor.

As you've likely noticed, I never miss an opportunity to hide green things in what my kids eat. And what are smoothies, if not a ripe chance to do just that? I go for spinach because it has the least aggressive flavor in its class. Plus spinach is softer and easier to blend than the smoothie king, kale. But take this pro tip and choose dark fruit, like blueberries, grapes, or cherries when you're going sneaky. It's easier to hide the flavor of spinach than its color.

1   cup packed fresh spinach

1   cup frozen blueberries

½   frozen banana

2   tablespoons Sweet Potential (page 296)

¼   cup plain Greek yogurt

1   cup fresh orange juice

4 to 6 cubes of ice

1   Throw everything in your blender and let it rip.

Wrapmagic

makes 2 large wraps

I never leaned into the wrap craze. I loved a good burrito, but a waxy wrap spun around turkey and Swiss just didn't turn me on. Perhaps I'd seen too many lifeless, loveless wraps in airport kiosks and in deli cases next to the hot buffets in supermarkets. For me, wraps always seemed like the lackluster step cousin to a good sandwich. Then a wrap changed my mind.

I had joined a friend for lunch at one of those salad shops that builds, tosses, and sometimes chops your salad before your eyes. I wasn't thrilled by the idea of salad that day and when the salad artist offered to make my salad a wrap I agreed, but kind of wondered how that would work and why it was even an option. She tossed the salad and mounded it right in the center of an oversized spinach wrap. I watched, confused, as she folded it up, opened the panini grill, and laid my wrap inside. I worried my salad would become a wilted pile of mush, but I didn't speak up. Instead I just decided to see what would happen.

The transformation was more spectacular than a cheese sandwich's journey to grilled cheese. The arugula wilted a bit, the chicken soaked up the dressing, the goat cheese oozed, and two sides of the pale green envelope crisped up. I was so moved by my hot salad wrap I bought a panini grill that very day.

I've made a lot of wraps since. I've stuffed and rolled blue cheese, cheddar, bacon, kale, nuts, anything you can imagine into what I now call a salad sleeve. And all my favorite combos call on fruit preserves as a definitive component. Something about the way they mingle when slightly warmed with the wilting leaves and the melting cheese is panini press brilliance I can't explain.

3 cups packed arugula

½ cup shredded chicken

½ cup diced crisp apple

⅓ cup seedless grapes, sliced

⅓ cup fresh goat cheese

¼ cup Sweet Potential (page 296)

3 tablespoons fresh orange juice, squeezed from an actual orange

2 tablespoons extra-virgin olive oil

1 teaspoon kosher salt

¼ teaspoon ground black pepper

2 large (10- to 12-inch) spinach wraps

1 Preheat your panini press if you have one, or heat a 12-inch skillet over low heat. In a large bowl, toss everything but the spinach wraps. What you have should look and taste like a proper salad at this point.

2 Divide the mixture between the two wraps and roll them up as you would a burrito. Put the wraps seam side down on your panini press or in your skillet. Close the top of the press. (If you're using a skillet, put a heavy-ish lid on top of the wraps to weigh them down.) After about 3 minutes, you'll hear the sizzle of arugula as it wilts and the first sides will be toasted. Flip the wraps over and toast on the opposite sides. Slice the wraps in half and ogle at the creamy warmish salad inside.

Sweet Heat Side of Salmon

serves 6

One of the oddities of Southern food I'm most fond of is hot pepper jelly. It perfectly sums up our love for sweet heat. But far too often my Southern brothers and sisters fail to take creative liberties with one of our canon's most creative concoctions, and we sentence pepper jelly to marrying a block of cream cheese. It's shameful to put baby in the corner that way and I'm here to demonstrate how we can do more with her sweet hotness.

First of all, you don't need to buy pepper jelly at all. Often what you find in the market is far more sweet than heat, more looks than flavor, more money than value. All you need to do is add jalapeño heat to the Sweet Potential you already have and suddenly you've got sweet heat realized and even improved by the likes of peach, pear, citrus, or whatever flavor your Sweet Potential happens to be. Then follow the rules I've laid out plenty of times before: Push back on the sweetness with acid for balance. Deepen it with umami for dimension. Partner with Mr. Rich and Robust for an apt companion. Finally, pat yourself on the back, you've freed hot pepper jelly from her cream cheese prison.

I've chosen a side of salmon here, smoked on the grill because we don't do that enough and because salmon loves a glaze. But this is amazing (I never use that word by the way) on chicken wings, duck anything, and pork in all forms.

1½   cups Sweet Potential (page 296), pureed in a blender

3 to 4 small jalapeños, sliced thin

3   garlic cloves, roughly chopped

3   tablespoons soy sauce

½   cup white wine vinegar or cider vinegar

4   tablespoons fresh lemon or lime juice, divided

1   (3-pound) side of salmon, skin on

¼   cup extra-virgin olive oil

1   tablespoon plus ½ teaspoon kosher salt, divided

2   cups radishes, shaved on a mandoline or sliced thin with your knife

3   cups packed arugula

20   or so fresh mint or chervil leaves (about ¼ cup packed), torn

1 In a medium saucepan, stir together the Sweet Potential, sliced jalapeños, garlic, and ¾ cup water. Bring it up to a boil over medium heat and cook for about 15 minutes, or until most of the water has cooked out and things look glazy. Add the soy and vinegar and boil for several minutes, until reduced and glazy once more. Take it off the heat and stir in 2 tablespoons of the lemon or lime juice.

2 Preheat your grill to medium high or about 400°F. You can do this in the oven too, but it will lack a little of the spectacular. As your grill or oven heats, let your side of salmon come to room temperature. Rub the salmon all over with the olive oil and use a paper towel to rub the grates of your grill with oil as well. Just before you put the salmon on the grill, season it with 1 tablespoon of the salt.

3 Lay the fish skin side down on the grill and cover. Cook undisturbed for 20 minutes. Check the salmon. It should be fully cooked along the edges and appear more rare toward the center. I'm a fan of this because we have some rare-lovers and some well-doners in our brood. Here there's something for everyone.

4 Taking the salmon off the grill will be the most terrifying thing you do all day. Get some help and two of the biggest spatulas you have and by all means make sure you have a suitably sized platter nearby before you go about it. If you lose the skin or portions of it, even if you lose whole chunks of fish to the grill, it's okay. You're gonna cover it in glaze and salad so who cares.

5 While both the glaze and the salmon are still warm, slather the second with the first. Then in a medium mixing bowl, toss the radishes, arugula, herbs, remaining 2 tablespoons citrus juice, and remaining ½ teaspoon salt and spread that glory all around the salmon.

A HERO IS BORN

The seed for this book, in fact the entire philosophy for the way I cook, began with a woman named Rose and a jar of pear preserves. It was June and Chef and the Farmer was about to turn two. Rose worked garde-manger, the station that preps and plates salads and desserts during service. She struggled at it. The hours were long. The pace was frenetic and, at roughly sixty, Rose was the oldest member of any kitchen I had ever been a part of.

Rose had also never worked in this sort of setting. She knew how to cook; she just didn't know how to cook in a restaurant. That's not a criticism. The two skills are as much alike as brushing your hair and commandeering a chair at a salon. However, when the running joke became that Rose was a tornado and our kitchen was her trailer park, I knew I had to make a change.

Honestly, I didn't have it in me to fire anybody, much less a grandma figure, so when Rose brought me a jar of her homemade pear preserves I created a job for her out of thin air. I told Rose I wanted to learn to make that kind of thing and that it would be more helpful for me and the restaurant if she would stop tossing salads and start pickling and preserving.

It's embarrassing to think about now, but I had no idea what this job opportunity would really lead to. I had zero experience with "old fashioned" techniques. Pickling and preserving are now en vogue, but back then my interests were immersion circulators, foams, and microgreens, not hot water baths and Ball jars. The only toe I'd dipped into the canning world was the spring prior when I stuffed radishes into a Mt. Olive pickle jar, poured vinegar overtop, and screwed on a lid. I honestly thought it was that simple. And while the pear preserves

Rose brought me were delicious, I wasn't sure how something sweet and syrupy could elevate what I cooked. Savory food was my jam. The only thing I could think to do with fruit preserves was slap them on a biscuit.

But that's my thing...at least one of my things. I make decisions like hiring a canning guru because my gut tells me to and I figure out later how those decisions make sense. I'm all emotion and enthusiasm. In most cases I get to the practical stuff eventually.

Rose started canning. She made jams, relishes, preserves, and pickles. I invested in jars and canning equipment and we designated an entire wall in the kitchen to display the fruits of her labor. I watched from my perch in the prep kitchen as she sterilized jars and plucked two-piece lids out of boiling water with a magnet. I held my breath as our resident tornado employed something akin to forceps to lift scalding hot jars of sealed mysteries out of a giant black pot she called a bath, and crossed my fingers as she painstakingly placed them inches apart on towels to cool. My favorite part of Rose's ritual was listening for the pop of their lids as the sealed treasures cooled. She described the subtle symphony as sweet music to a canner's ears, a sign she had done her work well. The slow, rhythmic show seemed to me like cooking in a different language.

By the end of summer Rose had attached sugar or vinegar to every variety of fruit and vegetable that crossed our kitchen's doorstep. Shiny, colorful, and impossible to ignore, Rose's wall was like a giant jewelry box. Although I found it remarkable and was certainly proud of Rose's feat, the wall became a stressor for me. From the looks of it, she had really done something—but I didn't know what to do with it.

All that would change in September, when the health inspector made her surprise quarterly visit. Naive and proud, I led her over to Rose's wall and did my best Vanna White all over it. She met my enthusiasm with a stern look and the words, "You know, you have to throw all that away."

I was 80 percent dumbfounded. Truthfully, there was always 20 percent of me that questioned whether we were allowed to preserve stuff in jars without any special certification, but that was just enough doubt to play dumb. So dumb and devastated is what I was. She said she would usually make someone in this situation throw everything out while she stood there, but she would do me the courtesy of being alone with the wall when I said goodbye to it.

I didn't get into trouble, but there wasn't a chance in hell I was gonna throw the jars away. I'm betting our sensible, kind health inspector knew that too, but rather than risk another jar discovery I decided to dump their contents into plastic containers and put them in the walk-in fridge for near-future use. With the jars' innards laid bare, I suddenly saw the possibilities locked inside the cornucopia of pickles and relishes—a million ways to balance braised meat, hearty stews, and rich gratins. I had been so intimidated by the canning process that I failed to see the ready-to-use potential of what Rose had made.

I also saw that none of this stuff truly *needed* to be canned. The pickles and relishes were packed with so much vinegar they'd be happy for half a year at least in the fridge, and the fruit preserves and jams were suspended in enough sugar to do the same. I had a plan for the former but didn't see the potential in the sweet sticky fruit, so I offered a lot of that to Rose. After all, she had put in the effort to make the mountain before me. She said thank you and added she loved fruit preserves with pork chops.

The mere mention of pork turned me on my heel and I took back my offer. I realized I had a jewel-toned goldmine of future pan sauce on my hands, and Rose was about to walk out the door with it.

Since then, sauces based on fruit preserves have become a thing I'm known for, and I've got Rose to thank for that. They're a trick you can take anywhere. They represent another skill in your repertoire, confidence up your sleeve, resourcefulness in your kitchen game. And best of all, they require ingredients you likely already have. I've walked into beach rentals and found everything I need to instantly pull off a sauce that tastes like it took a lot of skill and a long time to make.

An unctuous, sweet-and-sour glaze that builds off the pan drippings from searing a piece of meat or a swath of vegetables, this sauce is by far the best and easiest way to capitalize on the half-eaten jars of jam, jelly, and proper Sweet Potential you've got in the fridge. Follow the recipe the first time, but remember the formula so you can get all Picasso with your Back Pocket in the future. Before you know it, you'll be swapping in vinegars, adding herbs, blooming spices, and playing with fats to make an array of simple sauces on the fly.

I've chosen a streamlined, simple interpretation to lay out the basics, and paired it with pork because pork generally plays well with a little something sweet. All the ingredients listed as optional are just that. They give the sauce more dimension, but not having them on hand should not prevent you from simmering up the four things you need to make a delicious pan sauce. And because sometimes we struggle to see outside the lines, I've offered some additional brain-candy combinations to consider once you've got this technique tucked firmly in your Back Pocket.

Back-Pocket Pan Sauce

serves 4

2 tablespoons extra-virgin olive oil

1 pound pork tenderloin

2 teaspoons kosher salt, plus more for seasoning

2 tablespoons unsalted butter, divided

2 tablespoons minced shallot or red onion (optional)

1 tablespoon minced fresh ginger (optional)

¼ cup plus 1½ tablespoons vinegar of your choice, divided

¼ cup white or red wine (optional)

½ cup Sweet Potential (page 296)

2 tablespoons Dijon mustard

½ cup chicken or pork broth (optional)

1 Preheat your oven to 400°F. In a 10- to 12-inch ovenproof skillet, heat the olive oil over medium heat. Season the pork with the salt. Brown the pork carefully on all sides. This should take about 8 minutes. Transfer the skillet to the middle rack of your oven and roast for 12 minutes, until an instant-read thermometer registers an internal temp of 145°F. Put the tenderloin on a plate to rest and place the skillet back on the stovetop. This next part is gonna go really fast so make sure all your ingredients are at the ready.

2 Heat the skillet over medium heat. Add 1 tablespoon butter, the shallot or onion (if using), and the ginger (if using) to the skillet and sizzle for about 30 seconds. Then stir in the ¼ cup vinegar and the wine (if using), taking care to scrape up any browned bits stuck to the bottom of your pan.

3 Once this comes to a fervent simmer, add the Sweet Potential, Dijon, and broth (if using). Let that cook down for a couple minutes until it's glaze consistency. Swirl in the remaining 1 tablespoon butter and the remaining 1½ tablespoons vinegar. The sauce should be shiny and thick and should smell like honed kitchen skill. Taste it and add a pinch of salt if necessary.

4 Return the pork plus all its accumulated juices to the pan just to coat. Let the pork rest off the heat for about 5 minutes before you slice it.

SOME OTHER BACK-POCKET PAN SAUCE COMBINATIONS YOU MIGHT LIKE TO TRY
(and the order in which they should be added)

1
butter + minced ginger + peach, apple, or pear Sweet Potential + bourbon + lemon juice + butter

2
coconut oil + minced ginger-shallot + coriander seeds + watermelon, blueberry, strawberry, or citrus Sweet Potential + rice vinegar + lime juice + coconut oil

3
butter + shallot + garlic + red wine or sherry + red wine or sherry vinegar + fig or grape Sweet Potential + broth + lemon juice + butter

I Wish I Was a Cheese Baller

serves 4 to 6

I've gotten a lot of mileage out of the cliched yet adored cheese ball. Aptly named the Party Magnet, it was one of the most talked about recipes in my first book. Readers' attraction was so strong and their enthusiasm so wide I shrunk my cheese ball's size and decided to serve miniature magnets in my restaurant. I've given lectures on cheese ball science and was approached to write a whole book on the subject. Basically people know that I know what to do when it comes to spheres of spreadable dairy. So when we decided to sell mail-order cheese balls through Handy & Hot for Christmas, I knew I had to improve on the original and make the best cheese ball the planet had ever known.

But it was hard. I came up with a lot of good balls, but nothing that was distinct or measurably better than the original. Seeing I was stumped, my friend Baxter made a timid suggestion—one she thought I'd sneer at. Why don't you bake it? I did not sneer.

The beauty of the baked cheese ball and the reason it speaks to me is because I could never trust that people followed my instructions and served their Party Magnets under a torrent of fruit preserves. I've seen pictures on the Internet and I know that beyond the basic steps and ingredients in my recipes, people go ahead and do what they want—no fruit preserves in sight. So in this recipe, with everything I intend you to taste baked inside, you eat it like it should have been in the first place. Except now it's in a dish and decidedly not a ball. And it's hot. But those are just details.

3 scallions, green parts only, sliced thin

⅔ cup Sweet Potential (page 296)

4 ounces blue cheese, at room temperature

8 ounces (1 package) cream cheese, at room temperature

5 ounces fresh goat cheese, at room temperature

2 teaspoons hot sauce

2 teaspoons kosher salt, divided

1½ cups roughly chopped pecans, or V's Nuts (page 266) if you're feeling extra

1 tablespoon unsalted butter, melted

Chopped fresh parsley for garnish (optional)

Butter crackers, for serving

❶ Preheat your oven to 400°F. In a medium bowl, stir together the scallions, Sweet Potential, blue cheese, cream cheese, goat cheese, hot sauce, and 1 teaspoon of the salt. You're not looking for a homogenous mixture. It's okay if there are distinct pieces of blue cheese in places and lumps of cream cheese in others. Transfer the gloopy group to an 8 x 12-inch baking dish. Slide that onto the middle rack of your oven and bake for 20 minutes.

❷ While that bakes you'll need to toast your pecans. Toss the roughly chopped nuts with the melted butter and remaining 1 teaspoon salt and toast them on a baking sheet on the top rack of your oven for 8 minutes.

❸ After 20 minutes, your cheese should be bubbly and a bit brown on top. Shower it with the pecans and parsley if using, and serve warm with your butter cracker of choice.

Cocktail o'Clock

serves one too many

Forgive me for stating the obvious, but Sweet Potential is especially suited for cocktails. She's half syrup that's fruit flavored so you can inject drinks like sours, gimlets, and daiquiris with the sweet element they require and at the same time add an elegant fruitiness without watering any of the hard stuff down with juice. And as I've mentioned, one of Sweet Potential's most magnetic qualities is that her syrup tastes more like the bubble gum flavor of the fruit it's made from than the fruit itself. The fruit's personality is amplified,

so stirred into cocktails it stands out. I've made strong suggestions around the type of Sweet Potential to use for each of the following cocktails, but most combinations work. Just make sure you balance the boozy sweet stuff with acid or bitter. That's really the whole trick of it.

Forgive me again for stating something else obvious, but what's good for cocktails is also good for non-alcoholic drinks. In any of these recipes, replace the liquor quotient with club soda and call it a morning.

①

WATERMELON MINT GIMLET

- 2 ounces gin
- ¾ ounce syrup from watermelon Sweet Potential (page 296)
- ¾ ounce fresh lime juice
- 5 mint leaves

Combine everything in a cocktail shaker with ice. Shake like hell. Strain into a chilled glass. Garnish with a lime wedge and a cube of Sweet Potential watermelon flesh.

makes 1

②

PEAR OR APPLE SOUR

- 2 ounces rye whiskey
- ¾ ounce syrup from pear or apple Sweet Potential (page 296)
- ¾ ounce fresh lemon juice
- 1 egg white

Combine everything in a cocktail shaker with ice. Shake like hell for a full minute. Strain into a chilled glass.

makes 1

③

CHERRY BOULEVARDIER

2 ounces bourbon
1 ounce Campari
1 ounce syrup from cherry Sweet Potential (page 296)
Orange peel

Combine everything but the orange peel in a cocktail shaker with ice. Shake like hell. Strain into a glass filled with ice. Squeeze the orange peel before dropping it into the glass. Garnish with a Sweet Potential cherry.

makes 1

④

STRAWBERRY DAIQUIRI

2 ounces white rum
¾ ounce syrup from strawberry Sweet Potential (page 296)
¾ ounce fresh lime juice

Combine everything in a cocktail shaker with ice. Shake like hell. Strain into a chilled glass. Garnish with a Sweet Potential strawberry and a lime wheel.

makes 1

Easy, Baby...Back Ribs

makes 1 slab ribs

I love a good baby back rib. I think most meat eaters do. When cooked appropriately, ribs tap into our carnivorous pull toward something both tender and gnawable. And no matter what kind of pig they come from or how much sauce they're slathered in, ribs always taste porky and rich. But unless we pluck them pre-cooked from under a heat lamp at the grocery store, most people don't think of ribs as weeknight dinner. Most people don't live with me.

Ribs are in my weeknight rotation because they make my kids happy and a slab easily feeds our family of four. Plus the effort-to-reward quotient of a slab of ribs is unmatched. Don't misunderstand me. I'm not in the backyard on a Tuesday over a smoker. I'm washing dishes, arguing with my editor, and doing my best not to be late to a basketball game. I need ribs that kind of cook themselves. To do this, I tuck the ribs inside an aluminum foil sleeve, pour in some Sweet Potential plus garlic and vinegar, and slide that sleeve in my oven. Trapped in the foil pocket, the ribs steam in their own juices. Those juices mingle with their sweet and tart pouch-mates, and lo and behold two hours later, succulent ribs plus sauce emerge and I am the amazing woman other people think I am.

1 slab baby back ribs

2 teaspoons kosher salt

2 teaspoons ground black pepper

⅓ cup Sweet Potential (page 296)

¼ cup red wine vinegar or apple cider vinegar

2 garlic cloves, smashed and peeled

1 Preheat your oven to 350°F. Season the ribs with the salt and pepper. Lay the slab, meaty side down, lengthwise in the center of a roughly 2-foot-long piece of aluminum foil. Fold one end of the foil up over the slab and fold the sides up around it. At this point you should have ribs in a sleeve with an opening at one end.

2 Lift the slab up and pour the Sweet Potential, the vinegar, and the smashed garlic cloves into the opening. Make sure the seams of your packet are facing up so that the liquid can't leach out from the bottom. Fold the open end up like closing an envelope. Put the slab on a baking sheet and slide it onto the middle rack of your oven.

3 Two hours later, pull the ribs out. Open up the pouch. Brush the ribs with the accumulated sauce and serve to folks who are grateful to have such a clever cook living in their midst.

Ugly Cake

makes one 8-inch round cake

I wouldn't call myself an avid baker, but I do know a few things when it comes to quick, unattractive homemade sweets. The thing is, I get satisfaction from whisking something together, dumping it in a pan, and baking it up. I just loathe stand mixers and kneading and trying to decorate with icing. That distaste limits what I'm inclined to do in the oven, so most of my desserts come out of a casserole dish and I'm okay with that. The interesting thing is that once I decided not to fret about how my baked goods looked, I realized I rather like baking. In my kitchen, the uglier the better.

For this particularly ugly cake, I call on three things that we think of together but in a different way. Fluffy corn cake, known to some misguided souls as cornbread, gets the soak treatment with fruit preserves and buttermilk. It's quick, it's gooey, it's sweet and tangy. It's like tres leches cake and corn muffins had a messy casserole baby.

Nonstick cooking spray

2 large eggs, separated

2 tablespoons plus ¼ cup granulated sugar, divided

3 tablespoons vegetable oil

½ teaspoon vanilla extract

½ cup cake flour

¼ cup cornmeal

1 teaspoon baking powder

1 teaspoon kosher salt

1 cup buttermilk, divided

¾ cup Sweet Potential (page 296)

1 Preheat your oven to 350°F and coat the inside of an 8-inch round cake pan with nonstick cooking spray. In the bowl of a standing mixer fitted with the whisk, beat the egg whites until they have doubled in volume. Then add the 2 tablespoons sugar and continue to whisk until the egg whites have reached soft peaks. Transfer the egg whites to a bowl and set aside.

2 Rinse out the mixing bowl and fit the mixer with the paddle attachment. Paddle the vegetable oil with the remaining ¼ cup sugar on medium for about a minute. Add the yolks one at a time and then the vanilla and continue to paddle until things are light and fluffy, about 2 more minutes. In a medium bowl, combine the flour, cornmeal, baking powder, and salt. With the mixer running, add half the dry ingredients followed by ½ cup of the buttermilk. Once that's fully incorporated, add the remaining dry ingredients. Do not overprocess. This is cake, not bread. Once the dry ingredients are incorporated, use a spatula to fold in the egg whites.

3 Dump the cake batter into the baking pan and slide it onto the middle rack of your oven. Bake for 15 to 20 minutes, till the cake is set and lightly browned on top. Once it comes out of the oven, poke it vigorously all over with a toothpick, knife, or fork. The more holes the better. Then pour the Sweet Potential and the remaining ½ cup buttermilk over the top. It will look like a general disaster, but after about 2 hours the buttermilk syrup will have sunk in and the cake will just be ugly.

Blintzed Breakfast Bake

serves 8

My favorite time to entertain is morning because breakfast comes with cues everybody understands. It suggests beverages like OJ and coffee that take the guesswork out of what liquid to offer. It has a distinct beginning and a quicker end than dinner parties or long lunches. And more than at any other meal, a buffet with its casual, help-yourself aesthetic seems most appropriate at breakfast. But my fondness for early-day entertaining has taught me a lesson. While I'm not a sweets-for-breakfast kind of gal, there are a lot of you out there. So in an effort to keep everybody happy, I always insert a sweet offering among the cheesy eggs and salty meats I select for my own plate.

This one says stuffed French toast, bread pudding, and cheese blintz with whispers of Danish in its depths. It checks the sugar-for-breakfast box but it's not gonna give anybody a toothache, because the cream cheese swoops into every bite to balance Sweet Potential's presence. And for those of us who aspire to that easy entertaining vibe, you can put this together the night before and bake it just before your breakfast buffet begins.

8   large eggs
2½   cups half-and-half
2   teaspoons vanilla extract
1   teaspoon ground cinnamon
1   teaspoon kosher salt

8   cups 1-inch cubed bread, such as ciabatta, sourdough, or baguette
8   ounces (1 package) cream cheese
1   cup Sweet Potential (page 296)
¼   cup granulated sugar
2   teaspoons ground nutmeg

1 In a medium bowl, whisk the eggs, half-and-half, vanilla, cinnamon, and salt into a homogeneous milky mix. Put half the bread in a 10-inch round or 8 x 12-inch rectangular baking dish and pour half the egg mixture over top. If you partially froze your cream cheese it will crumble easily, so crumble half the cream cheese on top of the bread mixture then top that with half the Sweet Potential. Finish with the remaining bread, egg mixture, cream cheese, and Sweet Potential. Cover with foil and refrigerate overnight, or up to 48 hours.

2 The following morning, preheat your oven to 350°F. Combine the sugar and nutmeg and sprinkle it over top of the bread. Refasten the foil, slide the whole thing onto the middle rack of your oven, and bake for 40 minutes. Remove the foil and bake an additional 20 minutes, until crisp and browned. Serve warm.

ATTENTION

To make things a little easier, put your cream cheese in the freezer for about 15 minutes before you get ready to assemble your Blintzed Bake. Once assembled, the unbaked breakfast bake can rest in your fridge for up to 48 hours before you bake it.

Acknowledgments

A thousand thanks to the heroes that made this happen—

Baxter Miller and **Ryan Stancil (aka Luigi):** I hate to lump the two of you together, but I can't fathom splitting you apart. You are a true team, and I thank all the stars (even the unlucky ones) y'all found your way into my life. You are students of our region with hearts and intellect as big as the world, and I've grown so much with your wind in my sails. Shooting this book with you has been both a professional and personal highlight in my life, and if anyone ever tells me not to mix business with pleasure again, I'll invite them to wine time so they can see how mutual respect and shared goals and ambition can be a great place to build lasting friendships.

Mike Szczerban: Because I said it all there and because you can't handle any more of my gushing, please see "This One's for Mike" (page 270).

To **Ben Allen, Jules Horbachevshy, Stephanie Reddaway, Kim Sheu, Nyamekye Waliyaya, Thea Diklich-Newell,** and **Gregg Kulick** at Voracious / Little, Brown: It's been a pleasure on my end. I hope it hasn't been too bad on yours.

Laura Palese: You perfectly personified the spirit of this book. With color, font, and funky marks, you made a novel idea look like a paradigm.

To the folks at **Haand:** I know you didn't design your dinnerware for my book, but it sure seemed like you did. Over and over I pinched myself at the perfection in each of your pieces. The colors, texture, and modern elegance of your plates, bowls, ramekins, and mugs fit the tone of what I wanted for this book like a running sock. I've never worn a running sock, but I know they are tight, breathable, and designed to push you as far as you can go. That's what your ceramics did here.

Andrea Weigl: I'm not sure if you knew I needed saving or you just wanted to test my recipes. Either way, your insight, sensibilities, and means of giving noninflammatory criticism made this book so much better. And your laugh—it makes my day better every time I'm lucky enough to hear it. Your neighbors and I thank you.

Kim Adams: We've worked together a long time, and although sometimes you worry me to death, you're the first person I call when I need something done right and done right now. Thank you for showing up, going all the way and often even further, and believing in me and what we do for going on fifteen years now. I know I worry the shit out of you too, so we're good.

Nicole Scronce, Nikki Takemura, and **Laura Vinroot:** As I wallowed on Nikki's white faux-fur jacket in that silk Chloé top sweating like a pig, I wondered who I must have fooled to have the elegant, warm women from Capitol Shop style the portraits for my book. The thought made me sweat more, and I worried I might have to pay for the ruined blouse. But your grace, thoughtfulness, and enviable class eventually convinced me that what you do is less about the clothes and more about the people who wear them. Thank you for the week-long Cinderella moment. I'll always remember it.

David Black: Always there for me, always supportive, always honest. I couldn't ask for a better advocate, sounding board, or shoulder to cry on. Now that I've listed all the clichés, I'll admit you make a good bulldog too.

Mom, Dad, Leraine, Currie, and **Johna:** You've certainly given me a lot to write about! I used to think our family was disjointed, awkward, even cold. But the older I get the less I compare our family rhythms to others, choosing instead just to wallow in the comfort of siblings, nieces, nephews, and parents who are still in my life. Howard hugs and backhanded compliments may be our love language, but I'll take it.

Flo (aka The Flo): My favorite thing about this book so far was watching you flip through the first pass. You pointed out the photo of asparagus being tossed in a bowl and said, "That's when you were struggling to get that picture with the green stuff. You tried so hard and here it is!" When you said that, it made me happier than a million awards. To know you paid attention and then connected that moment with the actual book showed me so much about you and your desire to connect the dots. Thanks for paying attention to what I do. You and your brother are two of the main reasons I do it.

Theo (aka Boogie): My favorite moments of quarantine...the twenty or thirty minutes every morning you joined me on the couch while the rest of the family slept. I wrote and you watched, and we were quiet and snuggled together. Thank you for the peace found in those minutes.

Jennifer Sinclair (aka Ms. J): Simply put, you have been a gargantuan gift to my family. Your ever-positive attitude, consistent discipline, and level-headed nature are just what the Howard-Knight family would have ordered if we knew it was possible.

Kristen Whitfield (aka The Sheriff): In a bevy of ways you made it possible for me to step away and write this book. Commitment, trust, real-talk, and a willingness to do the hard stuff all come to mind when I think of you.

Lesley Davis (aka Crushherr): Sometimes we look so desperately for the thing we need, we fail to see her right in front of us. Thanks for coming back. It's gonna be good.

Ben: This life may not be what we planned, but I'm glad I get to build a family with you. Let's have more dinners around the table and more family bike rides and walks on the beach. Thanks for hanging on to the roller coaster that is life with Vivian and for always being the parent that plays with the kids.

Index

About the Author

Vivian Howard is the *New York Times* bestselling author of *Deep Run Roots,* which was named Cookbook of the Year by the International Association of Culinary Professionals. She co-created and stars in the public television shows *Somewhere South* and *A Chef's Life,* for which she has won Peabody, Emmy, and James Beard awards. She runs the restaurants Chef and the Farmer, Benny's Big Time, Lenoir, and Handy & Hot. Vivian lives in Deep Run, North Carolina, with her husband, Ben, and their twins, Theo and Flo.